PORTSMOUTH'S
WORLD WAR ONE HEROES

PORTSMOUTH'S
WORLD WAR ONE HEROES
Stories of the Fallen
Men and Women

JAMES DALY

The
History
Press

For Mum, Dad, Scott and Nicola

Cover illustrations: *Front Top:* British tank crossing no-man's-land. (GWPDA) *Bottom:* A Portsmouth Pals battalion leaving for active service. (Gates) *Back:* Machine gunner sculpture at the entrance to the Cenotaph. (Author)

First published 2013

The History Press
The Mill, Brimscombe Port
Stroud, Gloucestershire, GL5 2QG
www.thehistorypress.co.uk

British Library Cataloguing in Publication Data.
A catalogue record for this book is available from the British Library.

ISBN 978 0 7524 9149 3

Typesetting and origination by The History Press
Printed in Great Britain

Contents

Acknowledgements

This book has been several years in the making – begun even before my previous book, *Portsmouth's World War Two Heroes*, had been completed - and I have received the help and assistance of many people, for which I am very grateful.

In particular I would like to thank the many ancestors of Portsmouth's First World War servicemen whom I have been lucky to correspond with, and those who commented on my blog. Members of the First World War Forum eased my initial forays, particularly into some of the more specialist spheres of research. Michel de Gravel Tremco gave much advice on researching Lieutenant Colonel Dick Worrall.

I would like to thank my colleagues at Portsmouth Museums, Archives and Visitor Services, particularly John Stedman, Andrew Whitmarsh and Michael Gunton, who helped shape my thoughts during many an interesting discussion, often without realising it.

I would like to thank John Sadden, the archivist of Portsmouth Grammar School, for providing information about Old Portmuthians who were killed during the First World War, and students of the school, who produced this research. I would also like to thank Catherine Evans, the archivist at Charter House School; Paul Stevens, the archivist at Repton School; and Wendy Adams and Jo Outhwaite of the Temple Reading Room at Rugby School.

The staff at Portsmouth Central Library were as helpful as ever, especially in the Portsmouth History Centre – a remarkable resource with an unrivalled naval history collection for a public library. I would also like to thank staff at the National Archives and Chichester Library, and Jane Naisbitt, the head of the Military History Research Centre at the Canadian War Museum. A special mention is also due to the forward-thinking policy of both the Library and Archives of Canada and the National Archives of Canada for making their respective service records and war diaries available to download, for free, online, aiding the work of the researcher considerably.

I would like to thank Peter Higgins and Tim Backhouse for helping me to locate the Southern Grammar School Roll of Honour, and also the editor of *The News*, Mark Waldron, for permission to use images from the paper.

The authors of the Portsmouth Papers deserve recognition. The considerable body of work that they have produced over the course of almost fifty years is probably unrivalled for any city of Portsmouth's size and provides a rich tapestry of local history.

My father Peter Daly kindly proofread all of the chapters, as ever with an engineer's eye for detail and minutiae.

I would like to thank all at my publishers, The History Press, for their assistance and faith in me, in particular Jo de Vries, Ross Britton and Chrissy McMorris for their help with my previous work.

Finally, and most importantly, I would like to thank my family and friends for their unwavering support, throughout what has been at times a very trying process. Without their encouragement, and in particular my parents' nurturing of my love of history and reading, this book would not have been possible.

Abbreviations

ADM	Admiralty
AIR	Air Ministry
CAB	Cabinet
CO	Colonial Office
EN	*Portsmouth Evening News*
FO	Foreign Office
Gates	W.G. Gates, *Portsmouth and the First World War*
GWPDA	Photos of the First World War
LAC	Library and Archives of Canada
LG	London Gazette
NAA	National Archives of Australia
NATS	Ministry of National Service
PGS	Portsmouth Grammar School
PHC	Portsmouth History Centre
PRO	Public Record Office
SGS	Southern Grammar School
TNA	The National Archives
WO	War Office
YMCA	Young Men's Christian Association

Introduction

Having written about Portsmouth's Second World War casualties, it was a natural progression for me to look further back in history and tell the story of Portsmouth's war dead of the First World War. Both conflicts are, after all, part of the same broad history of the twentieth century. But although I had spent many years researching and studying the Second World War and knew much about what happened to my ancestors during that conflict, I knew very little about the First World War.

It quickly occurred to me that compared to the Second World War, Portsmouth's history of the First World War is barely known. Whilst most people in Portsmouth will be aware of the bombing of Portsmouth during the Second World War and of D-Day, few will have any knowledge of the Portsmouth Pals Battalions or of the Battle of Jutland. Yet, in terms of casualties and the sheer effect that the conflict had on the town, the First World War was one of the most defining moments in Portsmouth's history, and definitely the most costly.

I began by working through the names on Portsmouth's war memorial, of which there are over 5,000. Whilst many of the names were traced on the Commonwealth War Graves Commission's Debt of Honour Register online, a surprising number proved to be elusive. Whether this is due to a mistake on the memorial, the register or both can only be proven by extensive research on each individual. The war memorial proved to be just the start. A remarkable tool called Geoff's Search Engine allowed me to search the Debt of Honour Register for men who came from Portsmouth, and several hundred cropped up who, for whatever reason, were not included on the war memorial. The roll of honour in *'Portsmouth and the First World War'* by William Gates also added several hundred names to the database, as did the Portsmouth section of *The National Roll of the First World War*. Scanning local war memorials – parish churches, employers, etc – also provided more names. However, due to the nature of war memorials and how war casualties are recorded, it is difficult to know exactly how many men from Portsmouth were killed. It is likely to be more than 6,000.

Compared to researching Second World War servicemen, researching First World War dead is both easier and more difficult; easier, because the

Commonwealth War Graves Commission's online register includes house numbers and road names for many, but also because many useful official documents have been released into the public domain, allowing us to research individuals in more detail. The 1901 and 1911 censuses allow us to pinpoint war casualties in their communities, and for many, service records are readily available. But in many respects First World War casualties are more difficult to research because, due to the passage of time, their descendants are invariably less aware of their stories. Whilst there are Second World War veterans still alive, the last First World War veterans passed away some years ago. As a result, we are very much dealing with what is now history and not memory. And, tragically, the sheer number of men involved made the task a lengthy one.

In many ways the story of Portsmouth's war losses during the First World War tells the story of the city itself during those dark days, and indeed the preceding years. Portsmouth's war dead of the First World War were, in the majority of cases, born and educated in the Victorian era. In so many ways, the experiences of more than 6,000 men paint a vivid picture of life in Portsmouth. And a unique picture it is – nowhere else in Britain had anything like the social conditions that Portsmouth had in 1914. Portsmouth's status as a naval dockyard *and* a garrison town gave it a character all of its own; from the working-class slum neighbourhood of Landport, to the officers' enclave of Thomas Ellis Owen's Southsea; from the Portsmouth Pals to the sons of local politicians and the son of a brewing magnate, it is an incredibly diverse picture.

The largest contingent of men from the town were killed serving with the army, totalling 3,243, the majority of whom – around 2,000 – were killed on the Western Front. Over 1,700 of those who were killed from Portsmouth were serving with the Royal Navy, hundreds of whom were killed in one day at the Battle of Jutland. There were 374 men from Portsmouth in the Royal Marines and twenty-six serving with the Merchant Navy. The youngest servicemen from Portsmouth killed were 15, and the oldest was 72. Intriguingly for a war that is often perceived to have taken place solely in France and Belgium, Portsmouth casualties are buried in a remarkable forty-four countries, covering nearly every continent on the globe. Among the men from Portsmouth killed during the First World War, 240 are known to have held some kind of decoration for gallantry – 4 per cent of the total number of war casualties from the town. Men from Portsmouth served in all kinds of ships and units, performing every kind of role imaginable.

And yet whilst plenty has been written about the big events of the time, such as the Battle of Jutland, until recently there has been very little interest in uncovering what happened to the thousands of ordinary men from Portsmouth who died. In many respects, the sheer scale of the casualties meant that individuals were swamped in the sea of collective mourning. The First World War is now beyond living memory, and has in many ways been overshadowed by the Second

World War. Fortunately, an explosion of interest in family history in recent years has democratised military history, making it far more about the ordinary soldier than the well-known generals and politicians.

Public perceptions of the First World War have been irrevocably shaped and moulded by the historical and cultural trends that have waxed and waned since the armistice was signed on 11 November 1918. The massive losses engendered an attitude among the public and politicians alike that such a costly war must never be allowed to happen again. A reluctance to go to war led to the appeasement of Hitler in the 1930s, and the British experience during the First World War influenced how Britain subsequently fought the Second World War. Army casualties in that war, for example, were much fewer than during the First World War, as politicians and generals were determined to avoid the huge casualties suffered on the Western Front. Whilst casualty rates during the Battle of Normandy in 1944 were similar to those experienced on the Western Front, the British Army spent only a short period of time during the Second World War fighting the enemy on the mainland of Europe.

Alan Clark's *The Donkeys* is perhaps the best-known text that set the assumption that all British generals of the First World Wars were incompetent, a misconception that has been only partly dispelled by historians. The BBC documentary series *The First World War* heightened public interest in the conflict, as did the stage play *Oh! What a Lovely War*, which also reinforced popular perceptions. Although regarded as one of the best British comedies of modern times, *Blackadder Goes Forth* hardened the 'donkeys' perception among many and gave the impression that British soldiers on the Western Front spent the entire war living in muddy holes in the front line.

However, in recent years a growth of interest in family history has led many people to develop a closer knowledge and awareness of the experiences of their ancestors during the First World War. Series such as *Who Do You Think You Are?* inspired this growth, and it is noticeable that military ancestors feature prominently in such programmes. Novels such as Sebastian Faulks's *Birdsong* and Michael Morpurgo's *War Horse*, and the subsequent stage production and Steven Spielberg-produced film adaptation, have encouraged an interest in the First World War in general and – in the case of *War Horse* – the experiences of non-human combatants specifically.

As ever, the phrase 'from Portsmouth' is by no means simple, and deserves explanation. Many men were born in Portsmouth and either remained or moved away, and many were born elsewhere and moved to the town. Men were educated here, or worked here. A cursory glance at even a relatively small number of men from Portsmouth who were killed during the First World War suggests that local society was incredibly fluid and mobile, both nationally and internationally. Whilst the committee who submitted names for Portsmouth's war memorial applied

relatively strict criteria, history suggests that such a policy excludes many men who on reflection had valid claims to be remembered. Portsmouth was a place that saw a constant movement of people coming and going, and it is therefore wise to maintain an open mind as to what the phrase 'from Portsmouth' entails. Broadly speaking, in this author's opinion, if they spent more than a fleeting amount of their life in the town, and their loss affected local society and local people, then they deserve to be remembered here.

With the centenary of the First World War almost upon us, naturally much attention will be focused upon anniversaries. With the passage of time it is all the more important that we carry the torch of remembrance. They might be remembered on memorials, but is it really enough for us to look at their engraved names once a year on a particular date and ignore them for the rest of the year? No; we can and should do more, and hopefully telling some of their stories is a step in the right direction. We need to draw a distinction between recording a person's name, and remembering their life. A name is part of a life, but we should not limit ourselves to this. Remembering a name is one thing, but learning about a person's life and their experiences is quite another and gives remembrance a whole new dimension.

By focussing on the experiences of individuals, we can paint a much more vivid picture of a community as a whole. Many fascinating and unique stories emerge. Sadly, as with any book of this nature, it is not possible to tell all of their stories, but hopefully those who have been covered in the following pages stand as representatives of their comrades. Collectively it is a story of a city at war, a story of soldiers and sailors; of officers and men; of trenches, deserts and oceans; of emigrants and immigrants; of tanks, aircraft and submarines; of brothers, fathers and sons; of prisoners of war, of pals and horses.

Including the word 'hero' in the title of this book was not a step I took lightly. It is a word that is overused in many inappropriate ways and comes with considerable baggage. Whilst I have never heard any war veterans describe themselves as heroes, it is important that people of my generation recognise that we have never had to experience many of the testing, traumatic events that our ancestors had to live through. We have lived in peace primarily because they stood up to be counted when it mattered. The vast majority of soldiers during both world wars did not win medals for bravery, but if they had not served their country at such a critical time, our lives would be very different now. As Lord Moran wrote in his seminal work *The Anatomy of Courage,* very few men can be brave or courageous all of the time. And whilst it is important that we give recognition to the men from Portsmouth who were killed during the First World War, surely there can be no better tribute than to remember them as overwhelmingly normal men who served and died during one of the most traumatic events that Portsmouth has ever known.

I

Portsmouth Before the
First World War

As a city, Portsmouth has always owed its very existence to war, and its fortunes have always been closely tied to the role that Britain has played on the global stage. Indeed, the sheltered harbour made Portchester a key settlement from Roman times. The town of Portsmouth was founded in the late twelfth century in the area we now know as Old Portsmouth. Portsmouth was frequently a point of embarkation for medieval kings sailing to fight in France, most notably Richard the Lionheart, who granted the town its first charter in 1194.[1]

The naval dockyard in Portsmouth grew in importance, particularly when the first dry dock was built by Henry VII in 1494. Naturally, fortifications were built to protect such a vital facility, and the town became home to a sizeable army garrison. The dockyard expanded considerably during the eighteenth and nineteenth centuries with the growth of the British Empire and the Royal Navy. As the dockyard expanded, so too did the fortifications and garrison to defend it. The presence of so many large military establishments shaped the way the town developed, geographically and socially. Throughout its history Portsmouth has perhaps been more familiar with soldiers and sailors than any other town or city in Britain. Although the townspeople were used to sharing their town with servicemen – and usually happy to accept their custom – the relationship was not always an easy one.

Portsmouth's population grew at an incredible rate during the nineteenth century, increasing from 33,226 in 1801 to 188,123 in 1901, by which time Portsmouth was the fifteenth largest town in the country.[2] The great extension of the dockyard in the 1860s in particular drew many men to Portsmouth. In 1801 the population of the town was crowded mainly into the area of Old Portsmouth, with a growing settlement at Portsea and a number of farms inhabiting the rest of the island. Within a hundred years, rapid expansion had covered a large proportion of Portsea Island in housing. In 1911 the town – as it was then – had a population of 230,496 people. They lived in a total of 51,656 dwellings – a remarkable number for what was still a small island town. Much of the population was concentrated in

the south-western part of the town, in particular in Landport, Buckland, Portsea, Southsea and Fratton. There was serious overcrowding, especially in some of the inner-city areas.[3] Despite this overcrowding, Portsmouth was also a rural town, and areas such as Milton, Copnor and Hilsea were still relatively undeveloped villages. Apart from Cosham and a small number of houses in Drayton and Farlington, the mainland that would become part of the town after the end of the First World War was virtually untouched by development. Although Portsmouth was of national and international importance, in 1914 it was still only a town, with city status not being granted until 1926, and the Anglican Diocese of Portsmouth being created a year later.[4]

There was significant poverty and deprivation in some areas of the town, and one commentator, Rev. Robert Dolling of St Agatha's church in Landport, famously regarded naval towns such as Portsmouth as 'sinks of iniquity'.[5] Most families lived in small and basic terraced houses, in narrow streets. Children played in the streets due to a lack of space. Landport in particular was viewed as a slum area.

The large number of thirsty young men led to the development and prosperity of several local breweries such as Brickwoods, and in 1910 there were 742 licensed premises in Portsmouth.[6] Reflecting the nature of the town, many pubs boasted naval- and military-inspired names. Some of these names are still in evidence today – the *Artillery Arms* in Milton, the *Battle of Minden* in Kingston, the *Fifth Hants Volunteer Arms* in Southsea, the *Royal Marine Artillery Tavern* in Eastney and the *Wellington* in Old Portsmouth. There were also a large number of beerhouses in the area, which were in effect rooms of normal family homes given over to serving alcohol. Beerhouses were for many years more numerous than public houses – in 1900 there were 318 pubs in the town and 459 beerhouses.[7] They were frequently unsophisticated and rowdy; Robert Dolling investigated many premises, and alleged them to be hotbeds of gambling, betting, vulgar songs and bad characters.[8] Agnes Weston, the founder of the Royal Sailors' Rests, also campaigned fiercely against the number of pubs near dockyards, even to the extent of buying up troublesome premises and converting them to more sober uses. This was met with hostility from local publicans, who accused her of ruining their trade.[9] Placing the number of pubs and the role of alcohol in context, in 1851 Portsmouth had space for 8,700 people in seven churches, but over 650 pubs with space for 24,000 customers.[10] Not surprisingly, the owner of Brickwoods's Brewery, Sir John Brickwood, was one of the most influential men in the town and was also the founding chairman of Portsmouth Football Club in 1898.[11] The tightening of licensing laws upon the outbreak of war caused anxiety to local landlords and breweries alike.[12]

The large number of unmarried young men in the town also encouraged another vice, and roads such as Bonfire Corner, Blossom Alley, Yorkes Drift, Whites Row and Rosemary Lane were well known as notorious areas for

prostitution.[13] Not unnaturally, the prevalence of venereal disease amongst military personnel was a serious concern for the authorities, and in November 1914 the general officer commanding the Portsmouth Garrison complained that the large numbers of men in the town had encouraged prostitution, increasing the number of cases of venereal disease.[14]

In 1911 Portsmouth represented the largest concentration of servicemen in Britain. In fact, it was said that in the town 'everything looks, breaths and smells of soldiers, sailors and dockmen'.[15] The census of that year showed that 20,016 men resident in the town were serving in the Royal Navy and 3,236 were in the army. By comparison, Aldershot, the largest army garrison town in Britain, was home to 12,694 soldiers. The high concentration of servicemen also affected the gender balance of Portsmouth's population; there were 11,574 unmarried males aged between 20 and 25 in Portsmouth, compared to only 3,946 in Southampton, although both towns had a similar total population. The manner in which Portsmouth was geared up towards providing and housing men for the Royal Navy and the dockyard made the town's efforts in finding enough men to raise two Pals Battalions for Kitchener's 'New Army' all the more remarkable. Only thirteen other Pals Battalions were raised in the South of England, and no other city or town in Hampshire managed to raise its own battalion, let alone two.[16]

Portsmouth Football Club was only founded in 1898, but even in the short period between then and the start of the First World War the club made a habit of recruiting players from the local naval and military establishments. The armed services encouraged sports, and the great number of young men passing through the town gave the club a large pool of potential players to choose from. In 1904 a player known only as 'Archibald' joined the club via the 'Royal Navy Depot' – presumably the Royal Naval Barracks at HMS *Nelson* – and played four games for the club in two years. In December 1913 Pompey signed H. 'Wobbly' Matthews from the Portsmouth Royal Marine Artillery. Matthews only made two appearances, scoring one goal.[17]

Although many young men who were born in the town found their way into the armed forces, many more were drawn to the town from elsewhere, often at a very early age. Rev. Robert Dolling wrote about the experiences of young men who arrived in Portsmouth for the first time after joining the Royal Navy, and in particular the boy seamen who spent several years onboard training ships. Many of them had just left home for the first time and were lacking any kind of female influence. Dolling felt that with the vices on offer Portsmouth was not the best town for impressionable young boys to be in. Interestingly, he observed that sailors often remained childish, frequently marrying on impulse a girl they had known for only a few weeks.[18]

Until the nineteenth century, the Royal Navy and its sailors had spent most of their time at sea and very little time in port or ashore. The sailors of Nelson's navy

a century before had spent most of their time 'in port' living on ships anchored at Spithead, with ships only coming into the dockyard for repairs. However, health concerns led the Royal Navy to begin building barracks onshore in the 1890s, including the main naval barracks at HMS *Nelson*, which opened in 1903.[19] The increasingly technical nature of naval service led to the construction of specialist schools. The gunnery school at HMS *Excellent* opened on Whale Island in the 1880s and the torpedo school at HMS *Vernon* in 1876.

Portsmouth's history as an army garrison has often been overshadowed by its naval heritage. In 1914 an Infantry Brigade was stationed in Portsmouth. There were many army barracks in the area: Clarence, Victoria, Cambridge and Colewort Barracks in the town – all bearing suitably royal names – and the Royal Artillery camp at Hilsea.[20] A visitor to the town would have struggled to walk very far without seeing some kind of army establishment. For example, a visitor disembarking at the town station and walking towards Clarence Pier would have seen the Connaught Drill Hall of the Hampshire Regiment's local territorial battalion, the drill halls of the Hampshire Royal Artillery and Royal Engineers, the garrison commander's residence at Ravelin House and other senior officers' residences in Ravelin Park and Clarence Barracks. In many respects, the army was in fact a more visible presence in Portsmouth than the Royal Navy, which was largely afloat or ensconced behind the dockyard walls. That Portsmouth Football Club was born out of a Royal Artillery team hints at how quietly prominent the army was in local society.[21]

Connaught Drill Hall, the headquarters of the Portsmouth-based territorial battalion of the Hampshire Regiment. The building is now a nightclub. (Author)

The Royal Artillery Volunteers
Drill Hall in St Paul's Road,
now a University of Portsmouth
gym. (Author)

Of the rest of the population, a large proportion was made up of dockyard workers. In fact, in 1911, between a third and half of all industrial workers in the town – some 15,000 men – were employed in the yard.[22] Increasing naval budgets in the pre-war years and an increase in the naval construction program made the yard busier than ever before, typified by the remarkable completion of HMS *Dreadnought* in only a year and a day.[23] War only increased the demand for workers, given the urgent need to repair ships and make modifications such as fitting torpedo bulges and extra armour.[24] By 1918 the workforce had swelled to 21,000.[25] The introduction of ironclad ships and steam propulsion led to the growth of a number of new trades. In 1911, for example, there were 962 boilermakers in Portsmouth, virtually all of whom would have been working in the yard, and in 1914 there were 655 riveters and drillers working there.[26] Many dockyard workers were mistakenly presented with white feathers, despite the vital role they were playing in contributing to the war effort.[27] Although the dockyard was largely self-sufficient, local traders also profited from being a part of the yard's supportive infrastructure, either supplying goods for use in the yard or sustaining the vast workforce.

The presence of a large military population also shaped Portsmouth's social and cultural history. As the Royal Navy, the dockyard and the army were the main

The Royal Engineers Drill Hall in Hampshire Terrace, now home of the University of Portsmouth Music Department. (Author)

forces in the town, Portsmouth was frequently at the forefront of national and international events, particularly in the lead-up to the outbreak of war.[28] Events such as fleet reviews and the launches of dreadnought battleships were major social occasions. The first of each class of dreadnought battleships was built in Portsmouth: HMS *Dreadnought* was launched in 1906, HMS *Iron Duke* in 1912 and HMS *Royal Sovereign* in April 1915. Portsmouth could therefore firmly lay claim to being 'the home of the dreadnoughts'.[29] The launching of HMS *Dreadnought* in 1906 by King Edward VIII drew thousands to the town.[30] In July 1914 a test mobilisation of the reserve fleet took place, and the fleet was reviewed by the King at Spithead. Such was the immense size of the Royal Navy that the whole fleet took six hours to pass the royal yacht.[31] Thousands viewed the event from the shoreline and also saw a *feu de joie* fired by soldiers lining the Solent from Southsea to Fort Gilkicker.[32] Parades were a common sight, and the movement of so many soldiers and sailors meant that military uniforms were ever-present around town. Visits by members of the Royal Family and other dignitaries were relatively common, and the German Kaiser visited Portsmouth on 11 November 1907.[33]

As the navy, the army and the dockyard – and by extension the government – dominated employment in the town, this left very little room for other industries. One notable exception was corset making, with 10,373 people – mostly women – employed in this sector in 1911. The large number of women who

lived alone whilst their husbands were serving overseas, often for years on end, meant that there was a large potential workforce in the town for such labour. In addition, naval pay was usually not enough to support a family on its own, leading many navy wives to take on jobs. Despite the importance of alcohol retailing in the town, only 226 people were employed in brewing in the same year.[34] Although the dockyard was a big employer in the town, it was largely self-sufficient, meaning that there were few opportunities for local businesses to supply it. A town such as Southampton, by contrast, was home to commercial shipping rather than the state-controlled industries present in Portsmouth, and this encouraged the development of private business. The presence of the naval dockyard and the control of local waters by the navy inhibited the growth of Portsmouth's commercial shipping trade until after the Second World War.[35]

As a result Portsmouth was by no means a rich town, and this poverty increased in many quarters with the coming of war. While Thomas Ellis Owen's Southsea boasted many fine streets and avenues, it was Portsmouth's only middle-class suburb; the other areas of the town were grossly overcrowded.[36] In fact, Portsmouth has often been described as a northern industrial town, only in a southern setting.[37] In 1914 it was estimated that 2,000 poor children were in need of shoes. Working-class children born in Portsmouth in the years prior to 1914 faced an uphill struggle to survive into adulthood, with infant mortality as high as 8.9 per cent.[38] Even into adulthood, life could be trying, and the life expectancy

Ravelin House, formerly the residence of the Portsmouth Garrison commander and now owned by the University of Portsmouth. (Author)

of adult males in Portsmouth was 51.5 years between 1910 and 1912.[39] Such a tough background probably helped men joining the armed forces to cope in harsh conditions, however, as they were used to enduring long hours and hard work with few luxuries.

Given the poverty in the town and the number of women who were left to struggle alone with young families, charity sustained many through the difficult war years. With very little state provision for those suffering hardship, most assistance was of a voluntary nature. After the start of the war, ten soup kitchens were established around the town, serving 4,800 pints of soup daily. Portsmouth also had a long heritage of voluntary aid organisations, such as the YMCA, and several determined women, notably Sarah Robinson and Agnes Weston, who opened her Royal Sailors' Rest in 1881.[40] The Royal Sailors' Rest provided sleeping accommodation, food and sober entertainment for hundreds of sailors as an alternative to the countless pubs in the town.

Portsmouth was indelibly shaped by its status as a naval, military and dockyard town, and the thousands of young men working in these occupations. The social, economic and cultural conditions in the town had evolved over many years as a result of these forces, and as a result Portsmouth was deeply affected by the First World War. Whilst the consequences of the Second World War were more physical and visible due to aerial bombing, the effects of the First World War were more socially and demographically severe.

2

The Armed Forces:
The Royal Navy

They that go down to the sea in ships, that do business in great waters.

Psalm 107:23

As the driving force of the largest maritime empire that the world had ever seen, sea power was literally a matter of life and death to Britain.[1] In 1914 the Royal Navy was the most powerful fighting force that the world had ever seen. Since long before Trafalgar the navy had been the primary instrument of Britain's foreign policy, with the army being seen by many as a 'projectile to be fired by the navy'.[2] During the later years of the nineteenth century, the British government had adopted the 'two power standard', which ensured that the Royal Navy was always larger than the fleets of the two next largest navies combined. The launch of HMS *Dreadnought* also placed the Royal Navy, outwardly at least, at the forefront of global naval technology.[3] The navy entered the war with confidence and a sense of destiny; naval power was believed to be a war-winning formula.[4]

The First World War is not often thought of as a naval war. Popular culture may be well aware of the Somme and Ypres, but the Battle of Jutland is much less well known. Whilst there were very few set-piece naval battles during the First World War – much to the disappointment of a British public that had inherited the legacy of Nelson and Trafalgar – the Royal Navy was in action from the first day of the war until the last. The first sailor from Portsmouth was killed on 3 September 1914, and the last to die during the war was on 10 November 1918.

A total of 1,776 sailors from Portsmouth are known to have been killed during the First World War. Portsmouth had been a naval base for hundreds of years and had long been home to a vast number of sailors. Its status was cemented in 1893 when the Admiralty permanently attached sailors to one of the three main ports – Portsmouth, Plymouth or Chatham.[5] These ports also became the basis for mobilisation of reservists and the re-activation of reserve ships in the event of war. A remarkable number of ships received their crews via Portsmouth during

the First World War – no fewer than twenty-eight battleships, three battlecruisers, sixteen cruisers, twenty-four light cruisers, seventy-eight destroyers and a plethora of other small ships.[6] The home port system engendered an individual culture in each town and gave sailors the security to settle in one place, but also compounded the impact of losses when ships were sunk[7]. As such, not only did Portsmouth, Plymouth and Chatham have a higher proportion of sailors amongst their populations, but this proportion was also reflected in their war dead.

The origins of Portsmouth sailors tell us much about just how mobile and fluid local society was before and during the First World War. The birthplaces of 1,541 of these sailors are known; out of those, just under half – 711 – were born in Hampshire and 527 were born in Portsmouth itself. These figures suggest that just over half of all sailors who were regarded as 'from Portsmouth' were born elsewhere and moved to the town to join the Royal Navy. This suggests that Portsmouth society was highly diverse, probably more so than the majority of comparable towns and cities in Britain at the time.

Of the sailors who were not born in Portsmouth, the majority came from two kinds of backgrounds: southern maritime counties or urban areas of large population. The South Coast had traditionally provided the majority of recruits, and large numbers of young men from counties such as Cornwall (13), Devon (43), Dorset (22), Isle of Wight (44), Kent (63) and Sussex (98) joined the Royal Navy and settled in Portsmouth[8]. Statistics suggest that the Royal Navy relied on recruits from coastal areas; a naval career was no doubt an option for young men who grew up near the sea and may have had experience of seafaring, and young men from the south and south-east of England in particular were likely to be based in Portsmouth, whereas men from the south-west were more likely to be sent to Plymouth.[9]

In the late nineteenth century, constant expansion of the Royal Navy led the Admiralty to widen recruiting efforts into non-traditional areas. As a result, a considerable proportion of Portsmouth sailors originally came from areas of high urban population such as London (136), and from predominantly inland industrial counties such as Yorkshire (28) and Lancashire (27). Sailors from these counties seem to have come mainly from large industrial cities, including Leeds, Liverpool and Manchester. Other smaller areas also had a high percentage of sailors settling in Portsmouth: thirty-one sailors came from Ireland, perhaps as a legacy of unemployment during the late nineteenth century, and eighteen sailors came from the Channel Islands.[10]

The lower decks of the Royal Navy were overwhelmingly manned by working-class recruits, for whom civilian life could be insecure and naval service provided a relatively safe alternative.[11] Ratings were provided with regular pay, food, clothing and a roof over their heads – things that could not necessarily be taken for granted in civilian life in an age before the welfare state and council housing.

The Grand Fleet at sea. In 1914 the Royal Navy was at the height of its power. (GWPDA)

Conditions were steadily improving, with the introduction of professional cooks, canteens and modest pay rises. Life in the Royal Navy could also be fraternal, with 124 different friendly societies established by 1910.[12]

We know the addresses of 1,311 Portsmouth sailors at the time of their death, and this helps us to identify areas that were particularly strong naval communities. Not surprisingly, the majority of sailors living in Portsmouth lived close to the dockyard, in areas such as Portsea (48), Buckland (104), Landport (160), Stamshaw (56), Kingston (50), North End (112), Fratton (98) and Southsea (275). The presence of so many sailors shaped the nature of these communities, in particular poor, densely populated urban areas such as Landport. By contrast, only six sailors lived in Cosham and one in Farlington. Outlying areas such as Paulsgrove were still rural in nature and sparsely populated.

The dates of enlistment of 296 sailors are known. Of those, sixty-six men enlisted after the start of the war, and the other 230 were pre-war sailors, and 102 had actually joined the Royal Navy in the nineteenth century, the earliest back in January 1885. Service in the Royal Navy was clearly a long-term career for many Portsmouth sailors. It could be argued that the longer sailors served in the Royal Navy, the more likely they were to make Portsmouth their home rather than living elsewhere in Britain. In 1884 the Admiralty had extended the standard term of enlistment to twelve years, which could be extended further, and hence many sailors were extremely experienced, particularly when compared with army recruits, who were enlisted on much shorter terms of service.[13]

The Royal Navy received very few wartime recruits compared to the army. The navy's peacetime role – not least in securing the British Empire by policing the world's oceans – was in many respects as active as its wartime role would be.[14] As a result, for the navy war did not call for the same huge expansion in manpower that the British Army required, apart from the recalling of reservists to fill gaps and man ships re-activated from the reserve fleet. A total of 116 sailors were recalled from the Royal Fleet Reserve, which had been formed in 1901, or

mobilised from the Royal Naval Reserve or the Royal Naval Volunteer Reserve. This suggests that sailors from Portsmouth who retired tended to remain living in the town and that many young men in Portsmouth joined the Royal Naval Reserve or the Royal Naval Volunteer Reserve.

In terms of age, Portsmouth sailors covered an incredibly wide spectrum. The oldest sailor to die was 63 and the youngest were 15. Although many sailors were in their twenties, there were also significant numbers of Portsmouth sailors of an older age. Service in the Royal Navy was a relatively long-term career, and older, longer-serving ratings were probably more likely to settle in Portsmouth. Although many Portsmouth sailors were leading rates, petty officers or warrant officers, the town seems to have been home to relatively few naval officers – fifty-eight – only one of whom was of a rank above commander. It seems that few Portsmouth-born men were able to pursue a career as a naval officer, due to their low social standing and poor income. Aside from Thomas Ellis Owen's Southsea, Portsmouth was evidently not a fashionable place for officers from elsewhere to reside, as proportionally fewer officers from Portsmouth were killed than in the Royal Navy as a whole. For example, the fifty-eight officers from Portsmouth killed represent only 3 per cent of the town's sailors who were killed. By comparison, when HMS *Queen Mary* was sunk at the Battle of Jutland, her fifty-seven officers constituted 4.5 per cent of her crew.[15]

Of the 1,776 Portsmouth sailors killed, an overwhelming majority – 1,434 – were lost at sea and have no known grave, and are remembered on the Portsmouth, Plymouth and Chatham naval memorials. That so many men were lost at sea suggests how dangerous naval service was; when ships were sunk in action, few men survived. However, naval ratings also died of illness and other natural causes whilst they were in uniform. Of the sailors from Portsmouth who died during the First World War, 213 are buried in Portsmouth. The majority of them seem to have died of illness whilst ashore or were serving at shore bases such as HMS *Victory*, the name for the main naval barracks, or HMS *Excellent*, the naval gunnery school on Whale Island.

Although new weapons such as the submarine and the torpedo were used during the First World War, the Royal Navy was still overwhelmingly a big-gun, big-ship force, and the vast majority of sailors were lost when battleships were sunk. The launching of HMS *Dreadnought* in 1906 heralded a new dawn of naval construction and arguably accelerated the pre-war arms race[16]. Battleships were crewed by more than a thousand sailors, and often when they were sunk there were very few survivors. Those who did survive the sinking often found themselves floating at sea hundreds of miles from safety, with little or no hope of salvation.

Once the war began, few major ships used Portsmouth. The Grand Fleet was stationed in the anchorage of Scapa Flow in the Orkneys to guard against the German fleet breaking out into the Atlantic. Anywhere between 60,000 and

100,000 sailors were at Scapa at any one time.[17] Life at Scapa was boring, and as ships were at constant readiness to put to sea, shore leave was rare.[18] The flow of naval ratings between Portsmouth and the Fleet was such that from 1917 onwards a naval special train ran from the town to London's Euston Station to connect with the train to Thurso in Scotland.[19]

Service in the steel-hulled, steam-powered Royal Navy was very much of a manual and technical nature, and stokers and engine room artificers outnumbered seamen ratings.[20] Stoking in particular was gruelling work, and stokers were constantly tired even when off duty.[21] Agnes Weston, the founder of the Royal Sailors' Rest in Commercial Road, probably spent more time with lower-deck naval ratings than anyone else in Britain and was well placed to comment on how the Royal Navy had evolved:

Advertisements by Brickwood's brewery frequently referred to the war and current events. This one which appeared in the *Evening News* on New Year's Day in 1916 reflected the British public's perceptions of the invincibility of the Royal Navy. (*EN*)

The Grand Fleet at sea, seen from the flagship HMS *Iron Duke*. (GWPDA)

> The sailor pure and simple has disappeared with the sails that he used to manage... education has advanced enormously, and has brought many advantages with it, and the clean, smooth-shaven face of the twentieth-century bluejacket has replaced the bearded, jolly, happy-go-lucky face of the man of older type.[22]

The 1870 Education Act had introduced comprehensive education for all, and most First World War sailors would have been far better educated than their Nelsonian predecessors. This improvement in the basic education of even the poorest of sailors was fortunate, for their duties had become much more technical. The manual labourers who had been the heart of the sail navy – hauling on ropes and sails – were outnumbered in the twentieth-century navy by stokers and artificers.

Contemporaries frequently commented on the unique character of the Royal Navy's sailors. Rev. Robert Dolling was surprised by their cheerfulness, and Agnes Weston recollected that 'there is a light side of Jack's life – merry Jack, as he is often called ...'. But Weston also noted that despite the sailor's often brash exterior, 'Jack is proverbially a "shy bird", and is apt to give a very wide berth to any place where he thinks that he will be preached at, or made a teetotaller.'[23]

By October 1917 there were 420,000 men serving in the Royal Navy and the Royal Marines, three quarters of whom were either regular ratings or recalled pensioners.[24] During the First World War 38,515 men were killed serving in the Royal Navy, around 2 per cent of all who served – a relatively tiny figure compared to the losses of the army.[25] However, not only were over 6,000 of these losses sustained in one day at Jutland, but 1,776 of them came from Portsmouth. It is surprising that just over 5 per cent of naval war casualties came from

Portsmouth, especially given the prominence of Portsmouth as a naval town. However, the Portsmouth naval memorial on Southsea Common records the names of around 10,000 Portsmouth-based sailors who were lost at sea during the First World War. This would suggest that many naval casualties who spent time in Portsmouth, lived in the town for a short time or had other links with the area were not officially recorded as 'from Portsmouth'. In any case, there cannot have been many of the 38,505 sailors lost during the course of the war who had not spent significant time in Portsmouth during their service.

The Royal Marines also came under the organisational aegis of the Royal Navy. In 1914 it consisted of two separate corps: the Royal Marine Artillery and the Royal Marine Light Infantry. The Royal Marine Artillery had barracks at Eastney, and the area was dominated by Royal Marines and their families.[26] The Royal Marines almost doubled in size during the war, from 23,662 officers and men in January 1915 to 44,010 in August 1917.[27]

In many respects the grand traditions of the Royal Navy and the high esteem in which it was held by all ranks of society made its task during the First World War virtually impossible. Public opinion longed for another Trafalgar, and for a new Nelson-like figure. In reality, the Royal Navy of 1914 was to fight a different opponent with different weapons in a completely different kind of war.

3

The Armed Forces:
The British Army

For it's Tommy this, an' Tommy that, an' 'Chuck him out, the brute!'
But it's 'Saviour of 'is country' when the guns begin to shoot.

Tommy, Rudyard Kipling

The First World War heralded the first time that Britain fielded a mass citizen army. Faced with very little option but to fight on the continent of Europe, the army recruited millions of men through voluntary enlistment and then conscription. Although there were a number of 'class corps', compared to the Royal Navy, the British Army had an unglamorous reputation, and prior to 1914 soldiering still had something of a stigma attached to it.[1] The Duke of Wellington's comment that his soldiers were the 'scum of the earth' might have been applied to the army of 1914 as much as it was to that of 1815. But equally, the Iron Duke's lesser-known follow-up comment, '… but what fine fellows we have made of them', might also well be applied to the British Army of the First World War.

Traditionally Britain had maintained a much smaller army than other European powers such as Germany and France, as society had resisted the idea of a large standing army. Even during the lengthy Napoleonic Wars she had relied on a powerful Royal Navy and a small volunteer army. Whilst the pre-war French Army could boast 3 million trained men, the British Army, Territorial Force and various reserves amounted to only 733,000.[2] British soldiers were, however, traditionally better trained than their continental counterparts and could boast impressive skills of marksmanship – a legacy of so many imperial campaigns during the latter half of the nineteenth century. The coming of war in 1914 had been preceded by almost a century during which Britain had not been involved in a major continental war and the army had been used almost exclusively in imperial policing, primarily on the Indian sub-continent and in Africa.

However, the British Army had been extensively reorganised in widespread reforms after failings during the Boer War around the turn of the twentieth century.[3] Shortcomings in that campaign led to great reforms in what has often

This appeal for men to join the army appeared in the *Evening News* on 5 August 1914, the day after war was declared. (*EN*)

Your King and Country need you.

Will you answer your Country's Call? Each day is fraught with the gravest possibilities, and at this very moment the Empire is on the brink of the greatest war in the history of the world.

In this crisis your Country calls on all her young unmarried men to rally round the Flag and enlist in the ranks of her Army.

If every patriotic young man answers her call, England and her Empire will emerge stronger and more united than ever.

If you are unmarried and between 18 and 30 years old will you answer your Country's Call? and go to the nearest Recruiter—whose address you can get at any Post Office, and

Join the Army to-day!

been described as a 'dynamic decade'.[4] The small size of the army, combined with the poor condition of many working-class recruits during the Boer War, meant that Britain was traditionally more concerned with the quality of its volunteers than the quantity.[5] It has generally been thought that the British Army contained a lower class of men than the Royal Navy, although they were perhaps not quite as low as the Duke of Wellington's 'scum of the earth' army in 1815, being better educated.

Although Portsmouth is often thought of as being a naval town, the presence of such an important national asset as the dockyard led in turn to a considerable military garrison being based in the town and the surrounding area to guard against attack. A visitor to Portsmouth in 1914 would have observed a sizeable army presence. An infantry brigade was headquartered in Portsmouth, along with two regular infantry battalions. There were also a number of engineer and artillery units, and a sizeable number of territorial units, such as the 4th Battalion of the Hampshire Regiment, whose Connaught Drill Hall was in Stanhope Road. The Royal Artillery also had a sizeable barracks at Hilsea.[6] As a result, Portsmouth represented one of the largest concentrations of army personnel outside of London and the major garrison towns such as Aldershot and Colchester.

The British working classes held a deeply rooted prejudice against military service, particularly compared to the glamour attached to the Royal Navy. Despite this, the overwhelming majority of British soldiers of the First World War were working class in origin.[7] Primarily, recruits to the army were unskilled labourers and mainly from poor urban areas. Although the pay and conditions were poor, this was something that working-class men were used to, and the army did at least provide regular pay and food. There was also an element of security and purpose that civilian life could not always provide.[8] Before the war

it was all but impossible for a working-class man to become an officer, due to the formidable financial obstacles and the social cachet required. Although standards were relaxed during the war due to the demand for officers, relatively few men from Portsmouth were commissioned. The notable exceptions to this trend were old boys of Portsmouth Grammar School and the Southern Grammar School, who with a higher standard of education and wealthy family backgrounds, were prime candidates for commissioning. The low number of officers in Portsmouth was probably due to the comparatively humble social and economic background of the majority of men in the town.

The rapid expansion of the British Army during the First World War had a marked effect on British society.[9] Army casualties were considerable, as the British Army was in constant action virtually from the start of the war in August 1914 until the armistice in November 1918, in particular on the Western Front. During the First World War, 3,244 men from Portsmouth are known to have been killed serving in the British Army; as with most counts of war dead, the true figure is likely to be much higher. A total of 1,917 soldiers from Portsmouth are known to have been killed on the Western Front – 1,331 in France and 586 in Belgium. In the various campaigns in the Mediterranean and the Middle East, 294 men were killed – in Greece (35), Iraq (114), Israel (39) and Turkey (106).

At home in Britain, 293 Portsmouth soldiers died, probably due to the effects of wounds or of natural causes. Despite improvements in military medicine and nursing, far more men became ill during their service than were wounded. A number of other countries were host to significant British Army garrisons, even though they saw little or no fighting. Twenty-four soldiers from Portsmouth died in India, and twenty in Egypt – both strategically important parts of the British Empire. Portsmouth soldiers also died in a number of other countries around the globe that are not usually associated with the First World War, such as Uruguay, Tanzania, Sierra Leone, New Zealand, Latvia, Ireland and Iran.

By far the largest contingent of Portsmouth soldiers were killed serving in the infantry. In particular, a significant number of men – 908 – were killed fighting with the Hampshire Regiment. After the Cardwell reforms of the late nineteenth century, recruiting into the army, and in particular the infantry, was on a local basis, in order to foster stronger bonds with communities and loyalties between men. But Portsmouth men did, for a variety of reasons, join other regiments, including county regiments with which they might be thought to have little or no connection. The Rifle Brigade and the King's Royal Rifle Corps included ninety-eight Portsmouth men between them, perhaps because their headquarters were nearby at Winchester. Thirty-one men from Portsmouth died serving with the various foot guard regiments.

However, the demands of industrial, static warfare meant that more men actually served in supporting arms than in the 'teeth'. Whilst in 1914 the ratio of

'tail to teeth' was roughly one to one, by 1918 it was three to one, an indication of how the technological nature of warfare had evolved even in that short space of time.[10] This ratio was reflected in the number of losses among Portsmouth soldiers. A large number of gunners were killed serving with the Royal Field Artillery, the Royal Garrison Artillery and the Royal Horse Artillery – 309 men in all. A total of 155 Royal Engineers were killed, and also men in other services that often found themselves under fire, such as the Army Service Corps (50) and the Royal Army Medical Corps (41). The First World War was arguably the first 'industrial' war in history, and as a result of technological innovations, various new weapons were introduced. Fifty-five men died with the Machine Gun Corps, and twelve men in tanks. The Royal Flying Corps was also formed from the Air Battalion of the Royal Engineers.

By comparison with infantry losses, very few Portsmouth men were killed serving with cavalry units – only thirty-one men. Whilst there were cavalry units on the Western Front, trench warfare was not an ideal landscape for cavalry charges, and they spent much of the war awaiting a breakthrough to exploit. Some cavalry troopers fought on foot in the trenches. Cavalry also fought in other campaigns, in particular in Palestine.

Although major battles tend to capture the imagination, statistics suggest that the majority of men – an average of 634 per day – were killed in routine trench warfare, as part of what the high command euphemistically referred to as 'wastage'.[11] Major offensives were certainly the exception rather than the rule.[12] Units did not spend all of their time in the front line, but alternated between reserve, support and the front-line trenches. Spells of more than seven days in the front line were unusual, four days being more the norm. Apart from when major offensives took place, life in the front lines could be dull, particularly on quiet sectors.[13] Longer periods could be spent out of the trenches training or

Men of the Hampshire Regiment on the march somewhere in France or Belgium. The wagons in the foreground are carrying cookers. (Gates)

recovering after arduous operations. However, even time spent out of the trenches was not necessarily spent in rest, as work parties were common.[14] Divisions were frequently rotated between different sectors, often being sent to quiet areas to recover after heavy losses in a major offensive. Quiet sectors such as Ploesteeert could be relatively safe, even comfortable, for their inhabitants, sometimes to the point of boredom.[15] One historian has estimated that on average less than half of all tours in the front-line trenches could be regarded as active, and that for some battalions this figure was as low as 10 per cent.[16]

Men did not just die in battle, but through a number of other causes. Illness was a particular problem in the often unhealthy conditions of trench warfare. The military historian Richard Holmes estimated that for every man who was wounded on the Western Front, 1.3 men were admitted to hospital sick.[17] Men died of a variety of illnesses, such as influenza, heatstroke, pneumonia, meningitis, empyema and the effects of being gassed. In more tropical theatres, dysentery, malaria and typhoid were common. Many men died of wounds after being evacuated home – explaining why so many are buried in Portsmouth cemeteries – and some died years after they had been demobilised. Men also suffered from shell shock. With so many men in uniform, it is possible that some may have died from natural causes or illnesses that may not have been caused by the war. Accidents were also common in wartime, and Portsmouth men were killed by horses, when grenades exploded accidentally, or were drowned whilst swimming.

The soldier of 1918 in many respects was more akin to an industrial worker. He carried 61lb of equipment,[18] and although long journeys were made by rail, marching was an occupational inevitability. Marches of 15 miles in a day were not uncommon.[19] Rest billets frequently consisted of rudimentary bivouacs or farm buildings. It could be argued, however, that most working-class men were well used to hardship, physical labour, long hours and trying conditions.[20]

It is hard to draw general conclusions about the kind of men who served in the front line. It is tempting to regard all soldiers as being brave, but the majority of soldiers were simply keen to see out the war and avoid death or serious injury. A minority sought glory and rewards, but such individuals were rare and frowned upon by their comrades. The constraints of human endurance meant that men could not be brave constantly even if they wished to be. The number of cases of shell shock during the war inspired research that suggested that men had a finite reserve of courage and that this reserve could be used up without timely rests and careful supervision.[21]

Those who served on the front line tended to resent those who served further back, in particular staff officers. In an environment where small groups of men lived closely together, primary group loyalties could easily form. Comradeship was a key motivation for many men to keep fighting. The British Army has always been unique in that it consists of a loose band of 'tribes', in the form of regiments,

hence the loyalty of most men in the army was to their regiment first and the army second.[22]

The famous Christmas Truce of 1914 is the best-known example of how men who were ostensibly on opposing sides could arrange an informal truce, unsanctioned by higher command, which would provide a brief respite from danger. The 1st Battalion of the Hampshire Regiment was in the front line on 25 December 1914 and engaged in a truce with the 133rd Saxons until the New Year.[23] On quieter sectors throughout the war, troops frequently engaged in a 'live-and-let-live' policy, with each side tacitly agreeing to refrain from causing what they perceived to be unnecessary violence. Such a policy was not condoned by higher commanders. From 1916 onwards, headquarters ordered battalions to carry out raids on the enemy lines, in the belief that this would inculcate in them an offensive spirit. Nevertheless, there is much evidence that few British soldiers were aggressive all of the time, with cold-blooded hatred of the enemy being unpopular. Indeed, many soldiers on both sides realised that the common enemy was trench warfare and the conditions it entailed.[24]

Richard Holmes has suggested that the majority of pre-war regular soldiers were unemployed when they enlisted.[25] Many were escaping hardship, difficult social situations, and a very few were looking for adventure or were attracted by the uniform. Once the war began, the social composition of the British Army widened greatly. Men enlisted to fight from all sections of society, many of whom might previously have been hesitant about entering military service.[26] Discipline in the army could be harsh, but given the extreme conditions it had to be. However, no Portsmouth men were among the 346 men executed during the First World War.[27] Despite the broadening of the social make-up of the army, officers were far more likely to become casualties than other ranks. 15.2 per cent of all officers who served in the British Army were killed in action, compared to 12.8 per cent of other ranks.[28] Lieutenants and second lieutenants, the junior leaders of the army, had the most dangerous jobs on the Western Front.[29]

The participation of more people and a broader section of society changed widespread perceptions about the army and military service. For the first time since the Napoleonic Wars, large numbers of soldiers in uniform were visible throughout Britain, although the people of Portsmouth were probably more used to this sight than most other towns.[30] When Britain went to war again in 1939, the young men of Portsmouth were well aware of the experiences of their fathers a generation earlier.

4

A Man of Three Armies: Lieutenant Colonel Dick Worrall DSO and Bar, MC and Bar

Not many soldiers throughout history have served in two armies. Even fewer have served in three. But one First World War soldier from Portsmouth did just that and had one of the most remarkable careers in military history in the process.

Richard Worrall was born in Woolwich on 8 July 1890.[1] He joined the Hampshire and Isle of Wight Royal Garrison Artillery Militia on 3 September 1906. He was aged 17 years and 11 months and was an unapprenticed domestic servant to a Mr Williams. At the time of his attestation he resided in St Thomas parish, Portsmouth. He was 5ft 5¼in tall and weighed 107lb. He had a fair complexion, grey eyes and brown hair. Interestingly, he bore two tattoos – clasped hands on his right wrist and a girl's head on his left wrist.[2]

Intriguingly, Worrall only served for just over a month with the Hampshire and Isle of Wight Garrison Artillery; on 24 October 1906 he enlisted as a regular soldier with the Dorsetshire Regiment. We can only presume that he had joined the militia to wait until he was able to join the regular army. Dick Worrall served a total of eight years with the Dorsetshire Regiment. However, he does not seem to have served out the usual term of engagement, as at some point he emigrated to the United States of America. Although he later claimed that he had been working as a steward, it is thought that he had served in the United States Army.[3]

However, with the outbreak of war Worrall answered the call of his homeland and decided to travel to Canada to join up. As a Dominion, in 1914 Canada was automatically at war with Germany.[4] Undeterred by the fact that he was a member of the United States Army, he simply deserted by jumping off a train. On 21 September 1914 Dick Worrall enlisted with the Canadian Army; he was 24 and unmarried. In the years since he had joined the British Army he had grown to 5ft 10in tall. By now both arms were extensively tattooed, and he also had a tattoo on his right leg. His next of kin was a Mr Pennel, of Glenholme, Green Road, Southsea.[5]

The pre-war Canadian Army was tiny, numbering a total of 3,110 men of all ranks. Given that Canada had committed to send an expeditionary force to aid the mother country, rapid expansion was needed, and experienced soldiers such as Worrall were welcomed with open arms.[6] Worrall was posted to the 14th Battalion of the Canadian Infantry, a battalion of the Royal Montreal Regiment. Apparently, Worrall had simply walked into the regimental armoury and joined the battalion via the Canadian Grenadier Guards, who had provided a contingent to serve with the 14th Battalion.[7] As an ex-regular soldier among volunteers, Worrall's experience was recognised and he was quickly promoted to sergeant.

The battalion gathered at Valcartier near Quebec, along with the many other new recruits to the Canadian Army.[8] The battalion left Canada on 25 August 1914 and arrived in England on 14 October 1914; they were among the first Canadians, or indeed the first men of any imperial contingents, to land in Britain since the start of the war.[9] As Worrall had only joined the Canadian Army in September, it seems likely that he arrived in England later. Nevertheless, it must have been a strange homecoming for a man born in Britain, who had emigrated and was now wearing yet another different uniform. The battalion was based on Salisbury Plain over the winter of 1914, before finally embarking for France from Bristol on 12 February 1915. Landing at St Nazaire in Brittany, the 14th Battalion first entered the front line on the Western Front on 3 March 1915, in the Fleurbaix sector, near Neuve Chapelle.

The Canadians were held in reserve during the battle of Neuve Chapelle in order to reinforce any breakthrough, but were not called upon.[10] In April 1915 the battalion were in the front line between Langemarck and St Julien, in the north of the Ypres Salient. On 22 April there was a violent attack on the Canadian sector, on the battalion's immediate left flank. French colonial troops in the vicinity were shelled with gas, and after they broke and retreated, the Canadians were sent to fill the dangerous gap that had opened up.[11] Over the next few days the 14th Battalion was attacked repeatedly, coming under incredible pressure as they defended St Julien. The 3rd Brigade suffered a total of 1,500 casualties. To give some kind of impression of the intensity of the fighting, the 14th Battalion's Medical Officer, Captain Francis Scrimger, was awarded the Victoria Cross for treating then evacuating wounded men under shellfire and shielding a wounded officer with his own body.[12] The Canadians had suffered many casualties, but in the opinion of the official historian they had saved the situation.[13]

Dick Worrall had obviously distinguished himself in action, as on 12 May 1915 it was announced that he was being granted a commission as a lieutenant.[14] By the end of the war, although the British Army was commissioning men from the ranks, the Dominions were far more open to promoting men from non-traditional officer backgrounds. It is doubtful whether Worrall would have been commissioned in the British Army in 1915.[15]

The 14th Battalion was involved in the Battle of Festubert on 15 May 1915, being attached to the British 7th Division as a reserve. The battalion made a frontal attack across waterlogged fields devoid of cover. On 18 May the battalion attacked again, this time targeting what would become known as 'Canadian Orchard' and suffering heavy casualties from machine-gun fire.[16] Much of the summer of 1915 was spent in the front line around Ypres and Ploegsteert, a quiet sector often used for blooding newer units. On 24 August Worrall was awarded the Russian Cross of St George (4th Class).[17] Foreign medals were often used to reward deserving men who had not, for whatever reason, received a British decoration.[18] The winter was also relatively quiet, with the battalion serving in the front line in the Ypres and Ploegsteert sectors, particularly around Hill 63.

On 2 June 1916 the Germans launched an attack on Mount Sorrell. The battalion was moving up to reinforce the front line when it was bombarded heavily by German artillery. During a counter-attack on 3 June 1916, south of the Maple Copse towards Sanctuary Wood, every officer was killed, wounded, or buried by shell blasts. Worrall, recently promoted to captain, was among the wounded. He was evidently seriously wounded, as he was away from duty for almost four months.[19] Despite these heavy casualties, the battalion failed to drive the Germans from Mount Sorrell.[20]

Whilst Worrall was away, the battalion remained in the line around Ypres during July and early August 1916, maintaining what the official history referred to as a 'stationary but aggressive' policy.[21] Although some parts of the front line were regarded as quiet sector and some units were content to let things go quiet, the Canadians in particular seem to have kept up an aggressive approach and indeed pioneered raiding across no-man's-land.[22] On 13 August the battalion moved to St Omer, to begin training in preparation for a move south to the Somme. The 14th Canadians arrived on the Somme in early September, going into the front line near Mouquet Farm, north of Pozières, on 6 September.

The battalion took part in the offensive at Flers-Courcelette, again suffering heavy losses. More losses were incurred at the Battle of Thiepval Ridge on 26 September when the battalion attacked Sudbury and Kenora Trenches. After forty hours of continuous fighting, the battalion was down to only seventy-five men.[23] Worrall – now a major – rejoined as a reinforcement on 30 September, and no doubt his return was welcomed given his experience. Due to the heavy losses it had incurred, the 14th Battalion was not in the front line with the rest of the Canadian Corps when it fought in the Battle of the Ancre Heights on 1 October. By 17 October the battalion was in a quiet sector of the front line near Lens.

In November the battalion was serving in the Carency sector, north of Arras, and amidst what was a relatively quiet period played an important role when the 176th Tunnelling Company exploded a mine on 27 November 1916. Worrall was given the task of commanding two parties who would lay barbed wire

along the flanks of the crater. The mine was exploded successfully and the crater consolidated. Worrall earned high praise in the report of the operation, being recommended specifically for an award for his 'untiring support'. However, there is no evidence to suggest that he was rewarded for this action.

The end of the year was seen out relatively quietly, with spells in the line interspersed with training. For example, on 6 December Worrall gave a lecture to the non-commissioned officers of the battalion on discipline – fitting given that he was an ex-NCO himself. After the heavy losses suffered at Ypres and the Somme in 1916, the battalion received a large reinforcement of 452 men during December 1916. Worrall was awarded a Military Cross in the 1917 New Year's Honours List; sadly the *London Gazette* contains no citation for this award.[24]

Just as Gallipoli has become iconic for Australians, Vimy Ridge has attained an almost mythical status in Canadian history.[25] A nine-mile-long high feature, it dominated a considerable part of the Western Front. It was therefore important to drive the Germans from the ridge to provide a secure base for the launching of the Battle of Arras. The Battle for Vimy Ridge began on 9 April 1917, and the 14th Battalion were in the first wave of attacks south of Thelus. They saw vicious hand-to-hand fighting across difficult terrain but, in one of the most successful set-piece attacks of the war so far, the Canadians successfully took and held the ridge, suffering relatively light losses for what was a difficult operation against a prepared position.[26]

On 1 June 1917 Worrall was detached from the battalion and remained at the 1st Canadian Divisional School near Ferfay in order to train a large draft of reinforcements destined for the battalion. Whilst the battalion remained in the front line near Vimy, the reinforcements began to arrive in mid-June. Worrall does not seem to have been with his battalion for several months after this point.

In August 1917 the Canadians took part in more operations during the Battle of Arras. On 14 August Hill 70 was taken, and on 24 August the 14th Battalion was in reserve when the Canadian Corps captured high ground north of Lens. Worrall rejoined the battalion as acting commanding officer in October 1917, in the absence of Lieutenant Colonel Gault McCombe. He was in time to command during the key battle of Passchendaele, the climax of the Third Battle of Ypres. Although the benefit of hindsight suggests that the Third Battle of Ypres had run

Lieutenant Colonel Dick Worrall
(Author)

out of momentum by October, the battle for Passchendaele would assume great national importance for Canada. The 14th Battalion were not involved in the first phase of the battle on 26 October, but were involved in the second phase of attacks on 6 November 1917, which finally captured the village of Passchendaele.

Worrall wrote glowingly of the performance of the battalion during this period:

> I cannot speak too highly of the splendid spirits of all ranks throughout the operations. The Battalion lived under very adverse conditions and often without adequate shelter, and absolute cheerfulness and confidence in their being able to do even more than what was expected of them was the keynote throughout.

Worrall evidently left the battalion again during the winter, as in January it was being commanded by Major Powell before Lieutenant Colonel McCombe returned at the end of February 1918.

Worrall was commanding the reinforcement depot from February 1918, with the rank of acting lieutenant colonel.[27] As such, he was away from the 14th Battalion when the Germans launched their major 'Kaiser Offensive' on 22 March 1918. The battalion was moved up to the front line near Arras. During this period the battalion was under one hour's notice to move to reinforce the line. The Canadians, having gained a fierce reputation, were evidently being held in reserve in order to counter any German breakthrough.

Whilst the battalion was in reserve at Aubrey on 21 April 1918, its headquarters was heavily shelled. The commanding officer, Lieutenant Colonel McCombe, was seriously wounded; the second in command Major Powell was killed, as was the Adjutant Major Plow. Major Worrall was recalled to take charge of the battalion at a critical time. For a man who had joined the unit as a private and fought with it throughout the war in France and Belgium, the destiny of the situation surely cannot have escaped him.

Worrall quickly took charge of the battalion. Within days of his taking over, the rear details had been organised into an ad hoc unit ready to fight in the event of a German breakthrough. For his work in command of the battalion in the spring of 1918 Worrall was awarded a bar to his Military Cross, announced in the *London Gazette* on 18 July 1918:

> He moved about on open ground between his companies reconnoitring the position under heavy fire, and obtained information which was of the greatest value in the subsequent operations. His resolute and courageous conduct and splendid leadership were an inspiration to his battalion.[28]

However, the battalion was held back from the front line and underwent extensive training during May and June 1918. In June 1918 the battalion witnessed an

outbreak of influenza, but this did not hamper preparations for the role that the battalion, and the Canadian Corps as a whole, would have in the planned British offensive once the German attack had petered out. On 7 July Worrall was thrown from his horse while practising for a gymkhana. He was taken to hospital, where it was found that he had fractured his collarbone. Not to be deterred, he was back commanding the battalion by 20 July 1918.

By 1918 the Canadians were regarded as the storm troopers of the BEF and were destined for a prominent part in the coming battles.[29] The 1st Canadian Division – of which the 14th Battalion was a part – was by 1918 regarded as an elite unit, and was clearly being kept in reserve.[30] In early August, the battalion went up to the front line, assembling at Villers-Bretonneux near Amiens on 6 August. By this time in the war, the Canadians had such a formidable reputation among the Germans that an elaborate plan of deception was put in place to suggest that they were elsewhere on the Western Front.[31]

The battalion attacked at dawn on 8 August, shrouded in dense mist. At first the Germans put up very little resistance, but as the advance progressed their machine guns near Morgemont Wood and Tittle Copse sprang into action and inflicted many casualties; five officers were killed and four wounded. The Germans' first trench system was captured and consolidated, and the Canadians advanced beyond to capture the Germans' rear area. The battalion captured no fewer than ten field guns, forty-six machine guns and eight trench mortars – a remarkable achievement.

For his leadership during the attack on 8 August 1918, Worrall was awarded the Distinguished Service Order:

> Under difficulty of mist he personally led and directed his battalion in the attack and capture of the front line system of enemy positions, including the guns. He displayed great skill and courage in directing the operations on this and other occasions during which the battalion had lost 23 officer casualties.[32]

General Ludendorff would later regard 8 August 1918 as the 'black day' of the German Army, and the 14th Battalion, under Dick Worrall's leadership, had played a prominent part in it.

Twenty-three officer casualties had occurred in a short space of time, and represented almost a 100 per cent loss rate of officers. Commanding a battalion when it had lost so many of its officers must have seriously tested Worrall's leadership and speaks volumes about both him and the men under his command.

The next day, the battalion supported an attack by the 6th Canadian Battalion, beginning at 1.00 p.m. There was a heavy enemy barrage, and once again heavy casualties occurred. Although the objective was reached, the enemy threatened to counter-attack from Fouquescourt. Worrall, going forward and finding men of several battalions, quickly took command and organised them in defence.

The enemy attack was repulsed. One officer was killed, another died of his wounds and ten more were wounded. The fighting was so bitter that at one point Worrall took matters into his own hands and 'requisitioned' two horses from a major commanding a whippet tank detachment. One of the horses ran away when its rider was wounded, causing the tank major 'some inconvenience and considerable annoyance'.

After the battalion was relieved and went back from the front line, two more officers were killed on 11 August 1918 by a German artillery shell. However, the assaults spearheaded by the Canadians had been successful; on 16 August the Germans in front of them began to retire. Given the serious losses that it had experienced, no doubt the battalion was grateful to receive a large draft of reinforcements. The war diary records that whilst on a march, 'Some of the new draft showed a disposition to whine but the Commanding Officer soon cured them of that.'

Between 8 and 20 August the Canadian Corps had penetrated up to 14 miles, a remarkable achievement given the static nature of trench warfare for the past four years of the war.

On 20 August 1918, Worrall, whilst still a temporary major, was promoted to acting lieutenant colonel.[33] The battalion was in action again very soon after this. On 1 September the 3rd Canadian Brigade attacked the Drocourt-Quéant Line. Attacking at 4.50 a.m., the assault was completely successful, with between 200 and 300 prisoners being taken. The next day the battalion attacked again, this time targeting the Buissy Switch trench. Losses were again heavy; 250 men were killed, wounded or missing.

For his leadership during the attack on 1 September Worrall was again decorated:

He advanced his line half a mile, and under heavy fire maintained his position all day. The following day, though his left was exposed to withering machine-gun and artillery fire, he captured a village, taking prisoner a whole battalion. Still pushing on, he took the final objective, and established his position, having advanced some 5,000 yards from the jumping off line. He displayed fine courage and leadership.[34]

Worrall was awarded a bar to his Distinguished Service Order, just weeks after he had earned the DSO itself, this time for his leadership in the attack on the Drocourt-Quéant Line.

After such grievous losses the battalion was in no state to take part in further attacks and went back from the front line. Reorganisation was difficult due to the lack of officers and NCOs. On 8 September, Worrall departed on some well-earned leave. Whilst he was away the battalion was launched into yet another attack, this time on the Canal du Nord. Even without boats, the canal was crossed at 5.45 p.m. The second-in-command was wounded, and Worrall once again rushed back to resume command.

After reorganisation, the battalion attacked once more, near Cambrai on 1 October 1918. In heavy rain and cold, and without the usual rum issue that was customary in such inclement weather, the battalion attacked towards Bantigny. By 7.30 p.m. the town was taken. However, soon after, a German aeroplane flew over and the enemy artillery opened up. Machine-gunners filtered through on the flanks and a counter-attack was launched. Without support on either side, Worrall decided to withdraw rather than be surrounded and cut off in the town. At one point he sent two runners back to pass a message to brigade, but both were killed. Undeterred by this, Worrall eventually went back with the message himself – and got through safely. By the end of the day losses had stretched the battalion; having started the day with thirteen officers, it ended it with just nine. There was no regimental sergeant major and no company sergeant majors, and in two cases NCOs ended up commanding companies. Few commanding officers can have been so sorely tested yet prevailed so splendidly.

After fighting almost constantly from early August until October 1918, the battalion was taken out of the front line, and were at Fernain in training when the Armistice was signed on 11 November 1918. The Canadians had played a prominent role in the Hundred Days Offensive, and Dick Worrall had been in the thick of the fighting.[35] The next month Worrall had the honour of leading his battalion into Germany, crossing the border on 7 December 1918. On 13 December, the Canadians crossed the Rhine in Cologne. Worrall received one more award, with a mention in Field Marshal Haig's final despatch in December 1918.[36]

Having served in the occupation of Cologne, the 14th Battalion returned to Britain in March 1919. On 27 March, Worrall attended an investiture at Buckingham Palace, where he was presented with his two Distinguished Service Orders by King George V. The battalion finally sailed for home to Canada in April 1919. Worrall's return in particular was heralded in a triumphant tone, with his career being described by the *Montreal Gazette* as one that 'will stand as an inspiration in the Canadian Army'.[37] Large crowds assembled at Halifax to greet the 14th Battalion, which was the second battalion to return to Canada from Europe.[38]

Sadly, Dick Worrall died of influenza in Montreal on 15 February 1920.[39] He was 29. He was buried at Mount Royal cemetery in Montreal with full military honours, with a firing party present and his coffin being borne on a gun carriage. His funeral was reported prominently in the local press in Canada.

A remarkable man, Worrall had served at Second Ypres, Mount Sorrel, on the Somme, at Vimy Ridge and Arras; at Passchendaele, and during the German and Allied offensives of 1918. He had defied the odds by surviving so long as an officer, and by 1918 there were very few men alive on the Western Front who had been fighting since 1915. An extensively tattooed Colonel, who had served in three armies, Dick Worrall certainly was a unique character.

5

The Portsmouth Pals Battalions

Upon the outbreak of war, recruiting offices in Portsmouth were overwhelmed with volunteers, and along with most areas the town experienced a peak of recruiting in early September 1914.[1] The usual peacetime structures for recruiting were unsurprisingly swamped by the masses of men eager to volunteer.[2] Early recruits were often motivated by propaganda and a significant amount of peer pressure, but also in some cases a desire to escape dreary or unpleasant lives, to see the world, or to escape troubles. And, crucially, volunteers could choose which unit they wished to join.[3] Despite the deluge of enthusiastic volunteers, the War Office was experiencing significant problems in coping with the influx of men, as the usual apparatus for accepting recruits was already hopelessly inadequate. As a result, the War Office actively encouraged local areas to recruit their own battalions and essentially manage the recruitment process. In the words of one historian, the forming of many of these units was 'effectively privatised'.[4] These units have been immortalised in British history as the Pals Battalions, and have become one of the most poignant aspects of the culture of the First World War.

Although the Pals Battalions were initially inspired by the individual efforts of men such as Lord Derby in Liverpool, the concept was warmly embraced by the Secretary of State for War, Lord Kitchener – the Empire's most famous soldier in 1914 – who had a low opinion of the Territorial Force and had opposed its creation in 1908.[5] And, almost uniquely amongst politicians and generals alike, he also foresaw a long and costly war, in which Britain's military manpower would have to expand exponentially.[6] As a result, Kitchener sought to bypass the Territorial Force entirely with the expansion of the army in mind, and the raising of local units by local areas gave rise to the term Kitchener's 'New Army'.[7]

Although it is generally thought that the Pals Battalions were recruited in the early days of August 1914, the first such units were not formed until later the same month[8]. Even before then, leading figures in Portsmouth had attempted to encourage would-be volunteers. A Portsmouth Citizens Patriotic Recruiting Committee had already been formed on 21 August, and a recruiting march was held on 29 August, beginning and ending at the town hall and with Boy Scouts distributing leaflets along the route.[9] However, the efforts of other towns

and cities in recruiting their own battalions, combined with a strong feeling of civic pride, no doubt inspired Portsmouth's town fathers to do the same.[10] The formation of a Portsmouth Battalion was announced in the *Evening News* on 31 August, even before the mayor had written to Lord Kitchener offering to raise such a unit.[11]

The following day, the mayor received a reply from Lord Kitchener thanking the town for its efforts in raising a Portsmouth Battalion.[12] Four honorary recruiting officers were appointed, assisted by lady volunteers. Recruits were presented with a special badge, presumably to indicate to onlookers that although they might not have been wearing uniform, they had in fact joined up.[13] On 3 September a mass meeting was held in the Town Hall, attended by Admiral Lord Beresford, one of the town's MPs, and was addressed by representatives of all religious denominations.[14] Such meetings were common throughout Britain. They were frequently attended by a range of other prominent figures as 'cheerleaders' and employed many other techniques aimed at exerting emotional leverage.[15] The meeting was so well attended that a subsidiary meeting had to be held on the town hall steps.[16] From the next day, the *Evening News*, perhaps as an indicator of the town's contribution to the war effort and to encourage other volunteers, began to feature a running total of the recruits for the battalion on the front page of each edition.[17] By 5 September almost 200 men had been recruited in less than a week.[18] Recruiting also took place at Fratton Park, and recruits were also sought outside the town's boundaries in places such as Portchester and Petersfield. Eventually a recruiting area was established covering the area from Emsworth to Warash and extending as far north as Liphook.[19] On 7 September the *Evening News* featured a list of the first batch of recruits. Letters published in the *News* suggested that a company of Corporation employees could be formed and others composed of teachers and athletes, but these ideas were not taken further.[20] By the end of September, the town had recruited 617 men for its battalion in less than a month.[21]

Although some at the time suggested that recruiting for the battalion was difficult due to Portsmouth's naval heritage, this may have been cunningly exaggerated to encourage hesitant recruits. A letter to the *Evening News* on 10 September 1914 wondered where the expected men were to come from, given the number of young men serving in the navy and the dockyard.[22] In any event, for a naval town like Portsmouth, where many young men of military age were already serving with the Royal Navy and in the dockyard, even to attempt to form a Pals Battalion was a significant achievement.[23] In the event, the town managed to exceed even this feat.

As towns were left pretty much to their own devices in forming their battalions, the appointment of officers was often left to the mayor or a committee of local figures. This was not necessarily viewed as an onerous duty, but a function of

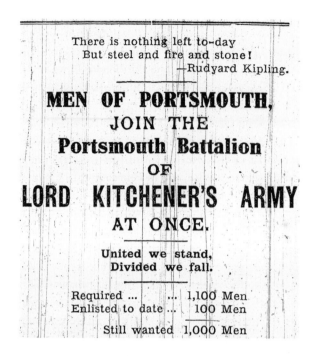

There is nothing left to-day
But steel and fire and stone!
—Rudyard Kipling.

MEN OF PORTSMOUTH,
JOIN THE
Portsmouth Battalion
OF
LORD KITCHENER'S ARMY
AT ONCE.

United we stand,
Divided we fall.

Required ...   ... 1,100 Men
Enlisted to date ...   100 Men

Still wanted 1,000 Men

An appeal for men to join the Portsmouth Battalion, published on the front page of the *Evening News* in September 1914. Such adverts appeared in the news regularly in 1914 and 1915, often showing a running total of recruits. (*EN*)

civic pride.[24] Expenditure in raising the battalions was initially borne by the town, but then refunded by the War Office once the unit was accepted into the army.[25] The sons of prominent citizens were prime candidates for commissions and many officers were simply recommended by the mayor, but many retired officers were also recalled to duty.[26] Many commanding officers were what were referred to as 'dug-outs', older officers who had retired some years before.[27] The first commanding officer, Colonel C.E. Ramsbottom-Isherwood, formerly of the York and Lancaster Regiment, was named on 15 September, along with Captain H.S. Orpen, formerly of the 3rd Royal Dublin Fusiliers, and Lieutenant G.M. Finaly, formerly of the Leinster Regiment.[28]

Clothing, equipping and training the hundreds of new recruits posed significant problems. With hundreds of thousands of men flocking to the colours, the War Office's peacetime stocks were rapidly depleted. There were few reserves of weapons, and many Pals units had to train with obsolete or even dummy rifles.[29] With barracks full, improvised camps sprung up all over Portsmouth, and ever-increasing companies of men could be seen drilling on Southsea Common.[30] Given the lack of accommodation, the War Office specifically requested that the town house the Battalion's recruits, and source clothing locally.[31] With so many men in uniform it is not surprising that some died of natural causes before they even left Britain. Private H.L. Hollick, of Asylum Road in Milton, volunteered in January 1915. However he was found to be medically unfit, and was discharged. He died on 3 March 1915 and is buried in Portsmouth.

With so many men to train and equip, it took some time for all of the Pals Battalions to reach the front, and the Portsmouth Battalions were among the last of Kitchener's Army to depart on active service.[32] The 14th Hampshires, as the 1st Portsmouth Battalion was now known, left Portsmouth on 15 April 1915 to much fanfare and watched by large crowds, marching from Southsea Common through Town Hall Square to the train station.[33] At Witley, in north Hampshire, the battalion joined the 39th Infantry Division. Before the Pals Battalions left for the Western Front, it was found that many of the older officers who had come out of retirement were not fit for active service, and in February 1916 Colonel Ramsbottom-Isherwood was replaced by Colonel Hickie.[34]

Lord Kitchener was reportedly so pleased with reports from the 1st Portsmouth Battalion that through Lord Beresford he requested that the town form another battalion. Recruiting for a 2nd Portsmouth Battalion began almost immediately, on 26 April 1915, and progressed even more swiftly than for the first. By September 1915, 1,100 men had been recruited, and command of the battalion was given to Major H.P.C. Farrell, a former cavalry officer who had fought in Burma in the 1880s.[35] The 15th Hampshires, as the 2nd Portsmouth Battalion became, left Portsmouth on 20 October for a camp at Witley.

The 15th Hampshires left Portsmouth for Aldershot on 20 October 1915. The battalion formed on Southsea Common and marched to Town Hall Square, where they were cheered off to the town station by a large crowd. The *Evening News* described the occasion somewhat ominously: 'Au revoir, we hope it will not be goodbye, although we fear such must be the case.'[36]

When the battalion left Portsmouth, a large proportion of men were in their thirties and forties, and 59 per cent were married. Although it has often been thought that the Pals Battalions were comprised of working-class men, the battalion included three probationary clergymen, four university graduates, and an officer who was a doctor of music. The Commanding Officer was Lieutenant Colonel Malone, formerly of the 1st Worcestershire Regiment. Colonel O'Farrell was transferred to command the 3rd Battalion that had been formed in order to provide reinforcements for the other two battalions.[37]

Even before the 2nd Battalion had left Portsmouth, recruiting began for a 3rd Battalion. The 16th Hampshires, as the 3rd Battalion became, did not leave Britain and provided reinforcements for the other two battalions on active service. In just over twelve months Portsmouth had recruited three battalions of 1,100 men each, a remarkable achievement for a town with so many men already serving, particularly in the Royal Navy and the dockyard. For the town's efforts the mayor, John Corke, was knighted.[38]

The Portsmouth Battalions were among the last of the Kitchener Battalions to be sent to the front, having been attached to relatively late-formed divisions.[39] After completing their training, the 14th Hampshires landed at Le Havre on

6 March 1916. As with most battalions new to the front, the officers and NCOs were attached to more experienced units in the front line, in order to gain experience. After moving up to the Western Front, the 14th Battalion first went into the front line near Fleurbaix, a quiet sector, on 20 March. The battalion suffered relatively few losses over the next few months being in quiet sectors. The first casualty among the men from Portsmouth did not occur until 16 April 1916, when Private E.A. Ayland, aged 34 and from Charlton Street in Landport, was killed. He is buried in the Guards cemetery in Cuinchy. On 28 May, Company Quartermaster Sergeant Percival Graham, who was acting as Company Sergeant-Major, was buried by lumps of earth that fell on him after the Germans exploded a mine whilst the battalion was in reserve near Lille. He was 34, and is buried in Cambrin cemetery. The next day Privates Frederick Webber, A. Vallor and James Channing, all from Portsmouth, were killed by a trench mortar whilst working in a communications trench. All three are also buried in Cambrin cemetery. Although losses were not excessive, reinforcements joined the battalion throughout this period, with a draft of fifty-seven men arriving from the 16th Battalion on 30 April.[40] On 1 June a draft of twenty-six men arrived, most of them old soldiers, including men from the 1st and 2nd Battalions.

The 15th Hampshires, now commanded by Lieutenant Colonel Cary-Barnard, landed in France on 2 May 1916. They were among the last of the Pals Battalions to embark for service abroad.[41] After disembarking at Le Havre, the Battalion entrained for the Western Front, finally reaching their billets at La Crèche on 9 May. From 12 May ten officers and forty NCOs spent two days with the 11th Royal Scots in the front line. The prospect of active service evidently weighed heavily on the minds of some men, for whilst waiting to go into the front line one private sadly committed suicide. The subsequent court of inquiry later found that he was temporarily insane.[42]

The 15th Hampshires finally went into the front line on 30 May, at Ploegsteert Wood – a relatively quiet sector often used to 'blood' new arrivals before they were sent to more active parts of the front. The Battalion's first casualty was suffered on the same day; whilst their first spell in the front line was relatively quiet, on 1 June the battalion headquarters at Rifle House was shelled by the enemy, with the loss of one man, and six men being wounded. Thus Private Andrew Baillie, 20 and from Lynn Road in Buckland, was the first Portsmouth man from the 15th Battalion to be killed in action. He is buried at Rifle House cemetery.

The 15th Battalion spent June 1916 serving around the Ploegsteert sector, alternating tours in the front-line trenches with spells further back in billets.[43] Casualties were very light during this period. However several Portsmouth men were killed during a stretch in the front line towards the end of June, when artillery fire was very active on both sides: Private William Stephenson, aged 17 and from Twyford Avenue in Stamshaw, and Private Leonard Marshall, aged 19

SEPTEMBER 7, 1914

Left column

the Admiralty warned
...ect incidents of this
...hat steps were being
...m to a minimum.

unhappily, already in-
...cruisers with about
...and quite a large num-
...iant vessels and fishing
lish method of conduct-
ng the country to high
nation, and the Admi-
opinion in this respect
intention of adopting
...sures for dealing with
...all shore lights may
ll buoys removed, so
...have no guidance from
...e followed up by treat-
who are caught in this

...es have been rendered
...uining calamities, and
...nation goes forth to
...red loss. They enable
...y to realise the risks
by the brave fellows
...us and invasion,
...vation. Heroically as
...e fighting in France,
...rgotten that without
...the crossing they
...ed upon French soil,
...t to hold the sea and
...hind the mine-strewn
this Empire would be

...ation of three Naval
...vn as the Fisher, the
...ford—to assist if and
...troops engaged on
liveliest satisfaction
...service, and there
...ush of recruits to fill
The fact that after
...ent and immediately
quirements the Ad-
of 10,000 officers and
and chafing at their
...a most reassuring
...ry. If all goes well
Naval Brigades will
...t to the Army and
intimates that the
...distinction on the

ROLL OF HONOUR.

PORTSMOUTH BATTALION.

Town and District Recruits.

The following is the list to date of the non-commissioned officers and recruits of the Portsmouth and District Battalion of the Hampshire Regiment which is being formed to take part in the war. In cases where the place is not otherwise stated, the men belong to Portsmouth:—

Sergt.-Major Simms, 19, Commercial-rd.
Walter John Hurrell, Co. Q.M.S.
William Robins, Company-Sergt.-Major.
Alfred Thos. Green, Orderly-room Sergt.

Recruits.

Herbert Wigmore, East Liss.
Harry Gisborne, care of Mrs. Cook, West Liss.
Wilfred Payne, 36, Stubbington-avenue.
William Baker, Reeds, East Liss.
George Hodges, Langley Cottage, East Liss.
George Wm. Huish, 25, Netley-street, Fratton.
William Adams, Cliff Cottage, Harting Combe.
James Collins, Harting Combe.
Frederick Payne, 36, Stubbington-avenue.
John Crawford, 32, The Square, Winchester.
John William Walter Long, 8, Villiers-road, Southsea.
Walter Messingham, Chestnut Brow, Bramshott.
Albert Porter, Queen-street, Liphook.
George Henry Wright, Royal Sailors' Rest.
Arthur James Joiner, do.
Stanley Theodore Pead, 73, Kingston-crescent.
Edward Ernest Harding, 313, Lake-road.
Edward John Creswell, 123, London-road.
Henry Murly, 62, Cranleigh-road.
Walter Herbert Carter, 15, Heidelberg-road.
James Hurt, 2, Holybank, Emsworth.
John Clifford Langton, 15, Heidelberg-road.
Frederick Charles Pragnell, Oak Cottage, South Leigh-road, Emsworth

Right column

THE NAT

The following
commissioned o
mouth Battalio
who left to joi
shire Regiment

Major J. Ral
Non-Commiss
W. E. Abra
Anderson, A.
Bamber, H. Bi
Bidgood, R. W
Brummen, G.
Beale, S. Ha
Cunliffe, H. G
J. V. Champion
T. Dent, D. C.
Deeley, B. Do
Ferguson, C.
Fuller, C. B. F
J. Geeves, H,
Gissing, H. G
ton, E. Hickle
W. Hemlin, C
R. F. Jenning
Kelly, J. H.
Lineham, A. M
Marshman, F.
Muggeridge, W
O'Callaghan, J
H. E. Pass, C
J. Patey, T. Ri
J. W. Seager,
W. Shaw, T.
Smith, S. H.
Travers, W. C.
Trueman, F.
Webber, A. E.
A. Wiltshire
W. Winter, J.
J. Yates.

SUCCE

[TO THE EDITO

Sir,—In you
express some d
in recruits at t
the Town Hal
agrees with yo
that those wh
their country
ing and not fr
As one of the
flow meeting,
felt that the m
and after the

The *Evening News* regularly published lists of men who had volunteered for the Portsmouth Pals Battalions. (*EN*)

and from Hester Road in Milton, were both killed. Stephenson is buried at Bailleul cemetery, back from the front line, suggesting that he had been evacuated wounded; Private Marshall is buried in Berkshire cemetery, near the front line.

On the evening of 30 June both Portsmouth Battalions were in the front line, and took part in raids in order to distract the enemy from the impending Somme

offensive further south, due to commence the next day. The 14th Battalion was at Ferme du Bois in the Loos sector, and supported an attack by the 12th and 13th Battalions of the Royal Sussex Regiment. The enemy artillery was so fierce that they had to withdraw. The Hampshires lost five men, among them Private William Ambler, Private Henry Chalmers, Private Sidney Hoare and Corporal G. W. Hardy. Chalmers was 19 and from Rudmore, and had volunteered in September 1914. Hoare was 23 and from Westover Road in Copnor, and Hardy was 31 and from Hawke Street in Portsea. A reservist, Hardy was mobilised in August 1914. Ambler and Hoare were reported missing and are remembered on the Loos memorial, whilst Chalmers and Hardy are buried in St Vaast Post cemetery.

A major raid was planned by the 15th Battalion further north near Ploegsteert. Artillery fire in support of the raid began at 7.30 a.m., and continued until 5.00 p.m., in order to cut the German barbed wire, and at 10.00 p.m. gas was discharged. The raid itself began at 10.23 p.m. The raiding party left in three groups. One party reached the enemy trenches and threw in grenades. The second party's leader was wounded and its second-in-command gassed. Meanwhile, the third party had trouble getting through the barbed wire and returned. Among the dead were Private E.H.W Judd; Private Edward Sansom aged 40 of Wilson Road, Stamshaw; Private L. Johnson of Fairlea Court, Portsea and Private B. Harrison, aged 17, of Clock Street, Portsea. Private William Penfold aged 21 of Brookfield Road, Fratton, was gassed and although he made it back to the battalion's lines he died of the effects later. All of the dead from 30 June are buried in Berkshire cemetery.

Men of one of the Portsmouth Pals Battalions leaving for active service, seen off by a large crowd. (Gates)

Both Portsmouth Battalions were withdrawn from the front line in August and sent south to take part in the latter stages of the Battle of the Somme. The 14th Battalion arrived on the Somme on 26 August, and just over a week later, on 3 September, attacked during the Battle of the Ancre, north of Hamel. Although it had not yet taken part in a major offensive, the battalion was under strength, and down to around 500 men.[44] Final assembly was completed by 4.00 a.m., and shortly afterwards A Company attacked, taking the German front line with virtually no casualties. B Company then took the second line, but although C Company attacked the third line they were repelled by rifle and machine-gun fire. After C Company retired, an order to attack the third line again was received, but the attack was not successful and the commanding officer, Captain Skinner, was killed. The second line was held until 1.00 p.m., when the party holding the enemy trenches ran out of ammunition and was forced back. Although enemy casualties were recorded as heavy, the 14th Battalion's casualties were not reported in the war diary. However, the regimental history suggests that out of 570 men who went into action 17 officers and 440 other ranks were casualties.[45] Sixty-one men from Portsmouth are known to have been killed on 3 September. The vast majority have no known grave and are remembered on the Thiepval memorial. Only one was an officer: Second Lieutenant Gilbert Ash, the son of an Isle of Wight coal merchant, was a former pupil of Portsmouth Grammar School. He was commissioned into the 14th Hampshires on 11 May 1915. He has no known grave, and is remembered on the Thiepval memorial and the St Andrew's parish memorial. Among the other dead on 3 September were Private Frederick Shill, an employee of the City of Portsmouth Passenger Transport Department, and Company Sergeant Major John Brown, a Royal Mail employee who volunteered in August 1914. Among the wounded was Sergeant Ernest Butt, aged 35 and from St Stephens Road in Southsea. One of the original volunteers in September 1914, he was badly wounded and evacuated home, but died on 29 September 1916. He is buried in Kingston cemetery. After the losses of 3 September the battalion was reinforced with drafts from other regiments, including 327 men from the Essex and Suffolk Regiments, and thus lost much of its original Portsmouth character.[46]

The 15th Hampshires were not far behind in being sent to the Somme. On 6 September the battalion boarded trains for the Somme, arriving at Bernancourt the same day. After several more days of training, the battalion marched to Fricourt on 11 September, and the next day went into reserve behind the front line. On 13 September, the battalion went into the front line. The Battle of Flers-Courcelette, as it came to be known, was intended to be a re-run of the first day of the battle of the Somme, in an attempt to re-energise the offensive.[47] On 14 September, the day before the planned attack, artillery was very active and two platoon commanders were killed. The battalion went over the top and into no-man's-land at 6.20 a.m., with seven tanks in support. Although the preceding

The grave of Sergeant Ernest Butt, who volunteered in 1914 and died of wounds received on the Somme. (Author)

barrage was good, three machine guns on the left held the advance up for some time and caused many casualties. The accompanying tanks performed well according to the war diary, especially in smashing in enemy strong points, and gave the men much confidence. Flers was taken, but heavy losses were caused by the German artillery barrage. All of the company commanders and company sergeant majors were wounded. The attack had become very disorganised due to the loss of most of the officers, but all remaining men reinforced the captured objective against counterattacks. One tank had advanced through the centre of the village, while three had outflanked it and other units leapfrogged forward.

However, later in the day the New Zealand Division on the left withdrew and small bodies of men began to flood back through Flers, pushing the front line back to just north of the village. Flers was held, however, and later that evening the battalion was relieved. Although the capture of Flers on 15 September was one of few brighter moments of the Somme campaign, the 15th Hampshires had suffered horrific losses. The war diary records that thirty-nine officers and men were killed and 248 were wounded or missing. However, at least forty-eight men from Portsmouth alone are known to have been killed on 15 September. Thirty-one of those have no known grave and are remembered on the Thiepval memorial; the remainder are buried in Guards cemetery, Lesboeufs; Bulls Road cemetery, Flers and AIF burial ground, Flers. One of the wounded company sergeant majors was 38-year-old Richard Thompson, a policeman from Milton Road in Copnor. He later died of his wounds in Britain on 31 October 1916, and is buried in Kingston cemetery.

Heavy losses on the Somme have come to characterise the experience of the Pals Battalions, and the Somme proved to be the graveyard of many of the early

volunteers to the Portsmouth Pals. That so many men from the same communities and from the same social groups were lost in such a short space of time meant that what were already horrific losses had an impact on the town out of all proportion to their size.[48] As a result, the Pals Battalions also lost much of their local identity after the Somme, but they have still had a particular resonance, not only in history but also in British popular culture.[49]

After such heavy losses the 15th Battalion went back from the front line to rest and train, before going back to trenches at Mametz on 3 October 1916. The Battle of Transloy had begun on 1 October, and six days later, on 7 October, the 15th Hampshires took part in a major attack on Gird Trench. The objective was secured and consolidated. On 9 October the battalion was relieved and left the front line, and by 17 October was in the Abbeville area. Nineteen men from Portsmouth were killed at Transloy on 7 October. Among them was Private Sidney Palmer, a City Tram conductor.

The 14th Battalion was also in action again on the Somme. On 22 October the Battalion attacked at Wood Post near the Schwaben Redoubt, a key feature that had been captured by the 39th Division on 14 October.[50] Seventeen men were killed, ninety-five wounded and thirty-two declared missing. The only man from Portsmouth killed was Major F.R.F. Warren, who was from Southsea and is buried in Grandcourt cemetery. That only one man of the seventeen killed came from Portsmouth demonstrates how the battalion's original Portsmouth character had been diluted by losses and subsequent reinforcements from other areas.

After the massive losses of the Somme, the intake of new reinforcements and a change in War Office policy away from local recruiting for regiments, the identities of the Pals Battalions were eroded.[51] The 14th Battalion left the Somme soon after the end of the battle, arriving at Poperinghe near the Ypres Salient on 18 November. After training and receiving a draft of seventy reinforcements, the 15th Hampshires were back in the front line, at St Eloi, south of Ypres, on 29 October 1916. Both battalions spent the winter and spring relatively quietly in the Ypres Salient, with the 14th Battalion around Boesinghe and 15th Battalion in the St Eloi, Voormezeele and Dickebusch sectors.

Despite the winter and early spring being relatively quiet, losses still occurred during the day-to-day routine of trench warfare. On 1 February the 14th Battalion were in the front line at Railway Wood near Boesinge when an SOS signal went up at 5.00 a.m. An intense trench-mortar bombardment and artillery shelling was followed by a German attack. The attack was driven back, but with the loss of nine men. Among the dead were Private Reginald Neale, aged 32 and from Stamshaw Road, and Lance Corporal Laurence Kennedy, aged 26 and from Arundel Street in Landport. Both are buried in Vlamertinghe cemetery. On 28 March 1917, Private H.G. Stoneham of the 15th Battalion, from Maitland Street in Landport, was killed in the front line when a British shell fell short.

The grave of Colour Sergeant Major Richard Thompson, another Portsmouth man who died of wounds received on the Somme. (Author)

At 7.00 p.m. on 20 April the Germans launched a strong attack on the 15th Hampshires' lines in the St Eloi sector. After heavy shelling, the Germans attempted to raid the front line and although they were driven back, serious damage was done to the trenches. While this damage was heavy, it was repaired within twenty-four hours. Among the five men killed were Private Cecil Williams, aged 19 of Jervis Road, Stamshaw; Corporal Frederick Rogers aged 33 of Goodwood Road, Southsea and Private F.E. Viney of Highgate Road, Copnor.

The 14th Battalion was earmarked to take part in the opening phase of the Third Battle of Ypres – better known as Passchendaele – and was withdrawn from the front line for training on 1 May. The men were specifically trained in attacking in platoons, companies and as a whole battalion. Fitness training also took place, including route marches and sports activities. After a brief spell back in the front line at Wieltje in late May and early June, the rest of June was spent training, including rehearsing their part in the coming attack, practising digging trenches and shooting practice on the firing ranges. Training continued into early July.

Early June, meanwhile, found the 15th Hampshires in the front line near St Eloi. On 7 June the battalion took part in the Battle of Messines Ridge. At 3.10 a.m. a huge mine was blown under the German lines on the ridge, and the leading British troops advanced. The 15th Hampshires began the day in reserve, but after two hours moved up to Dammstrasse in readiness to attack. The Hampshires' attack began at 6.50 a.m., and although many casualties were sustained, the objective was captured and held against several counter-attacks. Six men from Portsmouth were among those killed, and at least one man died later of wounds.

Much of July was spent in training and taking in reinforcements, in readiness for the planned offensive in the Ypres Salient.

The 14th Hampshires were in their assembly trenches near the Canal Bank at Ypres by 30 July. Zero hour was at 5.20 a.m. The weather was particularly bad, with torrential rain. The attack towards Pilckem Ridge initially went well, taking the Falkenhayn Redoubt, and eventually reached a point east of the River Steenbeek. The German lines had been lightly held, but were reinforced by a number of pillboxes. The Battalion captured three German field guns and seventeen machine guns and took 200 prisoners. The vital village of Langemarck, however, had not been captured.[52] Two officers and seventeen men of other ranks were killed, and five officers and 156 men were wounded. Seven men from Portsmouth were killed – Lance Sergeant Joseph Wilkins, Private Henry Harnden, Private Ernest Shawyer, Private G. Jerrard, Private Frank Childs, Private Reginald Chamberlain and Private T. Fitzgerald. Wilkins, Harnden and Childs have no known grave and are remembered on the Menin Gate memorial in Ypres; Shawyer, Chamberlain and Fitzgerald are buried in Buffs Road cemetery, and Jerrard is buried in Gwalia cemetery. Lance Sergeant Wilkins had been awarded a Distinguished Conduct Medal on the Somme, and Second Lieutenant Denis Hewitt was awarded a Victoria Cross after leading forward the advance despite being wounded, before being killed by a sniper. The 14th Battalion was finally withdrawn on 2 August, and went back to Poperinghe.

The 15th Hampshires were in the front line near Hollebeke on the first day of the battle, but only suffered four casualties in the wet weather. The next day, however, eight men were killed in heavy shelling, including four men from Portsmouth: Corporal Frederick Burrow, Private Cyril Grant aged 21, Private Arthur Potter of Fratton Grove, Landport, and Private Benjamin Tribe aged 21 of Marylebone Road, Southsea. Corporal Burrow had been awarded the Military Medal.

Both battalions remained in action at Ypres, where Private Arthur Cook was killed on 17 September serving with the 14th Battalion. An old boy of Portsmouth Grammar School, Cook was unusual for a public schoolboy in that he served in the ranks rather than as an officer. It seems that as he joined the army relatively late he was conscripted rather than volunteering, perhaps suggesting why he was not commissioned. Cook was 19 when he was killed and is buried in Reninghelst cemetery. He lived at Wahroonga in London Road.

On 20 September the 15th Hampshires took part in the battle for the Menin Road Ridge, also known as the Gheluvelt Plateau. At 5.40 a.m. the battalion attacked, with the task of capturing the red and blue lines west of Bassevillebeke. The Hampshires were held up by a strong point five minutes after going over the top, but the obstacle was captured. Although both lines were captured, casualties were very heavy, including all four company commanders. After a german counter-attack was beaten off, the 11th Royal West Kents passed through.

The West Kents, however, failed to take their objective and at 5.30 p.m. orders were received that the Hampshires were to assist the Kents in their attack. The Kents were too disorganised and the attack was eventually made by 130 men of the Hampshires. The first officer to reach the objective was Second Lieutenant Montague Moore, who for some time only had one sergeant and four men.[53] Undeterred, he bombed a large dugout, taking twenty-eight prisoners. Eventually more men trickled forwards. The position was captured, along with forty prisoners. Ten Portsmouth men were lost on 20 September. Due to the chaotic nature of the fighting, none of them have a known grave and are all remembered on the Tyne Cot memorial.

Early the next day, Moore had to withdraw his men slightly in order to avoid being shelled by British artillery, which, through a lack of communication, began to shell the area. After the shelling had ceased Moore once again reoccupied the objective. Later in the afternoon the Germans counter-attacked using flame-throwers. Although the Germans were repulsed, the area was later shelled by German artillery and then again by British artillery, who thought that the position had been abandoned. Now down to about ten men and having lost their weapons and rations, Moore and his men armed themselves with German rifles and grenades and prepared to meet any counter-attacks. At daybreak on 22 September they withdrew, leaving behind an anti-tank gun and two machine guns that they had captured. For his gallantry Montague Moore was awarded the Victoria Cross, the only man from the 15th Hampshires to receive this honour.[54] In the evening of 22 September the battalion was relieved and went back behind the line. During three days of fighting the battalion lost a total of fifty-five officers and men killed, and 296 were wounded or missing.

Less than a week later the 14th Battalion were in action again, at Tower Hamlets on 26 September during the Battle of Menin Road. The attack began at 5.50 a.m. The men were greeted by intense

Private Arthur Cook, an old boy of Portsmouth Grammar School who joined the ranks and was killed during the Third Battle of Ypres. (PGS)

artillery, sniper and machine-gun fire, and took heavy casualties. Despite this the battalion captured and consolidated its objective at Tower Trench. Forty-one men were killed, among them four Portsmouth men – Private Alfred Peachey; Private Frederick Mundey, aged 35, of Church Road, Kingston; Private J.W. Short, aged 29 of Cambridge Street, Southsea, and Lance Corporal George Barley.

After the crippling losses experienced at Ypres and on the Somme, the Portsmouth Pals Battalions had lost most of the men who had originally joined up in 1914 and 1915. Although fresh recruits were arriving from the 16th Depot Battalion, it was decided to merge the 15th Hampshires with the Hampshire Carabinier Yeomanry, a territorial cavalry unit. There had been few uses for cavalry in static trench warfare, and it was decided to make better use of their manpower by drafting the cavalry troopers into the 15th Hampshires. The first draft of twelve officers and 307 men arrived on 25 September.[55] Much of October was spent resting and training, providing men for work parties and absorbing new men from the Carabiniers. Future events would show that the intake of men from the Carabinier Yeomanry probably saved the 15th Battalion from disbandment.

On 7 November the 15th Battalion, along with the rest of the 41st Division, learnt that they were being sent to the Italian Front. By the end of November they had taken over a section of the front north-west of Treviso. Only three men from the battalion died whilst in Italy: Private A.T. Hoit, of Cherry Garden Lane, Landport, died of sickness on 2 July 1918, almost four months after the rest of the battalion had left Italy. He is buried in Dueville cemetery near Vicenza. By 9 March 1918 the battalion was back in France.

Whilst the 15th Battalion was in Italy, the 14th Battalion had spent the winter in the front line in the Ypres Salient. As manpower shortages began to take hold, The army on the Western Front had to make drastic decisions and restructure the British Expeditionary Force. Part of this restructure entailed reducing infantry brigades from four battalions to three and disbanding the fourth battalion to provide reinforcements for other depleted units. As a result, in February 1918 the 14th Hampshires were notified that they were to be disbanded. A draft of five officers and 100 men left for the 11th Battalion on 6 February, and many of the remaining men were transferred to the 17th Hampshires, an entrenching battalion.[56] Entrenching battalions provided manpower for one of the most onerous and unglamorous tasks on the Western Front – digging trenches. After an inspection and farewell speech by the Commander of the 39th Division, the battalion formally disbanded on 23 February.

The 15th Battalion fought on, however. On 4 September 1918, the battalion was involved in operations during the Allies' final offensive, at Vierstraat near Ypres. Orders were given out at very short notice, probably due to the fluid situation during this phase of the war. The attack began at 4.30 a.m. Unfortunately a number of German machine-gun posts were untouched by British artillery

fire and able to fire on the Hampshires unmolested. Although the battalion took heavy casualties, it reached its objective. However, due to the losses suffered and increasing enemy machine-gun fire, the battalion had to withdraw. Sixteen officers and 307 men became casualties, including the commanding officer and the acting adjutant. Fourteen men from Portsmouth were among the ninety men of other ranks dead or missing.[57] By this stage in the war many of the men of the battalion were reinforcements who did not come from Portsmouth and had either volunteered later in the war or been conscripted. The attack on 4 September was the battalion's last major operation of the war, although it was in action almost continually until the Armistice took effect on 11 November 1918. The battalion went to Germany as part of the occupation force before being disbanded in October 1919.

The Pals Battalions have come to be recognised as a well-intentioned but ultimately flawed concept, a phenomenon deeply rooted in Edwardian society.[58] A noble experiment during a desperate and unplanned-for situation, their localised recruiting accentuated the impact of losses, harming civilian morale on the home front.[59] As John Keegan has so rightly stated, the Pals Battalions have no counterpart in the history of the modern English-speaking world.[60] For a town like Portsmouth, with its naval and dockyard commitments, to contribute three whole battalions of men was a remarkable achievement, unmatched by any other town in Hampshire. As popular opinion tends to associate the Pals Battalions with northern and midlands industrial towns, the Portsmouth Pals have been largely forgotten by history.[61]

W.G. Gates summed up the experience of the Portsmouth Pals in what were perhaps rosier terms than many of the men who fought, or indeed the relatives of those killed, might have felt: 'the spirit which prompted the men of Portsmouth to rally to the Colours upheld them through all the days of horror and the nights of pain.'[62]

6

'Those Magnificent Men in their Flying Machines': Portsmouth's First World War Airmen

The First World War saw many technological innovations, and was the first conflict in which all sides made extensive use of aircraft, giving warfare an added aerial dimension.[1] Although the Wright brothers had first flown on 17 December 1903, military authorities had been lukewarm about the potential for aircraft in war. As late as 1910, the Chief of the Imperial General Staff, the head of the British Army, described aircraft as a 'useless and expensive fad', and the First Sea Lord quoted the naval requirement for aircraft as two.[2] Britain therefore lagged behind many other countries in terms of military aviation and the Royal Engineers Air Battalion was only formed on 1 April 1911, before becoming the Royal Flying Corps from 13 May 1912.[3] Most early pilots were already officers who transferred from other regiments and corps, but first had to obtain a civilian flying certificate from the Royal Aero Club, before being reimbursed by the army.[4] Locally, Gosport Airfield became one of Britain's first military aerodromes when it was constructed in early 1914. No. 5 Squadron of the Royal Flying Corps moved onto the airfield in July of the same year, only weeks before departing for France.[5]

Military aviation began the First World War on a modest scale. Four Squadrons of the Royal Flying Corps went to France in August 1914, consisting of a total of 105 officers and 755 men of other ranks.[6] The Royal Flying Corps spent much of the early part of the war in reconnaissance work. After the conflict settled into trench warfare, the ability to fly high over trenches and avoid the deadlock on the ground made aircraft a valuable asset. Inevitably, the Germans had the same idea, and aerial combat became more common. In addition, both sides began to perfect anti-aircraft fire, making flying a hazardous business. What would now be called friendly-fire incidents were not unheard of either, with front-line troops tending to have a 'fire first, ask questions later' approach to targeting any aircraft.[7]

The first airman with Portsmouth connections was killed in action in 1915 and had a rather colourful story. Stanley Caws was born on the Isle of Wight on 22 March 1879.[8] Although he was the son of a successful land agent, and a pupil at Portsmouth Grammar School, unconfirmed sources suggest that Caws was a 'black sheep' who was paid by his family to stay out of Britain.[9] He subsequently emigrated to Alberta in Canada, where he served with the 19th Alberta Dragoons and the Canadian militia, and with Paget's Horse during the Boer War. He was also a senior founding member of the Canadian Legion of Frontiersmen, a group of pioneers and British citizens who had emigrated to Canada to build a new life. He re-enlisted into the Canadian cavalry on 23 September 1914, giving his occupation as 'prospector'. He apparently had tattoos on both forearms. He was immediately promoted to sergeant.[10]

Early in the First World War, however, Caws volunteered for transfer to the Royal Flying Corps.[11] Caws was granted his aviator certificate at the Brooklands Military Aviation School on 25 February 1915, and on the same day he was commissioned as a second lieutenant in the Royal Flying Corps.[12] Soon after, in June, he was promoted to flying officer (an appointment rather than a rank), and in September he was promoted to the substantive rank of lieutenant. Unsurprisingly for such a character, a fellow officer later remembered him as the life and soul of the mess, and 'quite the most popular man in the squadron'.[13]

On the Western Front, Caws flew with 10 Squadron of the Royal Flying Corps, making scouting flights over the battlefield. On 21 September 1915 he and his observer were flying a BE2c aircraft, and had shot down two enemy aircraft. A third German aircraft, however, managed to kill Caws with gunfire. His observer managed to land the aircraft behind German lines and was taken prisoner. Although Caws was buried with full military honours, the location of his grave was lost and he is now remembered on the Arras flying memorial. He was 36.[14] His service record suggests that he was recommended for a gallantry medal, but there is no evidence that one was awarded.[15]

A remarkable number of airmen were killed in accidents during training. Of the eleven Portsmouth men who died serving with the Royal Flying Corps, six died and are buried in Britain. This statistic is sad, yet unsurprising given that air flight was still in its infancy – the First World War beginning a mere eleven years after the Wright brothers' first powered flight. Flying was an inherently dangerous occupation, with landings and take-offs carrying a not insignificant risk of crashing. One historian suggests that such crashes took the greatest toll in terms of pilots' deaths.[16]

The early part of the war was spent largely flying reconnaissance missions and spotting for artillery batteries, as initially the aircraft lacked suitable armament for fighting other planes, and in any case aerial combat tactics were still rudimentary. There was still little in the way of specialist equipment or clothing.

By mid-summer 1916 the Royal Flying Corps had expanded from four squadrons to twenty-six and possessed 421 aircraft with 200 in reserve, but British aircraft were still largely inferior to the German Fokker. The rapid expansion of the corps had also led to a decline in the quality of training, with new recruits being rushed to the front in order to make up for losses.[17] Given the intense nature of military flying over the Western Front, a laid-back and fun atmosphere was positively encouraged in Royal Flying Corps messes. Although front-line troops might have imagined that pilots lived a comfortable life on the ground, theirs was an extremely dangerous and highly charged existence, with a short life expectancy.

Flying attracted a certain stamp of young men, many of them public schoolboys. One of them was Robert Vernon-Inkpen, who was born in Portsmouth in 1890.[18] The son of a prominent Portsmouth councillor, architect and surveyor, Vernon-Inkpen attended Portsmouth Grammar School between 1901 and 1905, and later studied at the Institute of Surveyors.[19] Upon the outbreak of the First World War he volunteered for the army, initially joining the Hampshire Royal Garrison Artillery. However, after attending the Oxford University Officer Training Corps, Vernon-Inkpen was commissioned as a second lieutenant in the 12th Battalion of the Royal Warwickshire Regiment on 11 July 1915. Before his battalion went to the Western Front, however, Vernon-Inkpen volunteered for the Royal Flying Corps. He qualified as a pilot at Wantage Hall near Reading, but was killed in an accident at Gosport on 21 October 1916. He is buried in Highland Road cemetery. The inquest into his death found that his machine had careered into the ground, after he had tried to climb too sharply.[20] His commanding officer said, 'He has always been most painstaking and zealous in the discharge of his duties', and 'he was a most promising young officer'.[21]

Albert Churcher was born in Cosham in 1889 and attended Portsmouth Grammar School between 1900 and 1907, where he excelled at maths and played cricket for the first and second elevens. After leaving the school he worked as a self-employed chartered accountant. Churcher joined the Royal Engineers, before transferring to the Royal Flying Corps. Churcher died on 23 September 1918, and is buried in Milton cemetery. He was 29, and living in Victoria Road, Southsea, at the time of his death.[22]

As a measure of how important air warfare had become, by the late summer of 1916 80,000 people were employed in Britain's aero industry, and the sector was considered key to Britain's war effort.[23] As a result of this new-found prominence, the Royal Air Force was formed on 1 April 1918. The Royal Flying Corps and the Royal Naval Air Service merged, and from that date recruits joined the new service.

Maurice Oakley was born in 1899, the son of Harry E. Oakley OBE, an Admiralty superintending civil engineer. Oakley attended Rugby School and in 1917 joined the Royal Naval Air Service, after having worked – fittingly –

The grave of Second Lieutenant Albert Churcher. (Author)

manufacturing aircraft engines. After training at Crystal Palace, Vendôme, Cranwell and at Lee-on-the-Solent, he was sent to Italy on 18 February 1918, where he joined 66th Wing of what was then the Royal Flying Corps. Upon the formation of the RAF in April 1918, he was automatically transferred to the new service. Oakley was killed in an accident during a trial flight prior to a bombing mission. He is buried in Otranto cemetery. His captain later wrote to his parents:

Your son had done extremely well here and had carried out some particularly difficult bomb attacks on naval air bases at great distances from his own base... His accident, I regret to say, was caused by a slight error of judgement resulting in a nose-dive into the ground. His machine caught fire at once, but there is no doubt that both Pilot and Observer were killed instantaneously. Your son was buried in the cemetery at Otranto. Lieutenant Oakley was a gallant Pilot and I am very proud to have had him in my Squadron.[24]

Basil Jones was born in Portsmouth in 1898 and lived at Waverley Road. He studied at St Davids College in Lampeter, Wales. He enlisted into the London Regiment, and was posted to the 14th Battalion. He served with the battalion for three years as a despatch rider before enlisting into the RAF in 1918. After undergoing training he was posted to 4 Squadron, and served as an observer flying in RE8 aircraft. On 28 September 1918 Jones was flying as an observer when he was hit by gunfire from a German aircraft during a dogfight. Although the pilot managed to land the aircraft, Jones was killed. He is buried in La Kreule military cemetery in France.[25]

Flying seems to have attracted a certain kind of young man. Particular skills emphasised were individuality, self-belief, solitude, exhilaration and a disregard for danger.[26] Public schoolboys were well represented among Portsmouth airmen. By and large, young airmen from Portsmouth seem to have been the sons of prominent, wealthy or professional people – Caws was the son of a land agent,

Vernon-Inkpen an architect and Maurice Oakley a chartered engineer. Wealthy, well-educated men from middle-class backgrounds certainly had an advantage in applying for the Royal Flying Corps, and until losses forced the Corps to open up its entrance policy, public schoolboys did dominate the officers' mess.[27]

However, one man joined the Royal Flying Corps from the much more working-class Portsmouth Pals. Percy Main was born in Portsmouth in 1892, and lived at Harrow, a house in Portsdown Avenue in Drayton. He joined the ranks of the Portsmouth Pals and was initially serving with the 16th Battalion of the Hampshire Regiment, which provided reinforcements for the two Pals Battalions on the Western Front. Before he could go overseas, however, Main transferred to the Royal Flying Corps, initially for clerical duties. On 12 January 1916 he was commissioned as a second lieutenant, transferring back to the Hampshire Regiment. He went overseas with the Hampshires on 11 July 1916, serving with the 15th Battalion. His time in the Flying Corps must have left an impression on him and he was not at the front for long; in August 1916 he began flying training at Northolt. He was sadly killed in an accident on 23 September 1916. He was 24 and is buried in Kingston cemetery.[28]

Although the Royal Flying Corps was intended to provide aircraft for the army and the Royal Navy, the Admiralty were clearly unhappy with their air support being under army control, and in July 1914 unilaterally formed the Royal Naval Air Service.[29] Locally, the naval air station at Lee-on-the-Solent was opened in July 1917, originally as a seaplane base.[30] The Admiralty was not confident that it could attract suitable recruits for air service from within the navy and subsequently targeted recruitment for aircrew and ground crew at civilians. The service expanded exponentially, from 708 ratings in 1914 to 41,597 in November 1917. Of these, only one thousand were recruited from the pre-war, regular Royal Navy.[31] Four Portsmouth men – two officers and two ratings – were killed whilst serving with the Royal Naval Air Service during the First World War.

Leonard Hodges was born in Portsmouth in 1892, the son of a gun fitter at the Gunwharf.[32] Although he was working as an articled clerk in 1911, his family moved to Camberley in Surrey before the start of the war. Hodges volunteered for the Royal Navy Air Service and was granted a probationary commission as a flight sub lieutenant on 6 May 1915. He then went to the seaplane school on Lake Windermere to undergo his initial flight training. From there he undertook further training at the London Aerodrome in Hendon and was presented with Royal Aero Club certificate number 1667 on 3 September 1915. After initially serving at the naval air station at Calshot in the Solent, Hodges was sent to the Persian Gulf to command the naval air service in Basra. He died on 31 May 1916 of cholera.[33] He was 23 and is buried in Basra.

Cyril Emmett was born in Portsmouth in 1899, the youngest son of Richard Emmett, a local doctor and magistrate who originally came from Devon.

The grave of Second Lieutenant Percy Main. (Author)

The Emmett family lived in London Road and had six servants – a governess, two nurses, a cook, a housemaid and a pageboy.[34] Emmett had attended Lytham Prep School in Oxford and Repton College, and later began an apprenticeship as a mining engineer and surveyor.[35] He joined the Royal Naval Air Squadron in May 1917, and in August 1917, during his training, he was slightly injured. He went overseas in January 1918 and served on the Western Front with 12 Squadron for only a few weeks before he was killed in a flying accident on 15 March 1918. His De Havilland 4 crashed in a field near the aerodrome and burnt out.[36] He was 19 and is buried in Dunkirk cemetery in France.

Like the Royal Flying Corps, the Royal Naval Air Service also attracted public schoolboys. John de Camborne Paynter was born in Portsmouth on 17 May 1898.[37] His father, William Paynter, worked for long periods in Algeria as a mining engineer, where his wife Louisa died between 1891 and 1895.[38] Paynter was absent from the family home in both the 1901 and 1911 censuses. In 1911 the family were living in Victoria Road North in Southsea, and John Paynter attended Portsmouth Grammar School from 1910, excelling at French, English, maths and science. After leaving the school in April 1914, he went to the Municipal College in Portsmouth, and afterwards became an apprentice motor engineer.[39] On 25 June 1916, at the age of 18, he joined the Royal Flying Corps. After training at Crystal Palace, Chingford and Cranwell, he qualified as a pilot. In November 1916 Paynter was posted to Dover, but must have gone to the Western Front soon after, for in April 1917 he was admitted to St Omer Hospital in France with German measles. He was admitted to hospital again in May with a back injury, which rendered him unfit for flying for several months. He returned to flying in the autumn of 1917, based near Dunkirk, and claimed his first kill on 27 October, shooting down a German Albatross.[40]

On 3 March 1918, Paynter took part in a bombing raid on a seaplane base in Ostend, Belgium. For the operation, Paynter was awarded the Distinguished Service Cross:

For good work performed by him during a bombing attack on Ostend Sea Plane Base on 3rd March 1918, carried out in spite of very adverse weather conditions. He has shown great zeal and courage as a fighting pilot, having destroyed several enemy machines, and been twice wounded in aerial combats.[41]

Paynter became an ace, shooting down a total of ten enemy aircraft.[42] He was clearly a very brave man in the air, but his bravery proved to be his downfall, ironically, on the ground. He refused to take cover during an air raid on his aerodrome whilst serving with 213 Squadron at Coudekerque and was hit by shrapnel, which perforated his liver.[43] He died of his wounds on 6 June 1918, at the age of twenty. He is buried in Dunkirk Town cemetery and is remembered on the Portsmouth Grammar School and St Peter's church memorials.

Air Mechanic Frank Ball was one of the first civilians to join the Royal Naval Air Service as ground crew. He was born in Portsmouth in 1893, and was educated at Taunton School in Somerset before volunteering for the RNAS in November 1914. He was serving at East Fortune Air Station in Scotland when he died on 16 March 1916 after his aircraft crashed during a training flight. He is buried in Hollybrook cemetery in Southampton.[44] He was living in Wilton Terrace, Landport.

Leading Mechanic Edward Smart joined the Royal Naval Air Service in 1915, directly from civilian life. He was born in Paddington, London, in 1886 and was living in Queens Road, Buckland, when he died whilst serving as an air mechanic at HMS *President* in London on 31 October 1918. He was 32 and is buried in Milton cemetery.

The First World War had begun with military aviation as a relatively small part of the British Expeditionary Force and with many senior commanders unsure at best about its use. Within four years, the Royal Flying Corps and the Royal Naval Air Service and their men had proven their worth to the extent that a completely new service had been formed in the shape of the Royal Air Force. The air had firmly become a dimension of warfare.

The grave of Leading Mechanic Edward Smart. (Author)

7

Comings and Goings:
Portsmouth's Emigrants
and Immigrants

As a port, Portsmouth has inevitably been a place of movement for thousands of years. People have been coming to and leaving from Portsmouth for as long as it has existed, and the backgrounds of many local people during the First World War demonstrate just how mobile and diverse local communities were.[1] In fact, Portsmouth society was probably more familiar with immigration and emigration than most other towns and cities in early twentieth-century Britain. Nor was it only in an international context that Portsmouth people were mobile, as servicemen naturally moved around within the country frequently: sailors often moved from their home towns to live near the naval base and soldiers moved around as their unit was transferred from place to place.

In particular, the birthplace of sailors provides an interesting illustration of geographical recruiting patterns. Of the 1,776 sailors with Portsmouth connections who died in the First World War, the birthplaces of 1,541 of them are known.[2] Of those, 710 men were born in Hampshire – less than 50 per cent. Large numbers of men also came from London (121), Sussex (100) and Kent (61), as well as neighbouring maritime counties such as Dorset. Large numbers of men also volunteered from areas with large urban populations, such as London, Lancashire and Yorkshire. By comparison, fewer men came from inland agricultural counties such as Berkshire (7) or Oxfordshire (12). Thirty-seven of the men were born in Scotland, thirty-one in Ireland, thirteen in Wales and eighteen in the Channel Islands. Although Jersey and Guernsey had relatively small populations, seafaring would have been second nature to many young Channel Islanders. The Royal Navy was therefore probably a popular career choice given the proximity of the sea and the seafaring experience that many a young Channel Islander must have had from an early age, and a lack of other employment in the area probably provided further encouragement.

Advances in transport technology during the Industrial Revolution had made long-distance travel easier and cheaper than ever before. During the later years of the nineteenth century, many people left Britain in order to escape poverty, to seek a new life or to flee other problems. Countries such as Australia and Canada in particular were a popular destination for emigration and provided opportunities for working-class people seeking adventure and opportunity. As a result, when the First World War broke out, many young men who had originally come from Portsmouth were living in distant parts of the world, and joined the armed forces of their adopted countries. This emigration meant that a significant number of Portsmouth men were killed serving with foreign military units. Ironically, war service brought many of them back to a Europe that they had left years before in circumstances that they may never have anticipated.

Twelve Portsmouth-born men were killed serving with the Australian Imperial Force, two with the Royal Australian Navy and four with New Zealand units. Many of these men's service records survive, and it is possible to research much of their careers and lives. Most were working in relatively low-skilled and low-paid jobs in Australia. Three were farm workers and others were working as blacksmiths, general labourers and a kitchenman – any who had emigrated seeking to make their fortune must have been disappointed. In any case, those who had emigrated and made a fortune might arguably have been less likely to join up. Half of them were in their twenties or early thirties and had obviously emigrated whilst relatively young.[3]

One Portsmouth man who emigrated to Australia had a varied military career. James Rolls was born in Portsmouth in 1876, the son of a sailor who retired from the Royal Navy and become a labourer in the dockyard. Rolls served in the Royal Navy for twelve years prior to emigrating to Australia. Enlisting in the Australian Imperial Force on 30 April 1917, he was sent to the 43rd Battalion of the Australian Infantry and served as a private. He was killed on the Western Front on 22 August 1918 and is buried at Daours in France; he was 43.[4]

The prospect of a new life overseas similarly drew many to Canada, and thirty-nine men from Portsmouth died serving with Canadian units. Like those who emigrated to Australia, most were working in low-paid and low-skilled jobs before they enlisted. Their service records show backgrounds of boilermakers, bricklayers, carpenters, chauffeurs, farmers, labourers, plasterers and plumbers. Most of these men enlisted in 1914 or 1915, early in the war.[5]

Several had also served in British military units prior to emigration, which no doubt inspired them to re-enlist and made them prime candidates for promotion. Originally from the Isle of Wight, Lance Corporal Phillip Western had served for twelve years in the Devonshire Regiment in Egypt, India and the Boer War. After the end of his service he went to Canada in 1906, where, after the start of the war, he joined the Canadian forces. He was serving with the 1st Battalion of the

Canadian Infantry when he was killed during the second Battle of Ypres on 22 April 1915; he was 43. He is remembered on the Menin Gate and on St Matthew's church memorial in Portsmouth.[6] Another Boer War veteran, Richard Griffiths, was born in Portsmouth and enlisted in the Dorsetshire Regiment in 1894. He was promoted to corporal and appointed orderly room clerk, but in 1905 was convicted of drunkenness on duty and reduced to the ranks. Griffiths spent almost five years' service abroad in Malta, Crete and in South Africa during the Boer War. After serving for twelve years he was discharged and he emigrated to Canada. He had been working as a plumber, but he volunteered for the Canadian forces in September 1914 and joined the 7th Battalion of the Canadian Infantry, where he was swiftly promoted to sergeant. He was killed on 15 August 1917, aged 39, and is remembered on the Vimy memorial in France. he was also awarded the Military Medal.[7]

Often officers' commissions could be easier to gain in colonial units, and of the six Portsmouth men killed serving in the Indian Army, all of them were officers. Lieutenant Colonel Samuel Cook of the 38th King George's Own Central Indian Horse died on 26 March 1918, aged 48, and is buried in Highland Road cemetery. He was the son of a professor and had attended Sandhurst in 1889 and 1890.[8] Captain Leopold Poynder of the 1st Battalion, 6th Gurkha Rifles, was killed in Iraq on 26 June 1916. The son of a lieutenant colonel in the Indian Army, Poynder attended Sandhurst in 1909 and 1910. He is buried in Basra and was awarded a posthumous Military Cross.[9] T.N. Gilder, a second lieutenant of the 47th Sikhs, died on 4 November 1918. Although remembered on the Madras memorial, he is actually buried in Bareilly in India. John Walcott had attended Christ Hospital School in Sussex before going to Sandhurst in 1912 and 1913, and was subsequently commissioned into the 2nd King Edward's Own Gurkha Rifles as a second lieutenant. He was aged 20 and living in Cavendish Road, Southsea, when he was killed serving on attachment with the 34th Sikh Pioneers at Neuve Chapelle in France on 2 November 1914.[10]

In a similar manner, African military units were primarily led by British officers, and a number of officers were among the six Portsmouth men killed with African regiments. Captain Frederick Batchelor was born in Portsmouth in 1891, the son of a grocer's assistant. Aged 27 and from Hampshire Terrace, Southsea, he died on 29 November 1917 in Sierra Leone, West Africa, whilst serving with the 2/2nd Battalion of the King's Africa Rifles. He is buried in Freetown cemetery and was subsequently awarded a posthumous Military Cross.[11] Lieutenant Archibald Warn, aged 45, was serving with the South African Service Corps when he died in Malawi, East Africa, on 29 March 1918. He was born in Portsmouth in 1871, and in 1891 was working in Tottenham, London, as a draper's assistant.[12] T.W. Cobb, a second lieutenant with the Egyptian Labour Corps, died on 15 December 1920 and is buried in Milton cemetery, suggesting that he was either on home leave at the time of his death or died of wounds.

Some African units also served on the Western Front. Gunner Charles Mitchell, aged 20 and from Southsea, was killed serving with the 73rd Siege Battery of the South African Heavy Artillery on 20 April 1917. He is buried at Ecoivres, France. A former pupil of the Southern Grammar School, Mitchell had emigrated to Rhodesia (modern Zimbabwe) and worked as a piano salesman before enlisting.[13]

Conversely, Portsmouth had long been home to numbers of immigrants from a wide range of places. Since the mid-nineteenth century, Portsmouth had been home to a sizeable community of Irish immigrants, many of whom had fled famine resulting from failed potato harvests between 1845 and 1850. Portsmouth seemed to have held a particular attraction, perhaps due to the prospect of employment with the Royal Navy, and by 1851 over 1,000 Irish immigrants were living in the town; by 1891 the number had swelled to 3,177.[14] Thirty-seven men from Portsmouth killed during the First World War are known to have been born in Ireland; thirty-one of them were serving in the Royal Navy. Many of them bore typically Irish names such as McGeady, O'Brien and O'Rourke. Many other men from Portsmouth had what appear to be more distant Irish roots, with surnames such as Murphy, McGuigan and O'Gara appearing. Irish regiments were particularly well represented among Portsmouth servicemen. The list of Irish units in which Portsmouth men served was extensive, including the Royal Dublin Fusiliers, Connaught Rangers, Royal Irish Fusiliers, Royal Irish Regiment, Royal Irish Rifles, and Royal Munster Fusiliers, as well as cavalry regiments such as the 4th Dragoon Guards (Royal Irish). However, service in an Irish regiment did not necessarily mean that a man was born in Ireland. Private William McGuigan, for example, was serving with the 8th Battalion of the Royal Inniskilling Fusiliers when he was killed on 16 August 1917. He has no known grave and is remembered on the Tyne Cot memorial near Ypres. He was 37 and lived in Beatrice Road, Southsea. McGuigan was born in Portsmouth in 1880, and in 1911 he was working as a house painter.[15] As with many with Irish roots, it is likely that McGuigan's parents or grandparents had emigrated to Britain in the nineteenth century.

Portsmouth was also home to a relatively small community with roots in Germany. Several men with German surnames died during the First World War; some of them possibly had Jewish roots.[16] Many immigrants in Portsmouth were subjected to anti-German harassment during the war, including some who had been British citizens for years and others with no German connections at all, such as Poles and Russians.[17] However, many men with German roots joined the armed forces, including Gunner Henry Berger of the Royal Field Artillery, Private John Hedicker of the 2nd Hampshires, Officer's Cook 1st Class Herbert Weitzel of HM Yacht *Zarefah* and Gunner Albert Rosser, a Royal Marine onboard HMS *Vanguard*.

Petty Officer William Koerner was a Portsmouth serviceman with German roots. Although he was born in Lambeth in London in 1873, Koerner's mother had been born in Germany in 1851. The family were living in Bradford in 1891,

at which time William was a butcher, but by the start of the war he was living at Fyning Street, Landport. Despite his clearly German name, he volunteered for the Royal Navy in October 1915. Posted to the Canadian Navy, he was serving onboard HMS *Niobe* when she was caught up in a massive explosion in the harbour of Halifax, Nova Scotia, in May 1917. Koerner was badly injured and although he returned to England he died of his injuries more than two years later on 29 October 1919. He was 47 years old, and he is buried in Kingston cemetery in Portsmouth.[18]

Given the relative proximity of France, it is perhaps not surprising that Portsmouth also had a number of families with French roots. Many French asylum seekers had come to Britain during the eighteenth and nineteenth centuries, including Huguenots escaping persecution. Among Portsmouth's well-known French immigrants was Marc Brunel, the father of the engineer Isambard Kingdom Brunel. By 1914 most of Portsmouth's French immigrants had integrated into local society.[19] Private Henry Bosonnet was killed serving with the 15th Battalion of the Hampshire Regiment at Flers on the Somme on 15 September 1916. Petty Officer Telegraphist Frederick De Barr, born in Portsmouth in 1889, was 26 when

he was killed serving onboard HMS *Natal* on 30 December 1915. He has no known grave, and is remembered on the Portsmouth naval memorial. Signal Bosun Arthur Mortieau was born in Chelsea, London, in 1872. He was killed when HMS *Hampshire* was sunk on 5 June 1916, and is remembered on the Portsmouth naval memorial. Interestingly, although all three of these men had French surnames, none of them had been born in France, nor had their parents. This suggests that their families had emigrated to Britain some years before and had become an integral part of local communities. Bosonnet, for example, was the son of a clerk in the Army Ordnance Corps and was born in Dublin.[20]

The grave of Second Lieutenant Robert Vernon-Inkpen. (Author)

A small but visible Italian community also made its home in Portsmouth. Many found work in catering, such as the restaurant trade, or as street entertainers. The 1891 census recorded a total of 102 Italians living in Portsmouth. Other Italians had arrived in Portsmouth in 1894 to work on the wood flooring and marble columns of St Agatha's church in Landport.[21] Sergeant Albert Petracca was born in Portsmouth. He was 36 and lived in Broad Street, Old Portsmouth, when he died serving with 372nd Horse Transport Company of the Army Service Corps. He died on 1 March 1917, and is buried in Ryde on the Isle of Wight. Both Albert Petracca and his father Joseph – a hairdresser – were born in Portsmouth, but his grandfather Antonio, who was born in Maraconova in Italy in 1855, was a confectioner. Hairdressing and catering were popular occupations for Italian immigrants.[22] Chief Engine Room Artificer William Lucia was born in Sittingbourne in Kent in 1873. He was killed when HMS *Queen Mary* was sunk at Jutland on 31 May 1916. He was 41 and lived in Balfour Road, North End. William Lucia was serving on HMS *Prince of Wales* in the Mediterranean fleet in 1911. He was born in Kent, as were both his father and grandfather, suggesting that his Italian roots extended beyond the mid-nineteenth century.[23] Officer's Cook Alfred Santillo was born in Plymouth in 1880. He was onboard HMS *Goliath* when she was sunk off Gallipoli on 13 May 1915. Remembered on the Portsmouth memorial, he was 35 and lived in Cardiff Road in North End. He was born in County Clare in Ireland in 1885, but lived in Plymouth for some years before joining the Royal Navy. In 1901 he was working as an errand boy and in 1911 as a switchboard attendant.[24]

Sick Berth Attendant Arthur Mazonowicz's surname suggests a Polish-Jewish ancestry. Born in Bethnal Green in East London in 1891, Mazonowicz joined the Royal Navy. He was serving at the naval barracks at HMS *Victory* when he died on 22 October 1918; he is buried in Haslar cemetery. Poles fled to Britain throughout the nineteenth century, escaping persecution and violent pogroms in central Europe during the period.[25]

Given the nature of the British Empire, with such a wide geographical spread and with naval outposts positioned around the globe, it is not surprising that men with roots in such places settled in Portsmouth. Eight naval ratings from Portsmouth who died were born in Malta, a key naval base in the Mediterranean. Maltese ratings seem to have taken on particular roles onboard ship: two were working in canteens (Canteen Manager Emmanuel Cacchia and Canteen Assistant Salvatore Cacchia), and two as officer's stewards (Officer's Steward Albert Coster and Officer's Steward Carmelo Buhagiar). Albert Coster was born in Valetta in Malta in 1873, and in 1901 was working on the Royal Yacht *Ophir* as a steward.[26] Carmelo Buhagiar was born in Malta in 1888, and in 1911 was a messman in the Royal Navy and living in Gillingham, Kent.[27] Maltese immigrants in Portsmouth seem to have been prominent in the local Catholic

community, and the Cacchias and Albert Coster are remembered on the St John's Roman Catholic Cathedral memorial.

Other men from Portsmouth were born in more exotic climes. All have distinctly British names, so it seems that their parents were serving abroad in the armed forces or had other reasons for living abroad. Notably, many men seem to have born in parts of the British Empire that had considerable military garrisons or naval dockyards.

Petty Officer George Temple was born in Bermuda on 31 December 1879. A British territory in the North Atlantic, Bermuda was home to a large naval dockyard. On 31 May 1916, Temple was onboard HMS *Invincible* when she was sunk at Jutland. He was 37 and at the time of his death was living in Knox Road, Stamshaw. In the 1911 census he gave his place of birth as Portsmouth. His father had served in the Royal Navy, which probably explains why George Temple was born in Bermuda.[28]

In 1914 India was still the jewel in the crown of the British Empire, and almost half of the British Army was serving in the Indian subcontinent at any one time. Hence many British citizens were born in India while their fathers were serving there. In addition, there were also naval bases in Bombay and Madras. Lieutenant George Walker-Williamson, who was killed onboard HMS *Chester* at Jutland, was born in the Punjab in India in 1888.[29] Cook's Mate William

Opie was born in Bombay in 1893. Opie was killed when HMS *Good Hope* was sunk on 1 November 1914. He was 25 and living in Durban Road, Buckland, and in 1911 he was working as a bricklayer's labourer.[30] Cook's Mate Frederick Shephard was born in 1897 in Nowong, a town in Central India that was an important administrative centre of British India. His father Harry had joined the Royal Artillery in 1888 and spent nine years serving in India between 1889 and 1898 before being discharged as a Wheeler Quatermaster Sergeant in 1909 and returning to his

The grave of Petty Office William Koerner, a Portsmouth man who had German roots and served in the Canadian Navy. (Author)

hometown of Portsmouth. Frederick Shephard was onboard HMS *Invincible* when she was sunk at Jutland.[31]

There was also a significant naval dockyard at Trincomalee in Ceylon, in modern day Sri Lanka. Petty Officer Samuel Greenway was born at Point de Galle in Ceylon in 1863. Aged 52 and living in Lake Road, Landport, he was onboard HM Yacht *Sanda* when she was sunk by German shore batteries off Zeebrugge on 25 September 1915.[32] Also born in Ceylon, in Colombo in 1897, was Able Seaman William Morrison. He joined the Royal Navy in 1911 at the age of 14. He was serving onboard HMS *Odin* when he died on 15 October 1916, and is buried in Basra, Iraq. He was living in Diamond Street, Southsea.[33]

Some sailors were born in even more exotic places around the world that had no connection with the British Empire. Leading Seaman Edward Williams' service record states that he was born in Campos Gabrielle, South America, in 1892. He joined the Royal Navy in September 1907 and was killed onboard HMS *Black Prince* at Jutland. He was living in Strode Road, Landport.[34] Chief Engine Room Artificer Stamper Wade was born in Boston in the United States. He was onboard HMS *Good Hope* when she was sunk. Wade's parents were both born in Halifax, Yorkshire, where they were living in 1871. The family evidently emigrated to Boston, for Stamper was born there in 1876, but by 1881 the family had returned and were once again living in Halifax.[35]

Compared to sailors, for many of whom service records survive, we know much less about where First World War soldiers were born. One Portsmouth soldier, however, had an intriguing background. Private Henry Hodge's entry on the Commonwealth War Graves register states that he was born in Barbados, a British island in the Caribbean. Venezuelan sources suggest that his father, Erconswald Walston Hodge, was prominent in the Caribbean Petroleum Company. He was 19 and living in Magdala Road, Cosham, when he died on 19 January 1916 of wounds received serving with the 1st Royal Fusiliers. He is buried in Menin Road South cemetery in Belgium and is also remembered on the Corpus Christi parish war memorial.[36]

That so many Portsmouth servicemen had such rich backgrounds suggests that although we consider cultural diversity to be a modern development, people in 1914 were much more travelled, diverse and broad-minded than might be originally thought. However, given Portsmouth's status as a port and garrison town, which saw people come and go on a regular basis, it is perhaps not surprising that its local society was more diverse than many other towns.

8

Sea Soldiers: The Royal Naval Division and the Royal Marines

Although it may seem like a contradiction, British sailors have in fact served onshore for centuries. Although the Royal Marines were formed in the late seventeenth century to provide the Royal Navy with an infantry force, sailors have frequently landed on shore to fight when the situation demanded it, such as in Nelson's navy. A naval brigade also famously fought in the Boer War, with naval guns being brought ashore.[1] The First World War saw a similar but even larger unit, the Royal Naval Division, being formed.

As part of their terms of service, sailors who were discharged from the fleet were part of the Royal Fleet Reserve (RFR), liable to being recalled in the event of a national emergency. Given the large number of ex-sailors who resided in Portsmouth, many local men were indeed liable for recall in August 1914. In addition, some civilian men also served voluntarily in the Royal Naval Reserve (RNR) or the Royal Naval Volunteer Reserve (RNVR). The RFR, RNR and RNVR were all automatically mobilised in August 1914, swelling the ranks of the Royal Navy.

When reservists poured into the naval barracks in the early days of the war, however, it was found that there were somewhere between twenty and thirty thousand more reservists than there were spaces that needed to be filled on ships. One historian has described reservists as waiting in depots 'for something to turn up'.[2] The Admiralty, however, had foreseen this surplus of manpower, and tentative plans had been made for the formation of a naval brigade to serve on land.[3] The Admiralty were keen to be seen to be contributing towards the war effort, and given that the Royal Navy had fulfilled its manpower commitments and the army was desperate for every man that it could get, it made sense for surplus sailors to be transferred to land service. A brigade of Royal Marines was formed for shore service as an advanced base force, and with the surplus of sailors it was eventually decided to form additional naval brigades, which were joined with the Royal Marines to form a Royal Naval Division.[4] The Royal Marine troops were regulars, and battalions were drawn from the Royal Marine Divisions

at Portsmouth, Plymouth and Chatham.[5] Also diverted from the army to the Royal Naval Division to fill out its ranks were 600 miners from the north-east.[6]

Although the traditions of sailors fighting on land were well established, it has been suggested that many of the original men detailed to form the Royal Naval Division were extremely unhappy at the prospect of what they perceived as being conscripted into the army: they had volunteered to serve at sea, and would have much preferred to do exactly that.[7] Opinion among senior naval officers was divided between those who saw the division as a misguided use of trained seamen and those who viewed them as not being proper sailors due to their reservist background.

The relationship between the army and the naval division was not always an easy one. The Royal Naval Division maintained a unique approach to war, retaining many nautical references in its everyday life. The officers' mess was referred to as the wardroom; men used 'the heads' rather than latrines and ratings going on leave 'went ashore'. Even the division's uniform was a combination of navy and army in appearance, consisting of navy blue with splashes of khaki.[8] Some aspects of naval culture proved exasperating for senior army officers. Royal Naval Division personnel, for example, were allowed to grow beards whilst the rest of the army was strictly clean-shaven.[9] The division also continued to receive naval pay rates.[10] These oddities went a long way to engendering solidarity amongst the sailors and marines, in defiance of military conventions.[11]

After a brief landing in an abortive attempt to defend Antwerp, during which a large number of Portsmouth Royal Marines were captured, the Royal Naval Division returned to Britain to await further employment.[12] Fortunately the division received khaki service dress to replace the naval uniforms they had worn at Antwerp[13]. On 28 February 1915 the division sailed from Bristol for the Mediterranean. At the time of departure the eventual destination was unknown, but the division was in the forefront of the Gallipoli landings on 25 April 1915, having been split up among the various landing beaches.[14]

Royal Marines landing at Gallipoli. Note the naval-style uniforms. (GWPDA)

Several Portsmouth sailors were killed with the Royal Naval Division at Gallipoli. Petty Officer Alfred Hutchings, 38 and from St James Road, Southsea, first joined the Royal Navy as a Boy Rating on HMS *St Vincent* in May 1893 and had fought at Antwerp. He was killed on 6 May 1915 serving with the Drake Battalion.[15] Leading Seaman William Bray, 20 and from Highland Road, Eastney, was killed on 4 June 1915 serving with Howe Battalion and had been mobilised via the Sussex unit of the Royal Naval Reserve in May 1914. Temporary Assistant Paymaster Harry Biles, 36, was serving with 2nd Brigade Headquarters when he was killed on 13 July 1915. Biles had served in the Royal Navy as a chief writer before being commissioned in 1914. Biles is buried in Skew Bridge cemetery, while Hutchings and Bray have no known graves and are remembered on the Helles memorial in Turkey. The men of the Royal Naval Division were among the last troops to be evacuated from the peninsula on 8 January 1916. At Gallipoli, 1,653 men in the Royal Naval Division were killed.[16]

After its return from Gallipoli, the future of the Division hung in the balance – not for the first or last time in its existence – while the Admiralty and the War Office contemplated how to utilise it.[17] Eventually the incessant demand for manpower on the Western Front led to the division being sent to France, but not before it came under the command of the army in April 1916.[18] The division first went into the front line in July 1916, at Bully Grenay – a quiet sector.[19] By the end of September, however, the division had gone south to train for their part in the final offensives on the Somme. On 13 November the attack on the River Ancre began, with the Royal Naval Division experiencing heavy casualties fighting near Beaumont Hamel – where the 1st Hampshires had been decimated on the first day of the battle over four months previously.

The Royal Marine battalions in the Royal Naval Division had naval medical staff. Chief Sick Berth Attendant Thomas Quartermain, 40, was from Clive Road in Fratton. Quartermain has been born in St Pancras in London in 1875. Serving in the Royal Navy on the outbreak of war, he was posted to the Deal Royal Marine Battalion in 1914. He fought at Antwerp and was wounded at Gallipoli in 1915. Quatermain was killed on 13 November at Beaumont Hamel. He has no known grave, and is remembered on the Thiepval memorial. The attack of the Royal Naval Division on the Ancre was successful, although heavy losses were experienced – some 100 officers and 1,600 men of the division were killed.[20]

The Royal Naval Division was also involved in the opening attacks of the Battle of Arras on 23 April 1917. Able Seaman Cecil Tytler, 38 and from Lindley Avenue in Southsea, was serving with the Drake Battalion when he was killed, and is buried in Orchard Dump cemetery in France. Tytler had actually joined the army on 25 July 1916, but was transferred to the Royal Navy on 3 March 1917 after arriving in France.[21] Although the division's part in the attack was a success,

it again took heavily casualties, with 170 officers lost and a total of 8,624 men killed, wounded or missing.[22]

The Royal Naval Division fought in the closing stages of the Third Battle of Ypres in October 1917. The mud of Passchendaele made the division's task an impossible one, and more than 3,000 casualties were experienced in just five days of fighting.[23] Soon after, in December 1917, the division was ordered to the Cambrai sector and took part in the closing stages of the Battle of Cambrai, in particular at Welsh Ridge on 30 December 1917 where two Portsmouth sailors were killed. Able Seaman John Murray, of Drake Battalion, came from South Shields in the North East and appears to have had few Portsmouth connections, having enlisted in the Royal Navy in November 1914. Murray fought at Gallipoli, where he was evacuated sick, and was later wounded at Arras. Able Seaman Arthur Brading, of Howe Battalion, was 25 and from Silverlock Street, Stamshaw. A gasworks labourer in civilian life, Brading joined the army reserve in December 1915 before entering the army fully in August 1916. However, he was drafted to the Royal Naval Division in March 1917. After only weeks on the front he was invalided back to England in April with an injured knee, before returning to France in November of the same year.

The Royal Naval Division was hit hard during the Germans' spring offensive of 1918, withdrawing and fighting hard for days on end. The division made an important stand at High Wood and Thiepval, and then counter-attacked shortly after at Mesnil. Several Portsmouth sailors were killed in the final offensive of the war in the autumn of 1918. Sub Lieutenant Cecil Attfield, 23 and from Bishops Waltham, was serving with the Drake Battalion when we has killed on 29 September 1918. He is buried at Proville in France. Attfield was the son of a naval lieutenant who was commissioned from the ranks, and was a painter and decorator before the war. Volunteering for the Royal Naval Volunteer Reserve in September 1914, he served with the Howe Battalion at Gallipoli, being evacuated with a gunshot wound and then a septic right hand. Serving on in France, he was wounded again on the Ancre on 13 November 1916. Whilst back in England recovering, he was commissioned as temporary sub lieutenant. Able Seaman Albert Payne of the Anson Battalion was killed several days later on 1 October 1918. Aged 19 and from Charlotte Street, Landport, Payne worked as a baker before the war and enlisted in the Royal Navy in July 1915. He was drafted to the Royal Naval Division in Gallipoli, but arrived after the evacuation. He then served in France. Albert Payne is buried in Proville cemetery.

The Royal Naval Division suffered a total of 44,829 casualties during its existence – more than four times its total manpower when it was first formed.[24] However, it had earned a fine reputation as a fighting division, proving wrong its many doubters. The division was finally disbanded at a parade at Horse Guards in London on 6 June 1919.[25]

Although Royal Naval Division was an ad hoc formation, the Royal Marines, the navy's dedicated infantry force, had had a presence in Portsmouth since 1755.[26] In 1914 the Royal Marines had consisted of 19,845 men of all ranks, of which 10,047 were serving at sea.[27] A total of 374 Royal Marines from Portsmouth were killed during the First World War. The youngest were a number of 15-year-old boy buglers, and the oldest was a 66-year-old colour sergeant. Of these, 187 were serving with the Royal Marine Light Infantry, 151 with the Royal Marine Artillery, thirty-four in Royal Marine Bands, one man with the Royal Marine Engineers and one in a Royal Marines canteen.

Compared to sailors, a considerable number of Royal Marines were killed while serving with the Royal Naval Division; a total of fifty-two men from Portsmouth died while serving with the Royal Marines units in the Royal Naval Division between 1914 and 1920. A significant number of them seem to have been long-serving ratings: of the thirty-four for whom enlistment dates have been found, twenty-two had enlisted prior to the start of the war.[28] The oldest had enlisted in 1888. Sources suggest that the Royal Marines battalions were formed from regular troops in Royal Marine barracks in 1914, and long-serving men were potentially more likely to have settled in Portsmouth. Although the Royal Marines were intended to be soldiers, the expansion of the Royal Navy in the later Victorian and Edwardian periods had led to Royal Marines being used as 'substitute sailors' in ships' crews.[29]

Possibly because the Royal Marines were thought to possess more experience of fighting on land than their sailor counterparts, men and units from the corps formed an integral part of the Royal Naval Division. Royal Marine officers and non-commissioned officers were appointed to some of the Royal Naval Battalions in the division. In particular, at any one time several battalions of sailors were commanded by Royal Marine officers, one of whom lived in Portsmouth. Norman Burge was born in Glasgow in 1877, and commissioned into the Royal Marine Light Infantry in February 1895. In 1901 he was living in the Royal Marines barracks at Forton, Gosport, and in 1911 he was a captain serving onboard HMS *Berwick* at Gibraltar. On the outbreak of war he was posted to the Royal Naval Division, and commanded a company in the Portsmouth Royal Marine Battalion at Antwerp in 1914. He later served as the second-in-command of the Royal Marine Cyclist Company before taking over command of the Howe Battalion in June 1915. Less than a month later he was transferred to take command of the Nelson Battalion, and after being Mentioned in Despatches in January 1916 for service at Gallipoli he led the battalion to the Western Front later in the same year. He was killed on 13 November 1916 leading his battalion during the Battle of the Ancre. He is buried in Hamel cemetery. At the time of his death he was 40 and living at South Parade, Southsea.

At the lower end of the scale, the Royal Marines provided other specialists for the Royal Navy. The Royal Marines took over the role of providing bands for the

Royal Navy in 1903, and in a short time made the role their own.[30] By August 1917 the Royal Marines School of Music alone consisted of 1,639 men.[31] Aside from their musical skills, Marine bandsmen had other roles in action, including serving as stretcher-bearers. Among the bandsmen killed in action was Musician Stanley Billings, of Albert Road in Southsea. Born in Battersea, London, in 1897, Billings was the son of a tailor. He lived in Goodwood Road in Southsea and worked as an errand boy prior to enlisting as a musician in the Royal Marines in September 1911. Billings was initially attached to the Marine Brigade Headquarters Band, and then in March 1915 he was attached to Drake Battalion as a stretcher-bearer. He served at Gallipoli before being evacuated suffering with enteric fever. He died in hospital on the island of East Mudros on 27 June 1915.

One Royal Marines officer from Portsmouth was decorated for bravery on the Western Front. Archibald Bareham was born in London in 1880, and enlisted in the ranks of the Royal Marine Light Infantry in 1898. He re-engaged for a further term of service in 1909, and in 1911 was a sergeant at the Royal Naval College at Osborne on the Isle of Wight. He was commissioned as a lieutenant in January 1916 before being posted to France in April 1918, joining the 1st Royal Marine Battalion in the Royal Naval Division.[32] Literally days after reaching the front, however, Bareham was seriously injured, slipping whilst going up to the front line and dislocating his shoulder. He was invalided back to England. He eventually returned to France in September 1918, and was in the thick of the action on 8 October during the allies' last great offensive when the battalion were counter-attacked by the Germans with tanks at Niergnies. Bareham immediately rallied the men, including some from other units, and formed a defensive line. He succeeded in pushing the enemy back and retaking the original positions. During the attack, however, Bareham was wounded and went missing, presumed to be killed. He has no known grave and is remembered on the Vis-en-Artois memorial. At the time of his death he was 38, and lived at Lawrence Road in Southsea. He was awarded a posthumous Military Cross for his actions on 8 October 1918, which was announced in the *London Gazette* in February 1919.

Aside from the Royal Marines units serving in the Royal Naval Division, The Royal Marine Artillery provided a brigade of howitzers for service on the Western Front. These 15in guns were amongst the heaviest in use by the BEF and had a range of 10,800 yards.[33] Ten Royal Marine Howitzer Gunners from Portsmouth died on active service, among them Sergeant Jonathan Heaton. Born in 1876, he worked as a labourer before enlisting in the Royal Marines in Leeds in September 1896. Re-engaging for a further period of service in 1909, Sergeant Heaton was onboard HMS *Invincible* during the first five months of the war, seeing action during the Battle of the Falklands. Heaton then served with the Howitzer Brigade on the Western Front, where he died on 24 September 1917. He is buried in Gwalia cemetery near Poperinghe in Belgium. Poperinghe is

back from the front line near the Ypres sector, suggesting that Heaton died of wounds or of illness. He was 40 years old and at the time of his death was living at Adair Road, Eastney, not far from the Royal Marine Barracks. He was awarded a posthumous Military Medal in December 1917.

Portsmouth's sea soldiers from the Royal Naval Division and the Royal Marines had performed valuable service, often in environments for which they had received little or no training. The forming of a naval division was not repeated during the Second World War, although the Royal Marines did go on to develop a role as commandos, particularly in amphibious warfare.

9

The Easterners: The War in the Middle East

Although the First World War was, from a British point of view, fought primarily in France and Flanders, fighting was by no means limited to this theatre. The Royal Navy, of course, fought wherever enemies were at sea, including off the Pacific Coast of South America and even in the South Pacific.

The importance of the Western Front was a bitter point of contention between the generals and the politicians. The generals, in particular men such as Field Marshal Sir Douglas Haig, felt that as the bulk of the German Army was on the Western Front, it was there that the Germans could best be defeated. The politicians, however, were growing weary of lengthy casualty lists and the apparent stalemate in France and Flanders and began to look for alternative, perhaps less costly, ways of defeating Germany and her allies.

Perhaps the best-known 'sideshow' was that of Gallipoli, the attempt in 1915 to force the Dardanelles Straits and capture Constantinople, the capital of Turkey. Other lesser-known campaigns were fought in Mesopotamia (modern-day Iraq) and Palestine against the Turks, and in Greek Macedonia against Bulgarian forces, better known as the Salonika Campaign.

The 2nd Battalion of the Hampshire Regiment was stationed at Mhow in India when war broke out. The government decided to bring home regular units from India and replace them with Territorial Battalions who had volunteered to serve overseas. The 2nd Hampshires returned to Britain in December 1914. Along with other regular battalions who had returned from India, they were formed into the new 29th Division and sailed for the Mediterranean on 29 March 1915.[1]

The Gallipoli campaign was conceived as an attempt to assist Russia by forcing a passage through the Dardanelles Straits and taking Constantinople, thus controlling the Black Sea. Initially it was thought that the Straits could be forced using ships alone, however several British and French ships were sunk by mines and fire from Turkish forts on land. Rather than lose more ships, it was decided to land troops and attempt to clear the Turkish defenders.

The 2nd Hampshires landed at V Beach on Cape Helles on 25 April. The main party of the battalion landed via the SS *River Clyde*, a collier hurriedly converted into a makeshift landing ship, whilst two companies remained offshore as a reserve. The men were heavily laden, carrying 200 rounds and three days' rations each.[2] The *River Clyde* ran aground 40 yards off V Beach at 6.22 a.m., and the troops were met by intense fire from the Turkish defenders as they transferred from ship to shore via small boats. Lieutenant Colonel Carrington-Smith, the commanding officer of the Hampshires, was killed on the *River Clyde*, and by the end of the day the battalion had suffered very heavy losses.[3] Among the dead was Private Lawrence Gilks, 24 and from Reginald Road, Eastney.

Heavy losses were also experienced the next day, when the Hampshires were ordered to attack on old fort at Sedd-el-Bahr on the right of the beach. Amongst the dead was Captain Alfred Addison, a 35-year-old from Queen's Crescent, Southsea, who had attended Portsmouth Grammar School. Addison had been commissioned in February 1899 and served during the Boer War, where he was Mentioned in Despatches.[4] Addison was killed by a grenade while leading the attack to capture Sedd-el-Bahr, which cost the Hampshires a further sixty casualties.[5] He is buried in V Beach cemetery.

The fighting at Helles was frantic and, after landing, the men were almost constantly in action. After V Beach had been consolidated, the Hampshires were part of the advance on the village of Krithia – which had been an objective on the day of the landings – and the high point of Achi Baba. The first attempt to capture Krithia took place on 28 April, with the Hampshires in the centre of the attack. The assault fell short of Krithia and incurred significant losses, including several men from Portsmouth: Private Charles Goldring of Highfield Street, volunteered November 1914; Private Ernest Horn, aged 18 of Strode Road, Stamshaw; Lance Corporal Arthur Dore, aged 21 of Town Street, Landport, who enlisted in 1908; Lance Corporal Frederick Roberts, aged 23 of Havant; Lance Corporal Frederick Oakshott, aged 25 of Queens Road, Buckland; and Private Frederick Denyer of 22 Maitland Street, Landport. Denyer is buried in Redoubt cemetery on Gallipoli; the rest of the men from Portsmouth have no known graves and are remembered on the Helles memorial.

A second unsuccessful attempt to take Krithia took place on 6 May, when the Hampshires advanced up Fir Tree Spur.[6] Although they very nearly made a breakthrough, their advance ended two days later.[7] Among the dead were Sergeant William Greenstreet; Company Sergeant Major William Godsell, aged 35; and Private Alfred Chittenden, aged 23 of Manners Road in Southsea. All are remembered on the Helles memorial. By 10 May the battalion had only 229 men remaining.[8] A final bloody attack was launched on 4 June, and although the Hampshires had some success, advancing almost a kilometre and achieving their objective, they were eventually forced to withdraw after the battalions on their

flanks had struggled.[9] Nine men from Portsmouth were killed: Lance Corporal Henry Griffin, aged 23 of Pervin Road, Cosham; Private Ernest Stone, aged 24; Private Ephraim Kill; Private George Mills of Ernest Road, Buckland, who had volunteered in August 1914; Private James Mason, aged 24 of Common Street, Landport, who enlisted in 1907; Private Reginald Cooper, of Holloway Street, Landport; Private Hartley Cox, aged 23 of Tokio Road, Copnor, who had enlisted in 1907; Private Alfred Bramble, aged 22 of Malthouse Road, Buckland; and Private William Pope, aged 22 of Byerley Street, Fratton. All are remembered on the Helles memorial. On 17 July the battalion withdrew to the island of Lemnos, where they were reinforced by a draft of 300 men.

The 10th Battalion of the Hampshire Regiment, on the other hand, was a war-raised unit, formed in Winchester in August 1914 as part of Kitchener's first New Army. The 10th Hampshires were quickly up to strength and were sent to Ireland in September 1914. They were attached to the 10th (Irish) Division, and after returning to England in early 1915 they sailed for the Mediterranean in July 1915. They were landed at Suvla Bay north of Helles on 6 August in an attempt to break the deadlock. The 10th Hampshires suffered heavy losses at Suvla, including fourteen men from Portsmouth. Ten men were killed in one day on 10 August when the Turks attacked in great force: Private Ernest Rowe, aged 30 of Trafalgar Place, Fratton; Corporal Herbert Adams, aged 28 of Gosport; Private Albert Goodall; Lance Sergeant Thomas Burnett, aged 29 of Diamond Street, Southsea; Company Sergeant Major William Groves, aged 44 of Winchester, who had been Mentioned in Despatches; Private Augustin Stephens, aged 23 of Lindley Avenue, Southsea; Private George Kent; Corporal John Knight; Private Frederick Ogden, aged 22 of Berkeley Street, Southsea; and Private Thomas Smith, aged 20 of Marlborough Row, Portsea. All are remembered on the Helles memorial. The landings at Suvla failed dreadfully, but not for want of bravery on the part of the ordinary soldier.

Although the line further south around Krithia settled down into stalemate after the June attack, a diversionary attack was made on 6 August, in the vineyard area south of Krithia, to draw attention away from the landings further north at Suvla Bay. The battle of Krithia Vineyard saw the heaviest losses of Portsmouth men at Gallipoli; among total losses of eighteen officers and 224 men of other ranks, fifteen Portsmouth men were killed: Private Albert Freemantle, aged 23; Private William Chalmers, aged 17 of Tipner Street, Stamshaw; Private Albert Marriage, aged 20 of Stanley Street, Southsea; Private John Hedicker; Private Frederick Jestins; Private William Keogh, aged 20 of Butcher Street, Portsea; Private Edwin Denyer, aged 24 of Maitland Street, Landport; Private James Hoare; Private Joseph Geeves, aged 18 of Fords Court, Landport; Private Hubert Bell, aged 21 of Collingwood Road, Southsea; and Private James Drain, aged 29 of Arnaud Street, Buckland, an employee of Portsmouth Gas Company. Bell is buried in Twelve Tree Copse cemetery, while the remainder are remembered on the Helles memorial.

Gallipoli has become symbolic in particular for Australians, and has been viewed by many Australians as representing the birth of their nation. Several men with Portsmouth connections served in the Australian Imperial Forces and two actually fought and died at Gallipoli.

William Woodhouse was born in Portsmouth in 1875 and lived for some years in High Street. A man of the same name had served in the Boer War as a lieutenant in the Imperial Light Horse. Woodhouse emigrated to Australia some time before the 1911 census. Although he was working as a commercial traveller in Brisbane, he enlisted in the Australian Forces on 24 August 1914. He had previously served for six months in the naval brigade and for five years in the Oxley Regiment, a Brisbane-based militia unit. He was posted to the 9th Battalion of the Australian Infantry and was swiftly promoted to corporal and then sergeant within a week of enlisting. He embarked for Europe on the SS *Omrah* on 24 September 1914, and landed in Egypt. Records show that he took his Masonic regalia with him. Woodhouse was killed at Gaba Tepe, south of ANZAC cove, on 20 May 1915. Unlike many of the dead of Gallipoli, his body was recovered, and he is buried in Shell Green cemetery, just 100 yards from ANZAC Beach. He left behind a wife and four children.

Another Portsmouth man serving with the Australians at Gallipoli died of wounds. Frank Scrivens was born in Portsmouth in 1891. The son of a dockyard labourer from Liverpool Road, he emigrated to Australia on 28 October 1910, sailing from London to Freemantle. After working as a farm labourer, on 6 October 1914 he joined the Australian Light Horse, a cavalry unit, as a trooper. He landed at Gallipoli in May 1915 and, after twice being evacuated suffering from diarrhoea and influenza, he was seriously wounded at Watkins Ridge, receiving a gunshot wound to his chest. Although he was evacuated to Malta, the wound became septic and turned to gangrene. Frank Scrivens died in hospital on 20 August 1915. He is buried in Pieta cemetery on Malta.

Gallipoli was finally evacuated on the night of 8 and 9 January 1916, with the 2nd Hampshires being among the last to leave. A total of 122 men from Portsmouth were killed in Gallipoli during the fighting on the peninsula, and seven men died in hospitals on the nearby Greek Island of East Mudros. Other wounded were evacuated further afield to Malta or Egypt, and some men died there. The campaign on Gallipoli was a daring plan that was executed badly and demonstrated the particular obstacles that amphibious operations presented. These would not be fully overcome until the Second World War. The evacuation, on the other hand, was brilliantly handled, and almost certainly prevented even heavier casualties. Nevertheless, the campaign was a lasting embarrassment.[10]

The Middle East was strategically important in 1914 for the same reason it is today: oil. The Royal Navy had recently begun to replace coal fuel with oil, hence it was important for Britain to guarantee the security of a vital

The 1/4th Battalion of the Hampshire Regiment entering Baghdad. The triumphant entry into the city went some way to making up for the calamitous fall of Kut. (GWPDA)

oil-producing region. The new Queen Elizabeth class of battleships were the first capital ships in the Royal Navy to be oil fired, and their commissioning intensified British interests in the oil-rich Persian Gulf region.

The first units in Mesopotamia came from the British Army in India, the first troops of which landed at Sanniya on 8 November 1914.[11] Basra was occupied on 24 November. The majority of the troops fighting in Mesopotamia were actually from regiments consisting of Indian men led by British officers. However among the first troops to land were the 1/4th Battalion of the Hampshire Regiment, a territorial unit that had originally arrived in India in November 1914 to relieve the regular battalions that had returned to Britain. In February the 1/4th Hampshires were in Rawalpindi when they were unexpectedly given orders to prepare to go to Mesopotamia on active service. They landed in Basra on 18 March 1915.[12]

Although the intention of the Mesopotamian campaign was to secure the southern oilfields, success advancing north along the River Tigris encouraged the commanders to advance on Baghdad. Although this was not achieved, Major-General Townshend, the commander of the advanced force, decided to allow himself to be besieged in the town of Kut, confident that relief would soon arrive. The siege started on 7 December 1915, and among the 13,076 troops holed up in Kut were half of the 1/4th Hampshires.[13] In the trying conditions, disease and illness were rife, including 1,050 cases of scurvy.[14] Although morale was high early in the siege, the failure of the relief force to make sufficient progress and the shortage of rations caused morale to fade. Men began to eat starlings, horses, donkeys and dogs, and the understaffed hospitals were overcrowded and poorly equipped.[15]

The remainder of the 1/4th Hampshires suffered heavy casualties in the relief force attempting to rescue their colleagues. The battalion left Amara on 31 December 1915 and fought in a long and arduous advance following the River Tigris, in particular losing many men at the Hanna Defile on 21 January 1916,

among them Private Alfred Tarrant and Private Alfred Leal from Portsmouth. The Battalion suffered a total of 239 casualties of all ranks. Losses were so heavy that on 14 February the surviving Hampshires were amalgamated into a composite territorial battalion along with men of other regiments.[16]

Also killed in the relief force attempting to relieve Kut were 20-year-old Private William Bryce of the Royal Army Medical Corps (attached to the 1/6th Devons), from Londesborough Road in Southsea, who was killed on 8 March 1916; Major Arthur Bickford, aged 45, who was serving with the 56th Punjabi Rifles and died on 9 March 1916; Private Edward Oram, aged 18 and from Fratton Grove, who had enlisted in the army in 1910 and was killed on 5 April 1916 whilst acting as a telephonist with the 6th Battalion of the South Lancashire Regiment; and Private G.W. Stallard, of the 9th Royal Warwickshire Regiment, who was killed on 23 April 1916.

Townshend finally surrendered the garrison on 29 April after almost five months of siege; the relief force – including the other half of the 1/4th Hampshires – were 12 miles away, but still being held up by the Turks. During the siege 1,025 men had been killed in action, 721 men had died of disease and 1,450 were admitted to hospital sick or wounded.[17] Among the men from Portsmouth to be killed fighting with the 1/4th Hampshires during the siege were Private Sidney Goad, aged 17 of Henderson Road, Eastney; Private John Barnes, aged 20 of Clarence Street, Landport; and Private F. Wilkinson. The senior commanders had seriously underestimated their Turkish opponents, and the defeat was a humiliation for the British Empire. Although General Townshend spent his captivity in some luxury, the other ranks of Kut suffered horrendously; 70 per cent of them died. Of the 178 men of the 1/4th Hampshires who had been in Kut, only fifty returned home.

Baghdad was eventually captured in March 1917. The fighting did not end there, however, and a total of 127 men from Portsmouth died in Iraq between 1914 and 1921. One senior officer with Portsmouth connections died in the last days of the war in the Middle East. Lieutenant Colonel Reginald Lynch-Staunton was awarded a Distinguished Order and a bar and Mentioned in Despatches four times during the First World War, whilst serving as a staff officer, a Brigade Major and finally

Private James Iggleden, who drowned in the River Tigris. (SGS)

Lieutenant Alfred Chatterton, who died of heat
stroke in Mesopotamia. (SGS)

a brigade commander in the Royal Field
Artillery. Lynch-Staunton is remembered
on St Andrew's parish church memorial
in Farlington.

There could also be unfortunate accidents
during wartime. Private James Iggleden,
of the 1/6th Battalion of the Hampshire
Regiment, drowned whilst bathing in the
Tigris on 27 June 1918, despite the efforts of
two of his comrades to rescue him. His body
was not recovered and he is remembered on
the Basra memorial. He had enlisted in the
army in November 1915 and had formerly
been a pupil at the Southern Grammar School before becoming a teacher at
Stamshaw School.[18]

The extreme conditions in the desert could also be problematic for men
more used to temperate climes. Lieutenant Alfred Chatterton, serving with the
215th Brigade of the Royal Field Artillery, died of heatstroke on 21 July 1917,
and is buried in Baghdad's North Gate cemetery. Chatterton had attended the
Southern Grammar School, and secured an apprenticeship in the dockyard. His
life took a dramatic turn in 1914, however, when he enrolled at the University of
Cambridge with the intention of becoming a priest. Before the end of his first
year though, he had volunteered for the army. A letter from his commanding
officer suggests that Chatterton had remained at his post for several days even
while he was sick, and that this might have hastened his death.[19]

Due to the instability in Iraq in recent decades it has been very difficult for
British war graves in the region to be maintained. However, the Commonwealth
War Graves Commission hopes to renovate cemeteries and memorials in the
country as soon as conditions permit.[20]

Even before the first troops had been evacuated from Gallipoli, British and
French troops had already landed in Salonika, Greece, in an attempt to reinforce
the Serbian Army in their war against the Bulgarian Army in Macedonia.[21] The
first troops landed on 5 October 1915, and the 10th Battalion of the Hampshire
Regiment followed the next day, after being evacuated from Gallipoli. The
conditions in Macedonia were harsh, with cold nights and incredibly hot
summer days. After an initial advance the British forces fell back towards Salonika
in December 1915, before advancing once more in April 1916. Significant battles

British and French troops behind the lines in Salonika. (GWPDA)

were fought around Lake Doiran in April 1917 and September 1918, before an armistice was concluded with Bulgaria on 29 September 1918. Thirty-six men from Portsmouth are known to have died whilst involved in the campaign in Macedonia. Salonika was not a particularly dangerous theatre in terms of enemy action – only 8 per cent of men who served there became battle casualties, compared to 55 per cent on the Western Front.[22] The real enemy in Salonika was disease – it is thought that for every man who died in battle, twenty more died of illness.[23] A total of 502,809 men were admitted to hospital during the whole Salonika campaign, with 161,559 admissions for malaria alone.[24] A large number of supporting troops died of illness in Salonika. Among them were men such as Lieutenant Charles Stubbs, of the Army Ordnance Corps. Born in Southsea, he died on 9 March 1918. He had previously served as a staff officer in the Boer War.

Although the Bulgarians were prevented from advancing further into Greece, Serbia was not saved from collapse. One historian has argued that the real war in Salonika was not against the enemy, but the malarial mosquito.[25]

Egypt was a major transportation centre for British forces in the Middle East, given the presence of the Suez Canal and its strategic position between Asia and Europe. Twenty-eight Portsmouth men died in Egypt, probably in hospitals and depots in the region. Many of them may have been wounded in other campaigns, such as Gallipoli or Salonika.

Egypt had been occupied by British troops long before 1914. The Turks occupied the nearby holy lands of Palestine, and in 1914 and early 1915 British forces defended the Suez Canal against Turkish incursions. Fighting also took place in the Sinai Peninsula. By 1917 the British forces in Egypt had grown strong enough to advance into Palestine against the Turks. The 1/8th Battalion of the Hampshire Regiment were in the advancing army, and suffered losses at the

second and third Battles of Gaza in April and then in October and November. Jerusalem was finally captured in December 1917. In total, forty men from Portsmouth were killed in the war in Palestine. Among them was Rifleman Harry Hawes, aged 23 and from Gains Road, Southsea, who was serving with the 1/8th Battalion of the Hampshire Regiment when he died on 2 November 1917. He is buried in Gaza war cemetery, and was awarded the Military Medal. Another Portsmouth man killed in Palestine was Alan Steed. Although born in Glasgow, he had attended the Southern Grammar School for five years from 1906 before going to the Municipal College and becoming the president of the Student Union. After graduating he became a civil servant, rising to become a head of office in the National Health Insurance Department. Although he volunteered at the start of the war, he was not called up until late 1915, when he joined the London Regiment as a private. He specialised in musketry and went overseas with his battalion as an armourer, fighting at Arras on the Western Front, in Salonika and in Palestine. After taking part in the capture of Jerusalem in early 1918, he was killed by a Turkish shell in the Jordan Valley. He was 23 and is remembered on the Jerusalem memorial.[26]

10

Brothers in Arms: Portsmouth Families at War

Portsmouth society was well used to the role that many of its young men played in the armed forces, having been at the forefront of the development of the Royal Navy for hundreds of years. Children grew up with their fathers often away for long periods serving in the Navy, and then joined up themselves. But while Portsmouth families were used to the conditions of military service, the First World War represented the first time that thousands of Portsmouth families lost loved ones. Given the proportion of the population that served in the armed forces during the First World War – In 1911 Portsmouth had a higher proportion of servicemen among its population than anywhere else in Britain – and that military service was often a family tradition, it is not surprising that in many cases members of the same family were killed in action.[1] Sometimes more than two close relatives were killed. In the early days of the war, two Portsmouth soldiers were killed in the same unit on the same day, and in one Portsmouth family, four brothers were killed.

Walter and Elizabeth Ware married in Southsea in 1882. According to the 1891 census, they were living in Knapps Cottages, 1 Havant Road. This was technically outside Portsmouth, in Widley. Walter Ware was born in 1853, and was an employed labourer, originally born in the small village of Southwick north of Portsmouth. His wife Elizabeth was born in Southsea in 1858. They had six sons – Walter, William, George, Wynn, Jack and Wallace, and a daughter, Mabel.

Private George Ware was a regular soldier serving with the 1st Battalion of the Duke of Cornwall's Light Infantry. He had enlisted in Portsmouth. The 1st Duke of Cornwall's Light Infantry had been stationed at Curragh in Ireland, but went to France in August 1914, disembarking on 20 August. He was killed on 14 September 1914 during the Battle of the Aisne. He was 20 and is remembered on the La Ferté-sous-Jouarre memorial in France. He was entitled to the British War Medal, the Victory Medal and the 1914 Star.[2]

Wynn Ware was born in 1887. In 1901 he was living in Widley with the rest of the family and working in a brewery as a bottler, but in 1911 he was boarding

in Kensington in London and working as a chauffeur. He enlisted in St Austell in Cornwall into the Duke of Cornwall's Light Infantry, but at some point was transferred to the 5th Battalion of the Royal Irish Fusiliers. The 5th Royal Irish were a service unit, formed in Armagh in 1914 as part of Kitchener's New Armies. Sailing to Gallipoli in 1915 and by now a sergeant, he landed at Suvla Bay on 7 August 1915. Wynn Ware was killed on 17 September 191, and is remembered by a special memorial in Green Hill cemetery in Turkey. He was aged 29 and was entitled to the British War Medal, the Victory Medal and the 1915 Star.[3]

Jack Ware was born in 1895. He enlisted in the army in Gosport and was a medic serving at 33rd Casualty Clearing Station (CCS), part of the Royal Army Medical Corps. Jack Ware went to France early in the war, disembarking on 21 August 1914. The 33rd CCS were based at Bethune for most of the war. At some point Jack Ware was taken ill and evacuated from the front line to a base hospital in Calais. He died on 20 December 1916, and is buried in Calais Southern cemetery in France. He was 21, and was entitled to the British War Medal, the Victory Medal and the 1914 Star.[4]

Walter Ware was born in Eastney in 1884. In 1901 he was living in Widley and working as a bricklayer's apprentice, but in 1911 he was living in Cosford Stables, near Godalming in Surrey, and working as a domestic gardener. He enlisted into the Royal Garrison Artillery in Cosford, and joined the 136th Heavy Battery. He went to the Western Front relatively late in the war, probably from 1916 onwards. He was killed in action on 15 June 1918, and is buried in Canada Farm cemetery in Belgium. He was 36, and entitled to the British War and Victory Medals.[5]

Walter Ware Senior died in 1894 and his wife Elizabeth in 1903, but had they been alive they would have received four telegrams from the War Office informing them that each of their sons had been killed in action. One must have been bad enough, but to lose four sons in such a way would have been devastating. Three were pre-war regular soldiers, who died within the first year of the outbreak of war. Walter Ware Junior in particular must have been very aware of the fate of his three brothers when he went off to fight. In the film *Saving Private Ryan*, set in the Second World War, Tom Hanks's character went to save James Ryan as three of his brothers had been killed, but there was no similar ruling by the British Army during the First World War.

Staff Sergeant Arthur Hall. (SGS)

It is a sobering statistic that 291 sets of brothers were killed on the same day during the First World War,[6] one pair of which was from Portsmouth. Charles Roberts was born in Portsmouth in 1891, and his brother George was born in 1893. Their elder sister Alice was born in Mhow in India in 1880, with the 29th Regiment of Foot, suggesting that they were born into a military family. The 29th Foot had been in Templemore in Ireland in 1873, where the Roberts brothers' mother Ann had been born.

In 1901 both were living in Highbury Street, Armoury Lane in Portsmouth, but by 1911 George was serving as a drummer in the 1st Battalion of the Dorsetshire Regiment, based in Farnham in Surrey. He had enlisted in London. Prior to the outbreak of war he had transferred to the 2nd Battalion of the Royal Munster Rifles, into which his brother Charles had also enlisted in Gosport. They were both serving as signaller corporals.

The 2nd Munsters were garrisoned at Aldershot on the outbreak of war and were part of the Guards Brigade in the 1st Division. They landed at Le Havre on 14 August, and went straight up to the front. After the Battle of Le Cateau the British Army retreated. Along with the 15th Hussars, the 2nd Munsters fought a stiff rearguard action south-east of Le Cateau at Etreux. A single battalion was facing six German battalions.[7] Instructed to hold the ground around the town until ordered to withdraw, in a Rorke's Drift-style action the battalion fought for twelve hours and suffered severe casualties, until they were surrounded and virtually destroyed.[8] Out of the 1,008 officers and men who had landed in France, after Etreux only 201 remained.[9] Charles and George Roberts were both killed on the same day – 27 August 1914 – and are buried in the same grave at Etreux British cemetery in France.

The First World War also exacted a heavy toll on the Dugan family from Portsea. Private Wesley Dugan was part of the 15th Battalion of the Hampshire Regiment, the 2nd Portsmouth Pals. He was killed at Flers on the Somme on 15 September 1916, along with hundreds of other young men from Portsmouth. He has no known grave and is remembered on the Thiepval memorial. The 15th Battalion suffered incredibly heavy losses on this day, the first day of the Battle

Second Lieutenant Henry Hall. (SGS)

of Flers, an attempt to renew the Somme offensive that had started in July 1916. His brother Private James Dugan was killed just under a year later. Serving with the 2nd Battalion of the Hampshire Regiment, he died on 21 August 1917 at the age of 43. He has no known grave, and is remembered on the Tyne Cot memorial. He was killed during the Passchendaele offensive, between the Battle of Langemarck and the Battle of the Menin Road. The third Dugan brother fell in the spring of 1918. Private Edwin Dugan was killed on 19 April 1918 while serving with the 2nd Battalion of the Hampshire Regiment. He is remembered on the Ploegsteert memorial. This was during the Kaiser Offensive, the Germans' last-ditch attempt to turn the tide of the war on the Western Front in 1918. Thus the Dugan family lost three sons in eighteen months of bloody fighting.

Rifleman Albert Squires was serving with the 1/8th Battalion of the Hampshire Regiment in Palestine when he was killed on 19 April 1917. He has no known grave and is remembered on the Jerusalem memorial. He had originally enlisted in October 1915. Private Charles Squires was serving with the 4th Battalion of the Worcestershire Regiment in the Ypres Salient when he was killed on 9 October 1917. He has no known grave and is remembered on the Tyne Cot memorial. He had originally joined the army in October 1916. Lance Corporal Harry Squires was serving with the 2nd Battalion of the Hampshire Regiment when he was killed on 24 August 1917. He is buried in Dozinghem cemetery, near Poperinghe, Belgium. Dozinghem was used as a burial ground by CSS set up to treat the wounded from the 1917 offensive in Ypres, better known as Passchendaele. This would suggest that he died of wounds. Harry Squires was awarded a posthumous Military Medal, announced in the *London Gazette* on 16 October 1917, and was also Mentioned in Despatches.[10] He had joined the army in November 1916. Thus John and Ellen Squires of Landport lost three sons within the space of six months. All had joined up during the war and gone on active service from 1916 onwards.[11]

John Dennis, aged 24 and of the 2nd Battalion of the Rifle Brigade, was a regular soldier who, according to the National Roll, had joined the army in 1906. He landed in France on 7 November 1914 as a private, and during almost two years of service on the Western Front was promoted to sergeant. He was killed on 25 August 1916. He has no known grave, and is remembered on the Loos memorial. He was entitled to the British War Medal, the Victory Medal and the 1914 Star.[12] Corporal Arthur Dennis, of the 15th Battalion of the Hampshire Regiment, volunteered in 1914. He served at Gallipoli with the 2nd Hampshires, landing on 25 April 1915, and then in France. He was killed on 5 August 1917. He has no known grave, and is remembered on the Menin Gate memorial in Ypres. He was entitled to the British War Medal, the Victory Medal and the 1915 Star.[13] Neither the Commonwealth War Graves register nor the National Roll record his age; however, records show that an Arthur Dennis was born in Portsmouth

between January and March 1895, which would make him 22 at the time of his death. Private James Dennis, of the 1st Battalion of the Dorsetshire Regiment, joined the army in July 1917. Aged 19, he was killed on 28 August 1918. He is buried in Assevilliers New British cemetery, France. Their ages certainly suggest that all three men were brothers, and that John and Sarah Dennis of Amelia Street, Landport, lost three sons between 1916 and 1918.

Two brothers from the same family died serving with railway companies of the Royal Engineers, within a day of each other. Robert Hyson was born in Aldershot in 1886 and his brother Frederick in Portsmouth in 1894. Their father Joseph was a military messenger. In 1901, both were living in Goodwood Road in Portsmouth and Robert was working as a blacksmith's apprentice. Both seem to have enlisted in the army after the start of the war.[14] Frederick married in 1916 and enlisted into the army in Portsmouth. In December 1917 he went to Egypt with the 98th Light Train Crew Company, which had only been raised the same month. Robert, meanwhile, married in 1906 in South Stoneham near Southampton, and in 1911 was working as a signalman. He enlisted in Portsmouth and – unsurprisingly, given his occupation – he also joined a railway operating company, and went to Salonika. The railway operating companies were responsible for operating the tracks, stations and signalling, while the train crew companies, naturally, provided the crewmembers for the trains themselves. By 1917 Robert was an acting sergeant. He died on 30 December 1917, and is buried in Lembet Road cemetery in Greece. He was 32. Frederick was onboard the SS *Osmanieh*, a troopship liner, sailing to Egypt. He was killed when the ship was sunk by a mine entering Alexandria harbour on 31 December 1917, and is buried in Hadra cemetery in Alexandria. A total of 190 men and eight nurses were killed on the SS *Osmanieh*.

Already a prominent artist, William Lionel Wyllie purchased Tower House off Broad Street in Old Portsmouth in 1906. He subsequently became famous for his maritime scenes, including many of the Portsmouth area. All five of Wyllie's sons served in some capacity during the First World War, two of whom were killed. Robert Wyllie, known as Bob, was born in Rochester, Kent, in 1889. He served as a private in the Territorial 1/14th Battalion of the London Regiment, known as the London Scottish. Bob Wyllie first landed in France on 15 September 1914 and was killed in a bayonet charge at Messines, near Ypres, less than six weeks later, on 1 November 1914. Although his mother Marion went to the Western Front seeking news, his body was never found and he is remembered on the Menin Gate. He was 26. He was entitled to the British War and Victory Medals and the 1914 Star.[15]

Further tragedy struck the Wyllie family. William Wyllie Junior, known as Bill, was born in St John's Wood, London, in 1882. He married in Wiltshire in 1912, and lived in Purbrook. Initially serving with the 2nd Battalion of the Durham Light Infantry, including during the Boer War, he first went overseas in 1915 and

later acted as Brigade Major – senior staff officer – in the 13th Infantry Brigade. He was killed on 19 July 1916 at Montauban, near Mametz, on the Somme. He was 34 and is buried in Dantzig Alley cemetery. The 5th Division went into attack at High Wood the next day, suggesting that Bill Wyllie was killed whilst preparing for the attack. He was entitled to the British War and Victory Medals and the 1915 Star, and left a widow and three children.[16]

After the end of hostilities the Wyllies visited the Western Front in search of their sons' last resting places, but only William's grave could be found. Fittingly, William Wyllie Senior painted a watercolour of his son's grave. Whilst there, Wyllie also painted sections of the trenches. A memorial to Bill Wyllie is in Portsmouth Cathedral, a magnificent bronze effigy commissioned by his father. Bob Wyllie is remembered in his father's painting *The Miraculous Draught of Fishes*.

There were very few cases of fathers and sons both being killed. Regimental Sergeant Major Frederick Frampton, aged 46, of the 65th Heavy Group of the Royal Garrison Artillery, was killed on 24 August 1917 and is buried at Bard Cottage cemetery in Belgium. He lived in Chichester Road in North End. His son had evidently followed him into the Royal Garrison Artillery. Gunner George Frampton, aged 19 and also of Chichester Road, died on 29 September 1918 serving with 355th Siege Battery of the Royal Garrison Artillery. He is buried in Doingt cemetery in France.

Many more siblings – and indeed fathers and sons – were killed whilst serving in the army than in the Royal Navy. This was probably due to the higher proportion of men serving in the army and the higher casualty rates that the army suffered as it fought constantly in a number of theatres from August 1914 to November 1918. However, there were several instances of family members being lost at sea in the same battle, and even in the same ships.

Given the manner in which war casualties were recorded, it is likely that even more sets of siblings were killed than has been acknowledged. Only around 50 per cent of entries on the Commonwealth War Graves Commission's register have information regarding parents and home address, making it difficult to ascertain family connections, in particular with more common surnames.

However, it should at least be clear that some families paid a staggering price during the First World War, a price that would have seemed morbidly unbelievable in August 1914 when young men were joining up for adventure and expected to be home by Christmas. For parents to lose a child is against the natural order of life; to lose one son must have been bad enough; to lose two must have been incredibly difficult. But to lose three or four, or two sons on the same day, or even a husband and son or father and brother, must have tested the emotional resolve of more than a few Portsmouth families.

11

Portsmouth's Bloodiest Day: The Battle of Jutland

Ever since the Battle of Trafalgar in 1805, Britain could legitimately claim to have ruled the waves. Nowhere was the general public more conscious of this than in Portsmouth, the historic home of the Royal Navy and the port through which a large proportion of the Royal Navy's capital ships were manned. Not only were thousands of Portsmouth sailors onboard the fleet's ships, but many of those ships had been built by the hard labour of Portsmouth Dockyard workers. It was very much a fleet made in Portsmouth.

The British fleet that fought the war at sea had its roots in the nineteenth century, but had undergone rapid transformation in the decades before 1914.[1] The First World War had in part been caused by the volatile naval rivalry between Britain and Germany, a rivalry that was escalated by the launch of HMS *Dreadnought* in 1906. *Dreadnought* boasted a faster turn of speed, bigger guns and stronger armour than existing vessels. She had been built in Portsmouth, in the remarkably short time of a year and a day. The battlecruiser concept had been developed by the First Sea Lord, Admiral Sir Jacky Fisher, who also encouraged mixed progress in incorporating aircraft and the submarine into naval warfare. The size of conventional battleships, and with big guns, the battlecruisers sacrificed armour for speed – the idea being that their speed was to be their defence.[2] Battlecruisers were not initially intended to fight the enemy's main battleships but merely to act as a scouting force. Crucially, a lack of awareness of the failings of their weak armour and ambiguity over their role in battle prevailed well into the war.[3]

Although much of the fleet was manned from Portsmouth, and indeed many ships were based there in peacetime, upon the outbreak of war the Royal Navy's Grand Fleet moved to anchorages in Scapa Flow and the Firth of Forth. This enabled the fleet to react swiftly to any German forays into the North Sea. The Dover Straits were well protected by destroyer patrols, which guarded the never-ending stream of troop ships taking men to the army in France and Belgium. Public opinion in Britain longed for a climactic fleet action, a 'second Trafalgar'.[4]

Britons had been brought up on a diet of British naval supremacy, and expectations were sky high. The sailors of both fleets also keenly awaited battle, what the Germans referred to as *'Der Tag'*.[5] The commander-in-chief of the Grand Fleet, Admiral Sir John Jellicoe, was less keen to fight a major battle, however. The Royal Navy already controlled the seas, and a costly battle might damage this status quo. The German Navy, for its part, was also keen to avoid a major battle, and its few raids into the North Sea were designed to avoid any kind of contact.[6]

On the whole, Portsmouth does not seem to have produced many naval officers. One naval officer from Portsmouth, however, had a varied career, including royal connections. Reverend Henry Dixon-Wright was born in Islington in 1870 as Henry Wright and, after studying at Cambridge as an Abbot's Scholar, joined the Royal Navy as a chaplain in 1899.[7] He served onboard HMS *Resolution*, HMS *Ramillies*, HMS *Bedford* and ashore in Malta. He married his wife Annie Lawrie in Portsmouth in 1904, before becoming the chaplain at the Royal Naval College in Dartmouth in September 1907.[8] He was at Dartmouth when the Prince of Wales (the future King Edward VIII) was at the college. Wright assisted the Archbishop of Canterbury and the Dean of Windsor at the Prince's confirmation on 24 June 1910, having prepared the Prince spiritually, and composed a new hymn especially for the occasion.[9] In September 1911 Wright changed his surname to Dixon-Wright, and soon after accompanied the royal party as chaplain onboard HMS *Medina*, a loaned P&O steamer that took King George V to India for the Delhi Durbar in December 1911.[10] He must have been reasonably wealthy, as the 1911 census shows that he had two servants – a nurse and a cook.[11] He returned to Dartmouth in February 1912, and was made a member of the Royal Victorian Order, a personal gift of the sovereign, the same month.[12] Dixon-Wright joined the Battleship *Albermarle* in July 1914, and a year later he followed the commanding officer of the *Albermarle*, Captain Craig, to the brand new Queen Elizabeth class super-dreadnought HMS *Barham*.[13]

Another Portsmouth officer in the Grand Fleet was serving not in the Royal Navy but the Royal Marines. Francis Harvey was born in Kent in 1873, the son of a commander in the Royal Navy. The family had strong naval roots, going back to Captain Harvey who commanded HMS *Brunswick* at the 'Glorious First of June' in 1794. Harvey entered Portsmouth Grammar School in July 1884, where he was a prominent member of the debating society. During his time at the school, the Harvey family lived at Courtney Lodge off Clarendon Road in Southsea. In 1892 he took exams for Sandhurst and finished thirty-third out of 193 candidates, and for the Royal Marines, where he ranked second out of twelve. He eventually chose to join the Royal Marines Light Infantry and went to the Royal Naval College in September 1892. He became a specialist in gunnery, and served afloat in the Pacific and with the home and channel fleets. In 1910 he served as a gunner instructor at Chatham, before he joined the battlecruiser HMS *Lion* in February 1913.[14]

Admiral Scheer, the commander of the German High Seas Fleet, knew that he could not defeat the Grand Fleet in a pitched battle, and therefore planned to destroy the Royal Navy's big ships piecemeal and gradually improve the odds in his favour. On 31 May 1916, Scheer launched an operation to bombard Sunderland. This, he hoped, would draw out the battlecruiser fleet from the Firth of Forth, for whom German submarines would be waiting. Scheer was not aware, however, that his signals were being read by the Admiralty and analysed by naval intelligence, before being passed on to Jellicoe.[15] The battlecruiser fleet did indeed sail, to intercept Scheer before he had even left harbour, and the rest of the Grand Fleet was not far behind. The men onboard the ships leaving Scapa were not necessarily expecting a battle; the fleet had sailed many times before, on exercises or false alarms.[16] But, imbued with a national heritage of sea power, the sailors of the Grand Fleet were calmly confident.

Scheer's plan to bombard Sunderland, meanwhile, had been abandoned; instead the German fleet launched a foray north along the Danish coast. The Battle of Jutland almost began by accident when the two fleets stumbled into each other. Beatty's battlecruisers had been sent to search for the German fleet. At 2.20 p.m. on 31 May, ships from Beatty's fleet were sent to investigate a neutral Danish merchant vessel and encountered German destroyers on the same mission.[17] The first shots were fired by the light cruisers HMS *Galatea* and HMS *Phaeton* at 2.28 p.m. After a short exchange, the British and German ships withdrew towards their main fleets. Then, at 3.22 p.m., Beatty and Hipper's fleets came into contact in what would later be called the 'run to the south'. Beatty possessed six battlecruisers and four Queen Elizabeth class battleships compared to Hipper's five battlecruisers, and hence should have proved more than a match for his adversary. The first shots of the battlecruiser action were fired at 3.48 p.m. The fleets steamed a parallel course while firing at each other, with Beatty attempting to cut the Germans off from their bases while Hipper attempted to draw Beatty onto the guns of Scheer's High Seas Fleet, which was approaching from the south. The aggressive Beatty assumed that his role was to engage the German battlecruisers, rather than lure them onto the guns of the Grand Fleet's battleships.[18] Jellicoe, on the other hand, did not want Beatty to fight an independent action on his own, for fear of losing ships needlessly.[19]

Unfortunately for Beatty, the 5th Battle Squadron – containing four of the brand new Queen Elizabeth class battleships with 15-inch guns – missed a crucial signal and had not changed course. Therefore Beatty was lacking a significant amount of firepower that would have almost certainly decimated his opponent.[20] Beatty's flagship, HMS *Lion*, came under heavy fire early in the action. At around 4.00 p.m. a salvo of 12-inch shells from *Lutzow* wrecked the Q turret amidships. The fire threatened to engulf the nearby magazine, but by great presence of mind Major Francis Harvey, who was badly burnt and whose legs had been crushed, dragged himself to the voice pipe and ordered the magazine to be flooded, thus

removing the risk of a catastrophic explosion but drowning the survivors left in the turret in the process.[21] Eleven Portsmouth men died on HMS *Lion* during the battle, including Major Harvey, who died of his wounds soon after. For his brave actions he was Mentioned in Despatches and awarded the Victoria Cross. Events on other ships soon after would show how critical Harvey's actions were.[22]

At 4.02 p.m., after only fourteen minutes of action, HMS *Indefatigable* was hit by shells from *Von der Tann*, detonating her after magazine and forcing her to fall out of the line of battle. Shortly after, *Von der Tann* hit *Indefatigable* again; this time a shell plunged down through one of her forward turrets, piercing the thin armour and causing a huge explosion in her main magazine. She rolled over and then sank. *Indefatigable* was crewed mainly by Plymouth men, but nine Portsmouth sailors were lost when she was sunk, along with six Royal Marines. Among the men lost was Instructor Henry Wallis, 29 years old and from Southsea. Wallis was the holder of a Master's degree from Oxford University.

Shortly after, at 4.25 p.m., HMS *Queen Mary* was hit by a combined salvo from *Derrflinger* and *Seydlitz*. Both of her forward magazines exploded and a red flame was seen to rise up from her fore. Explosions then erupted forward and amidships, and she collapsed inwards and sank in a huge cloud of smoke. All but nine of her 1,275 men were lost. *Queen Mary* was a Portsmouth-crewed ship, and 152 Portsmouth men were among the dead, including fifteen Royal Marines. She had sunk so suddenly that HMS *Tiger*, the next ship in the line, had to steer wide to avoid colliding with her wreckage. Among the dead on *Queen Mary* were two brothers serving in the Royal Marines Band. Band Corporal Arthur Wood was born in Worcester in 1892 and enlisted in the Royal Marines in 1906; his brother Frederick, a musician, was born in 1889 and enlisted in 1905. Their parents, of Kimberley Road in Southsea, would have received not one but two official telegrams after the battle. Officer's Cook Edwin Palmer, aged 52, was the oldest Portsmouth man killed at Jutland. Born in Fareham, he lived in Brougham Road, Southsea. Electrical Artificer 3rd Class Leonard Major was born in Portsmouth in 1889 and lived in Teddington Road, Milton. After attending Southern Grammar School, Major became a ship and electrical fitter's apprentice in the dockyard, and after completing his apprenticeship served in the Royal Navy as an electrician. He was 27.

HMS *Princess Royal*, a Lion class battlecruiser, was hit by a German salvo around the same time, at 4.26 p.m. A huge explosion caused even Admiral Beatty to think that she had sunk. It was at this point that Beatty uttered his immortal words, 'there seems to be something wrong with our bloody ships today.'[23] In fact, the *Princess Royal* survived the battle but required extensive repairs in Portsmouth afterwards, her battered state upon arrival shocking onlookers. In total, seven Portsmouth sailors were killed onboard *Princess Royal* at Jutland, among them Gunner Ernest Gamblin, a Royal Marine reservist who had originally joined up in 1897 and was mobilised on the outbreak of war. Two more Royal Marines who were killed on

Princess Royal had joined up long before the First World War – Gunner Alfred Eburne in 1906 and Gunner Walter Pearson in 1908. Also killed onboard *Princess Royal* was Steward William Whitewood, who had been mobilised from the Mercantile Marine.

It would be very difficult to cast Beatty's 'run to the south' as a victory. The loss of two ships and thousands of sailors killed for no enemy ships sunk in return meant that he had squandered his numerical advantage, both by misusing the battlecruisers and by failing to communicate with the 5th Battle Squadron correctly. However, there was indeed 'something wrong with our bloody ships'. The battlecruiser concept was flawed, the armour that had been sacrificed for speed proving to be sorely missed. British ships also had inadequate anti-flash protection, increasing the risk of explosions spreading throughout the ship.[24]

After losing two of his ships so suddenly, Beatty ordered his escorting destroyers to make a torpedo attack. The destroyers managed to get close to the German battlecruisers, but HMS *Nomad* was disabled early on with a shell through her main steam pipe, and a shell hit HMS *Nestor*'s forward boiler room.[25] Several Portsmouth men were lost on the destroyers – Petty Officer George Hawkins on the *Nestor* and three men on the *Nomad*, including Able Seaman Walter Read. Read was Mentioned in Despatches and was also awarded the Romanian Cross of Military Virtue, 2nd Class. Both *Nestor* and *Nomad* were heavily damaged and later sank.

Several minutes after *Queen Mary* had sunk and *Princess Royal* was damaged, the main body of the German fleet was sighted. Beatty turned his remaining battlecruisers north, in order to rejoin Jellicoe and the rest of the Grand Fleet. The 5th Battle Squadron, for the second time in the battle, missed the signal to turn to the north and subsequently engaged the German fleet on its own for an hour.[26]

At 5.38 p.m., the brand-new light cruiser HMS *Chester*, screening the Grand Fleet, was intercepted by German scouting ships and suffered horrendous losses. Among her wounded was Boy Jack Cornwell, who died of his wounds and was later awarded the Victoria Cross for manning his gun after the rest of the crew had been killed. He was just 16. Lieutenant George Walker-Williams, 27 and from Southsea, was the most senior officer killed on the *Chester*. An officer of the RNR,

HMS *Lion*, Admiral Beatty's flagship, leading the battlecruiser fleet. *Lion* was heavily damaged at Jutland. (GWPDA)

Major Francis Harvey, who was mortally wounded
at the Battle of Jutland and posthumously awarded
the Victoria Cross. (PGS)

Walker-Williams was born in India, lived
in St Andrew's Road in Southsea and had
been Mentioned in Despatches when HMS
Alcantara had clashed with the German ship
SMS *Greif* in February 1916.

The three Invincible class battlecruisers
that had sailed with the Grand Fleet
were sent by Jellicoe to reinforce Beatty.
The commander of the squadron, Rear
Admiral Hood, mistakenly sailed towards
the German fleet and opened fire on the
German battlecruisers. As the lead ship
HMS *Invincible* took heavy fire and a shell penetrated her Q turret, a flash ignited
powder in the magazine, causing a catastrophic explosion. The ship broke in half,
with each end subsequently pointing out of the water and clear to onlookers on
nearby ships. *Invincible* was another Portsmouth ship, and of her crew of 1,032
men only six survived. Of those lost, 154 definitely came from Portsmouth. The
ship's senior rating, Master at Arms Thomas Peters, was among the Portsmouth
men killed. Born in 1879, he joined the navy in 1897 as a Boy Rating on HMS
St Vincent. He served on ships as an able seaman, a sailmaker and as a ship's
corporal, before being promoted to master at arms in January 1915. Peters served
on HMS *Invincible* throughout the war.[27] Carpenter Thomas Walls was born in
County Tyrone in Ireland in 1873. He was 42, and lived in Warren Avenue in
Milton. Although he is classed as a carpenter on the Commonwealth War Graves
register, his service record states that he had been promoted to warrant shipwright
in 1905. He was awarded a Distinguished Service Cross – an officer's award
– for bravery during the Battle of the Falklands. Ship's Cook Arthur Mansell
was born in Woking in Surrey in 1880. At the time of Jutland he was 31 and
living in Marylebone Street, Portsea, and had served ashore during the Boer War.
Engineer's Mate Samuel Self, the son of a retired engineer lieutenant commander,
was born in Portsmouth and lived in Festing Grove in Southsea. After attending
Southern Grammar School between 1902 and 1904, he enlisted into the Royal
Navy in 1904 as a boy artificer. Awarded the first prize among his intake on the
training ship HMS *Fisgard*, Self served as an engine room artificer before being
commissioned as an engineer's mate. The commander of HMS *Invincible*, one of
the few survivors, wrote of him, 'He was a popular officer in the wardroom and

HMS *Queen Mary*, another Portsmouth-based battlecruiser sunk at Jutland. (GWPDA)

an excellent messmate. The Engineer-Commander had also a high appreciation of his professional abilities.' The chaplain of his previous ship, HMS *Neptune*, wrote, 'Everyone formed a very high opinion of him. We all liked him very much and we all feel that the service has lost a keen and promising officer.'

Around the same time, the 1st Cruiser Squadron also managed to blunder into the German line. They bravely opened fire on the *Wiesbaden* but were devastated by Hipper's other battlecruisers. HMS *Defence* was sunk with the loss of all 903 of her crew, sixteen of them from Portsmouth, and HMS *Warrior* was heavily damaged.

Once the main fleets came within range of each other, the fighting reached frenetic proportions. *Barham* was seriously damaged, as was *Malaya*. Shortly after the main fleets engaged, however, Scheer turned towards the German coast, then swiftly turned back as if planning a last ditch attempt to take on the Grand Fleet. Before this climactic duel, however, Scheer turned 180 degrees yet again, this time for good, and ordered a destroyer torpedo attack. Jellicoe ordered the Grand Fleet to turn away to present a narrower target to the torpedoes. This order has subsequently been as evidence that Jellicoe was too cautious, but it undoubtedly saved more British ships from being sunk, not to mention the lives of thousands of sailors.

As dusk fell, the Grand Fleet was between the German fleet and its home bases. Despite the opportunity that this presented him, Jellicoe was eager to preserve his fleet and wanted to avoid a night action. In the confusion of darkness, several unexpected encounters occurred between the two fleets. The cruiser HMS *Southampton* came upon unknown ships in the dark and was heavily damaged. Five Portsmouth men were killed, including Canteen Manager William Barley, of Fordingbridge Road in Eastney.

The obsolescent armoured cruiser HMS *Black Prince*, which had already blundered into the German fleet early in the battle, did so again during the night. She received heavy fire from the German battleships and her main magazines exploded. All of her crew of 857 were killed, including 101 men from Portsmouth. Among the Portsmouth men killed were Bugler Cyril Tawney, at 15 years old one of the youngest to be killed at Jutland; Painter William Wearn, of Toronto Road

in Buckland; and Chief Petty Officer John Heath, who had enlisted in 1891 and lived in Stamshaw.

The Fourth Destroyer Flotilla also stumbled into the German fleet. The flagship HMS *Tipperary* challenged mystery ships, and after being illuminated by searchlights received fire from six German ships as a reply. Twenty-three Portsmouth men were killed, including Able Seaman John Wallis, a 40-year-old reservist who had been recalled in August 1914. Wallis had been born in Dorset but lived in Havant Street, Portsea. *Tipperary* fell out of the line, shattered and in flames. Led by HMS *Broke*, the remaining ships attacked. *Broke* was fired on by *Westfalen*, and after her wheel was destroyed, collided with HMS *Sparrowhawk*. The collision was so violent that several men from *Sparrowhawk* landed on *Broke*. *Fortune* was picked up by German searchlights and took heavy fire, and *Ardent* was also hit after taking on a division of German battleships. *Tipperary*, *Sparrowhawk*, *Fortune* and *Ardent* later sank. *Broke* miraculously survived, but with heavy casualties, including Chief Petty Officer John Rathmell, who was born in Newcastle and had been awarded the 1900 China Medal, and Leading Seaman Trueman, of Clive Road, Fratton.

HMS *Shark* was hit and severely damaged; unable to move, she eventually sank. HMS *Defence* was sunk by the *Lutzow*; there were no survivors from her crew of 903. Among the Portsmouth men killed on the *Defence* were another 15-year-old Royal Marines bugler, Alfred Rush, and Petty Officer John Barrett, who had served in the Boer War and in China.

Although many men were killed by shellfire and explosions, the majority of men who survived into the water died of exposure; only a fortunate few were rescued.[28] Although the vast majority of men were lost at sea, some bodies were washed ashore in Scandinavia and are buried there. These mostly seem to have been men whose ships were sunk in the night action. Leading Cook's Mate Audley Sealey, of HMS *Shark*, is buried in Egersund in Norway. Eight Portsmouth sailors are buried in Kviberg in Sweden: Petty Officer Stoker Charles Collins and Petty Officer Stoker Harry Hughes of HMS *Ardent*; Petty Officer Stoker Harry Reeves, Able Seaman Thomas Page and Able Seaman Sidney Bellchamber of HMS *Fortune*; Chief Bosun Frederick Mansbridge of HMS *Black Prince*; and Petty Officer Stoker Stephen Mayhew and Artificer Engineer Allan Hurst of HMS *Shark*.

Most of the men who died of wounds soon after the battle were buried at sea in the traditional manner; those who died nearer to home were buried ashore at Lyness cemetery.[29] Among them were Henry Dixon-Wright, who had succumbed to his wounds on 1 June, and Cook's Mate Frederick Watts of HMS *Malaya*, who died on the same day.[30] Onboard HMS *Lion*, Admiral Beatty began the funeral service, the chaplain having been killed. Among the men to be buried was Major Francis Harvey. Overcome by emotion, Beatty had to hand over to the ship's captain, Ernle Chatfield.[31] Several Portsmouth men died of their wounds

HMS *Invincible*, sunk at Jutland on 31 May 1916. (Gates)

Engineer's Mate Samuel Self, who was killed at Jutland when HMS *Invincible* was sunk. (SGS)

sometime after the battle. Engine Room Artificer William Dent, of HMS *Barham*, died on 2 June and is buried in Lyness, and Chief Petty Officer Henry Jones, of HMS *Malaya*, died on 11 June 1916. At 52 and a reservist, Jones must have been among the oldest seamen to fight at Jutland. He is buried in Kingston cemetery.

News of the battle was made public in the newspapers on 3 June. The ambiguous reports coming from German and British sources shocked the general public – they had expected nothing less than a crushing victory. Although the British had suffered heavy losses, the Germans had not achieved their objective and the strategic status quo still favoured Britain. The debate over who won the Battle of Jutland – and whether Beatty or Jellicoe was responsible for the lack of a more resounding triumph – has raged ever since.

On an infinitely more human level, Portsmouth was hit incredibly hard by Jutland. The battle caused what was, in all probability, the largest ever loss of life among Portsmouth people in one single incident. Portsmouth's dead from Jutland came overwhelmingly from the city's terraced houses. Seventy-eight were from Southsea, forty-nine from Landport and thirty from Buckland. Of the fourteen who died from Eastney, eight were Royal Marines. That few men were killed from Cosham (four) Drayton (two) and Farlington (one) suggests how sparsely populated these areas were in 1916.

A total of 6,094 British sailors were killed at Jutland.[32] Of the 534 Portsmouth men to die at Jutland, only eighteen, just over 3 per cent, were commissioned officers. Of these, most were relatively junior, the most senior being Major Harvey of the Royal Marines, along with three engineer commanders – Reuben Main of HMS *Invincible*, William Colquhoun of HMS *Tipperary* and Hubert Clegg of HMS *Indefatigable*. The low number of officers from Portsmouth would suggest that not only were young men born in Portsmouth less likely to gain a commission – probably given their lack of wealth, education and social

The grave of Henry Jones, who was wounded onboard HMS *Malaya* at Jutland and died after the battle. (Author)

The memorial service in Victoria Park for the many Portsmouth men lost at Jutland. (Author)

connections – but also that officers from elsewhere were less likely to take up residence in the town, perhaps preferring to live in more fashionable towns and villages nearby.

Of the other ranks killed in the battle, a large proportion of Portsmouth men were leading ratings, petty officers and warrant officers. Presumably such longer-serving men were more likely to settle in Portsmouth. Of the Portsmouth men killed at Jutland, 152 of their enlistment dates are known. Of these, only eight had joined up after the outbreak of war, and four had been mobilised from the reserves. Forty-two had enlisted in the nineteenth century, and the longest-serving rating had first enlisted in the Royal Navy back in 1891. Men with trades such as blacksmith, shipwright, cook, plumber and sailmaker were killed, indicating the range of skills required onboard ship in what was still in many respects a Royal Navy very similar to that of the Victorian era.

News of the Battle of Jutland was received with mixed emotions in Portsmouth. The first indication of the battle reached the town at 6.58 p.m. on 2 June, when a telegram reached the *Evening News* office stating 'Great Battle in the North Sea'. The Admiralty's official despatch on the battle, on which initial media reports were based, conveyed the impression of a loss for the Royal Navy and did nothing to dispel public distress, the terrible loss of ships and lives having a particular effect in Portsmouth. The streets rapidly filled with people. Two women in Commerical Road fainted with grief, not knowing if their menfolk were alive or dead.[33] The town's war relief offices opened later than usual to assist the bereaved. The next

EVENING NEWS, MONDAY, JUNE 5.

TOLL OF BATTLE.

THE CASUALTY LIST.

300 OFFICERS LOST.

TWO ADMIRALS INCLUDED.

The Admiralty has promptly issued a detailed list of the casualties among the officers serving in the ships which took part in the great fight. All those on board the Indefatigable, the Defence, and the Black Prince were lost; only four of the Queen Mary and two of the Invincible were saved. The list of killed numbers 333, and includes Rear-Admirals Hood and Arbuthnot, whose flags were carried on the Invincible and the Defence respectively. Among those who are returned as having died of wounds is the Rev. Henry Dixon-Wright, M.V.O., Chaplain of the Royal Naval College, Dartmouth. Many representatives of well-known families are to be found in the list, including the Earl of Denbigh's second son, Lieut.-Commander the Hon. R. C. Fielding; Commander the Hon. B. S. Bingham, the third son of Lord Clanmorris; Midshipman the Hon. Cecil E. Molyneux, the Earl of Sefton's youngest son; a son of Sir Thomas Esmonde, M.P.; and a son of the Rev. Dr. Gow, the Headmaster of Westminster School.

In a later list the Admiralty announces the names of the petty officers and men reported saved from the Queen Mary, Invincible, Fortune, Ardent, and Shark. It numbers only 43, of whom eight are returned as wounded. No men have been returned as saved from the Indefatigable, Defence, Black Prince, Tipperary, Turbulent, Nomad, or Nestor. A list of casualties on the Warrior comprises the names of 64 killed, one died of wounds, one missing, believed dead, and 27 wounded. A list covering casualties on other ships not named comprises the names of 106 killed, nine died of wounds, and 73 wounded, of whom five are returned as dangerous and 38 as severe cases.

OFFICER CASUALTIES.

H.M.S. Queen Mary.

KILLED.

Captain Cecil I. Prowse.
Commanders Sir Charles R. Blane, Bart., and

Francis T. Phipps, Griffith O. L. Owen, the Hon. Bernard M. Bailey, Malcolm A. M. Harris, John D'U. Scott, Meynell O. Hanwell, Trevor G. L. Hayles.
Clerk Cyril H. Adams.
Assistant Clerk Jack A. Kneel.

H.M.S. Black Prince.

KILLED.

Captain Thomas P. Bonham, R.N.
Commander John B. Waterlow, D.S.O.
Lieutenant-Commanders David W. S. Douglas and Charles S. Morris.
Lieutenants Robert I. Faulkner, Robert C. Chichester, William W. J. Fletcher, Geoffrey H. V. Bayfield, Harold Blow, R.N.R., and Charles F. Halliday, R.N.R.
Engineer-Commander George E. A. Crichton.
Engineer Lieut.-Commander James D. Niven.
Engineer-Lieutenant Ernest W. Caine.
Captain Alfred W. Delves-Broughton, R.M.L.I.
Lieutenant Geoffrey R. Steinthal, R.M.L.I.
Chaplain Rev. William F. Webber, B.A.
Fleet-Surgeon Herbt. L. Geoghegan, M.B.
Surgeons Thomas M. Wood-Robinson and John S. D. McCormac.
Sub-Lieutenant Arthur H. C. Barlow.
Sub-Lieutenant Thomas McL. Hutchinson, R.N.V.R.
Mates Thomas H. Clark and (E) Henry T. Cleare.
Assistant Paymasters John P. Rising, Harry H. Palmer, R.N.R. and Edgar S. Price, R.N.R.
Chief Gunner George F. Collingwood.
Chief Boatswain Frederick H. Mansbridge.
Gunners Donald Simpson and William A. Morrell.
Boatswain William J. Grier.
Signal Boatswain Henry H. Rowe.
Carpenter Ernest H. Mortimer.
Acting Artificer Engineer Albert Middleton.
Artificer Engineers William G. H. Pike, James Woodrow, and Thomas Cole.

H.M.S. Warrior.

KILLED.

Chief Carpenter James M. Richards. All the other officers were saved.

H.M.S. Tipperary.

KILLED.

Captain Charles J. Wintour.
Lieutenants Ronald I. Collier, E. N. G. Maton, J. A. Kemp and Gerald T. C. Collins.
Engineer Commander W. C. Colquhoun.
Assistant Paymaster T. B. Brooks.
Gunner J. Oates, Signal Boatswain Arthur W. Phillips, Warrant Telegraphist Edwin Dymott, Artificer Engineer C. E. Rees.

H.M.S. Turbulent.

KILLED.

Lieut.-Commander Dudley Stuart, Lieut. John A. Orr-Ewing, Engineer Lieut.-Commander Reginald G. Hines, Sub-Lieutenant John S. Kirkland, Gunner George Borthwick.

H.M.S. Fortune.

KILLED.

Lieut.-Commander Frank G. Terry, Lieut. Richard E. Paterson, Acting Sub-Lieut. Hugh B. Paul, Gunner John P. Hutchings.

H.M.S. Ardent.

KILLED.

Lieut. Charles E. F. Egan, Surgeon Probationer John E. MacIntyre, Chief Artificer Engineer Ernest Slack, Gunner Albert G. N. Livermore.

H.M.S. Nomad.

Extensive lists of Portsmouth casualties filled the pages of the *Evening News* for weeks after the Battle of Jutland. (*EN*)

MOURNING REQUIREMENTS.

The New Shop which we have added to-day to our MOURNING DEPARTMENT, on the opposite side of the road, we think will contribute to your comfort when shopping. We now have a separate shop for Black Costumes and Dresses. We were so crowded yesterday that we had to hurry our builders to give us the use of this new shop at once. The windows are dressed to-day, and there is a complete new show of all the newest productions in Black Tailor Made Costumes. There are models at 19/11, 21/9, 25/9, 29/6, 35/6, 45/6, 49/6, 59/6, and 63/- each. There is also a huge stock of sensible and serviceable Indoor Black Dress Skirts at 2/11, 3/11, 5/11, 6/11, right up to 16/11 each. We have also plenty of the extra large sizes in Black Dress Skirts. Simple and dainty Black Frocks are another feature; there is a nice choice at 10/11, 16/11, 19/11, and 25/9.

We also draw attention to a special line of Black Silk Taffeta Robes, which are worth 35/9 each, but which we can sell you at 19/11 each.

Black Alpaca Coats will be found to be very useful, and can be bought in this new shop at 10/11, 12/11, 16/11, right up to 35/6 each. Those requiring all Black Macintoshes will find our special Model at 25/6 most serviceable and dependable. We have every length in Stock.

BLACK FEATHER NECKWEAR

Will be shown at 3/11½, 5/11, 6/11, right up to 21/6 each. These are very fashionable this season and are a pleasing finish to the neck. Black Silk Sports Coats are very scarce, but to-day we have a varied assortment.

BLACK MOIRE COATS

Are always becoming, and have a rich good looking tone and finish. We have some exceedingly pretty styles at 16/11, 19/11, 25/9, 29/6, and choice productions up to 63/ each.

For slight Mourning we have a useful collection of Black and White Voile Robes, Black and White Check Coats, and Black and White Check Skirts. These two shops are devoted exclusively to every kind of mourning requisites all the year round.

MOURNING MILLINERY

Also has a shop to itself. We have an endless assortment in Hats and Bonnets, both trimmed and untrimmed. The choice includes not only the very smartest of shapes, but also a big selection in the more simple designs. Quite a lot of ladies give the preference to what we may describe as the plain and sensible shapes, and we cater for these with as much variety as the smart and stylish series of designs. The object of the two shops is to bring down the unnecessary expenses attached to mourning requirements, and to sell every item at a low rate of profit. In addition to this, we believe that the old-fashioned virtues of kindly service, of pleasing and obliging assistants, are valued more highly to-day than ever before. We are very confident that in these new shops our customers will not only find our goods cheaper and better, but that they will experience attentive service. The fact that the shops are detached from the rush and bustle of our bigger premises will also contribute to your comfort when buying blackwear.

AT

MARSHALL'S MOURNING

Adverts for mourning clothes increased in the *Evening News* in the aftermath of Jutland. (*EN*)

day the *Evening News* offered 'profound sympathy with the many families who are today mourning'. The *Evening News* appeared to share the belief that the battle had been a defeat, stating that 'the balance appears to be against us'. An absence of official casualty lists caused much anxiety. A list was eventually posted outside the town hall, and the *Evening News* dedicated pages to a special roll of honour, every day from the 8th until 17 June. The Post Office telegraph boy was busy delivering the dreaded telegrams in naval communities.[34] It was reported that at the Trafalgar Institute in Landport, the lockers of nearly a hundred dead sailors and marines had to be emptied.[35] Meanwhile, the government worked vigorously to convince the public that the Battle of Jutland had in fact been a victory, and in the opinion of contemporary local historian W.G. Gates the people of Portsmouth gradually came to share this view.

Jutland has perhaps become best-known in Portsmouth history for an often perpetuated belief regarding losses. Whilst the editor of the *Evening News* and Gates, wrote that there was 'scarcely a family that does not mourn a husband, son, brother or friend',[36] more specifically it has also been suggested that one unnamed street contained forty widows as a result of Jutland.[37] Research suggests that the streets with the highest number of casualties from Jutland were Chichester Road in North End, Guildford Road in Fratton and Telephone Road in Southsea, from each of which five men were killed. Four men were lost each from Adelaide Street in Buckland, Newcome Road in Fratton, North End Grove in North End, Queens Road in Buckland and Reginald Road in Eastney. Although these casualties do represent significant losses for one battle, each of the streets mentioned above consisted of considerably more dwellings. Even allowing for the small number of casualties for whom no address is available, it seems unlikely that any one street in Portsmouth lost as many men has been suggested. Although the losses were perhaps not as severe as some commentators have intimated, they were still extraordinarily heavy. The Bishop of Winchester stated that at Jutland Portsmouth had suffered losses three times as heavy as the whole nation had endured at the Battle of Trafalgar in 1805.[38]

Despite the public view that Jutland was a victory, the loss of life cast a dark shadow over the town. In the words of the *Evening News*, 'never before was prayer more needed, never before was it more expressed'.[39] Memorial services were held at St Mary's church and in Victoria Park, incongruously under a blazing June sun. The sinking of the Cruiser HMS *Hampshire* several days later, with the death of Lord Kitchener and ninety-four sailors from Portsmouth, only compounded the sense of loss in the town. Somewhat cynically, advertisements in the *Evening News* for mourning clothes increased dramatically.[40]

Jutland cast a shadow over Portsmouth for many years. HMS *Barham* was eventually lost during the Second World War, sunk by a U-boat in 1941 with the loss of many Portsmouth sailors.[41] The battlecruiser HMS *Hood*, commissioned

during the First World War and built to a similar concept as the battlecruisers that fought at Jutland, was sunk by the *Bismarck* in 1941 in a remarkably similar fashion to her predecessors, a single shell penetrating her poorly-armoured magazine and causing a catastrophic explosion.

On paper, the Battle of Jutland was a strategic victory for the Royal Navy. It still controlled the seas, and its losses were made good swiftly. The German fleet had scurried back to port and rarely ventured out again during the war. Yet public opinion and the traditions of the Royal Navy, somewhat unfairly, demanded more than a tactical victory.[42] Whatever the result, the Battle of Jutland represents Portsmouth's greatest loss of life in one day throughout its entire history. Perhaps due to the blurred nature of its outcome, and that the First World War is not generally perceived as a naval conflict, Jutland has largely been forgotten by history compared to battles such as Trafalgar. The fleet that fought in the North Sea on 31 May and 1 June 1916 was very much made in Portsmouth, and the hundreds of men killed from the town meant that regardless of the strategic outcome, Portsmouth bore the impact of the battle more than anywhere else. Perhaps William Gates best summed up Portsmouth's attitude to Jutland: 'Portsmouth will always remember Jutland with pride, though not without sorrow.'[43]

12

A 'Sink of Iniquity'? Landport:
A Portsmouth Community at War

Although middle-class Southsea boasted by far the most officers among Portsmouth's war casualties, most of the town's working-class neighbourhoods lost many hundreds of men serving in the ranks. Although the fate of the middle-class elite has been much more prominent in history, the deaths of thousands of working-class men from Portsmouth perhaps more accurately reflect the town's lost generation of the First World War. A total of 446 young men from Landport alone were killed, and the experiences of these men provide a useful cross section of Portsmouth society in general. It can be seen, from even a small handful of stories, that their backgrounds were remarkably diverse, and their experiences even more so.

The first dwellings in Landport – originally called 'halfway houses' – were built in the early nineteenth century as an overspill from the town of Portsmouth resulting from the influx of people during the wars with revolutionary and Napoleonic France. Its name derives from the gate on the land side of the old town fortifications, the 'land port'. Straddling the road from Portsmouth to London, among the first houses built in the area was that in Old Commercial Road in which Charles Dickens was born in 1812. The nineteenth century saw rapid change in Portsmouth, and by 1914, Landport was completely unrecognisable from the neighbourhood of Dickens's time. With the coming of the railway, Landport assumed a new importance. Due to the fortifications around Old Portsmouth, Portsmouth's main railway station had to be built some way to the north, next to the road to London. A number of hotels sprang up around the station, as well as the town post office. Commercial Road, slightly to the north, grew into the town's major commercial district, with the road occupied by department stores and public houses. Crowning the development of the area, the new neo-classical town hall was completed in 1890.[1]

Yet, despite these impressive developments, Landport was still predominantly a slum area. The medieval town of Portsmouth had expanded onto the east and north of Portsea Island, and Landport was by now bordered by new areas such as

Fratton, Kingston and Buckland.[2] Whereas in the early nineteenth century any part of Portsea Island outside of the town walls could be referred to as 'Landport', by 1914 developments in neighbouring areas led to Landport becoming smaller and more defined, broadly covering an area east of Anglesey Road, slightly south of the railway line, west of Fratton Road and roughly south of where Portsmouth's commercial port now stands. Nevertheless, old habits died hard and many people who lived in other areas of Portsea Island still gave their address as 'Landport'.

For a relatively small geographical area, Landport had a large population. In 1911, St Mary's electoral ward, which roughly reflected the boundaries of Landport, was home to 11,376 people in 2,570 separate households. There was a much higher proportion of men than women, due to the presence of so many young sailors.[3] Landport also had its notorious aspects. Many military wives took to prostitution to supplement the household income while men were away. Voller Street was a particularly rough area, which even the town police avoided, and Upper Church Path, Matrimony Row and the Arches were also infamous.[4] Children were encouraged to play in the streets due to a lack of space indoors. It has also been suggested that a high rate of juvenile crime was due to the absence of many fathers at sea, and that the lack of a 'firm hand' adversely affected the development of so many children. Poverty also went hand in hand with a lack of healthcare and slum housing.[5] Although diseases like cholera had declined since the 1870s and child mortality rates had improved steadily, for the most part conditions in Landport had barely changed between then and 1914, and many houses in the area were described as 'scarcely better than hovels'.[6] There was also a particularly large concentration of licensed premises in the Commercial Road area of Landport, a main thoroughfare for those travelling in and out of the town.[7] Agnes Weston was the founder of the Royal Sailors' Rest in Commercial Road, and her first glimpse of that thoroughfare left a lasting impression:

> I could not help but notice a densely thronged thoroughfare called Commercial Road. When the men left their ships they all made for it... It is still called the most crowded thoroughfare in the south of England, and it was and is a very Regent Street for the naval world.[8]

The poor were also at the mercy of private landlords, with few working-class people able to afford to buy their own homes and council housing still a generation away.[9] Landport was also home to a sizeable population of Irish immigrants, perhaps due to the preponderance of low-quality housing.[10]

Unsurprisingly, religious organisations approached the area with a missionary fervour. A particularly zealous Anglo-Catholic missionary priest, Rev. Robert Dolling, took up residence at St Agatha's church in the late nineteenth century, and his memoirs of his work in Landport provide us with a unique insight into

St Agatha's church, the epicentre of Landport in the early nineteenth century, now isolated among roads and the Cascades shopping centre. (Author)

life in the area at that time. He described seeing a 'Landport dance' upon his arrival in the parish, which consisted of women wearing men's trousers and men wearing only the girls' petticoats whilst dancing up and down the street.[11] Wages were low, temptation was at every corner, and the presence of so many sailors in the community drastically affected society. Dolling felt that a lack of menfolk – many fathers being at sea – affected not only the social development of boys, but also girls.[12] Although he had feared that sailors would present him with the most trouble in his work, he found them to be breezy and cheery, and that they relieved the monotony:'...sailors everywhere, sometimes fighting, sometimes courting, always laughing and good-humoured, except when afraid that they have broken their leave – our chief joy, alas, our greatest danger.'[13]

Furthermore, Dolling went as far as to suggest that the presence of sailors, and their nature, more than made up for the negative aspects of the neighbourhood: 'Their uniforms and rolling gait redeemed from its squalor and commonplace this poor little district, with its eleven hundred little houses and its fifty two public houses.'[14]

Dolling was not afraid to clash with authority, routinely accusing the town corporation of neglecting areas such as Landport in favour of its 'favoured infant' Southsea, which was certainly home to most of the town's wealthy and influential families and the majority of its naval and military officers.[15]

Dolling's concern over the number of public houses was shared by Agnes Weston, who followed a policy of purchasing licensed premises. One particularly troublesome Landport pub, the French Maid in Chandos Street, was well frequented by sailors and often the scene of fights. Weston purchased 'the Maid' and put it to more sober use.[16]

All Saints' church was built at the northern end of Commercial Road to serve the growing population of Landport by Jacob Owen and his son Thomas Ellis Owen,

who later became a prominent architect and builder of much of Southsea. The church was completed in 1827.[17] The parish memorial in All Saints' church records the names of 161 men from the parish who were killed during the First World War.

Perhaps the most striking statistic, and one that reflects the nature of Landport's social status, is that of the hundreds of men from the area who died during the First World War, only one was serving as an officer when he was killed, and even he had started his army career in the ranks. Captain William Corris lived at No. 95 Toronto Road in Landport, and was a parishioner of St John's church in Rudmore. He first enlisted in the Rifle Brigade in 1911, and began the war as a sergeant in the 1st Battalion.[18] He was later commissioned. After fighting at Bullecourt, Messines, Ypres, Lens, Aisne, the Marne and Amiens, Corris was fatally wounded at Bapaume on 30 August 1918 during the allies' final advance and died the next day. He is buried in Ligny-Saint-Flochel cemetery in Averdoingt, France.[19] That only one officer came from Landport is surely an indication of the extent to which social and economic factors could limit the social mobility of people born into such a neighbourhood in the early twentieth century.

Landport was a particularly densely populated area, with thousands of people crammed into rows of terraced houses, in conditions that could be compared to northern industrial towns. Some roads in Landport saw particularly heavy losses. Arundel Street and Commercial Road, both significant thoroughfares with hundreds of residences, shops and licensed premises, each lost eleven men.[20] Among those killed from Commercial Road were butcher's sons Driver Robert Billing and his brother Private Albert Billing. Robert was serving with 123rd Brigade of the Royal Field Artillery when he died on 24 April 1918, and he is buried in Kingston cemetery. He was 24. Albert had previously served in the Hampshire Regiment but was serving with the 1st Battalion of the Dorsetshire Regiment when he was killed at Ypres on 5 December 1917. He was 26 and is remembered on the Tyne Cot memorial.[21] Also from Commercial Road was Frank Dopson, who was serving as a private in the 1/2nd Battalion of the London Regiment when he was killed on 13 October 1918. His company had taken the village of Aubigny-au-Bas, north of Cambrai, when the Germans counter-attacked, and Dopson was killed by a machine gun as he pulled back. He was 18, and is remembered on the Vis-en-Artois memorial. A dockyard apprentice, Dopson had attended Southern Grammar School between 1911 and 1915.[22]

However, by far the highest casualty rates were experienced by the area's smaller residential streets. Eight men from All Saints Road were killed, an average of one out of every six residences – the highest proportion of losses out of any road in Landport. Intriguingly, two of them were unrelated but living in the same house. Petty Officer Richard Hand was killed when HMS *Invincible* was sunk at Jutland, and Leading Stoker George Marner was killed five days later when HMS *Hampshire* was sunk. Both were living at No. 11 All Saints Road. In 1914 the house was owned

by a Mrs Cass, suggesting that it may have been a lodging house.[23] Eight men were also killed from Amelia Street – an average of one for every eight dwellings in the street. Among them were three brothers, Arthur, James and John Dennis, who lived at No. 53. Next door at No. 55, Lance Corporal Ted Brady, aged 27, died serving with the 5th Company of the Machine Gun Corps in India in 1921. Wingfield Street, a mainly residential road, lost thirteen men, an average of one for every eleven households; twelve men were killed from Hertford Street, also an average of one for every eleven residences. It is not difficult to imagine that heavy casualties in a tight-knit community could be devastating, particularly if they occurred in one battle.

Many regular servicemen seem to have lived in Landport. Edward Breeze was a regular soldier who had first enlisted in the army in 1903. On the outbreak of war he was a sergeant in the 1st Battalion of the Lincolnshire Regiment, which had been part of the Portsmouth Garrison in 1914 before embarking for the Western Front on 14 August 1914. Breeze was awarded the Distinguished Conduct Medal for bravery at Hooge, near Ypres, on 16 June 1915:

> For conspicuous gallantry and ability at Hooge… when he collected a few men and attacked the enemy with bombs in their second line of trenches, destroyed two of their machine guns and took twelve prisoners.[24]

Breeze was killed on 4 June 1916 and is buried in Dartmoor cemetery, near Albert on the Somme front. At the time of his death he was living in Church Path. His wife remarried soon after the war, a not-uncommon occurrence. Entries on the Commonwealth War Graves Commission's register frequently record war widows as having remarried soon after the war. Although to modern sentiment this may seem insensitive, many war widows, lacking an income and with little or no provision for hardship, were forced to remarry in order to support themselves and their family.

A number of older men from Landport were killed, most of them either long serving ratings or naval pensioners who had been mobilised from the Royal Fleet Reserve. Naval pensioners from Landport in particular seem to have been used to crew smaller ships that were requisitioned at the start of the war, such as yachts and tugs. John Tarrant was a long-serving sailor on dockyard tugs; as far back as 1881 he was serving onboard the *Discovery* as a 22-year-old able seaman.[25] In 1891 he was a mate on the steam tug *Manly*, and in 1911 was a mate on the dockyard tug *Grappler*.[26] Tarrant was serving on the *Grappler* when she hit a mine off the Nab light vessel on 22 October 1915.[27] Tarrant was killed; he was aged 58. A resident of King Street, Tarrant is remembered on the Portsmouth naval memorial. Edward Winter was a leading stoker in 1901,[28] but by 1911 had left the Royal Navy.[29] He was living at Frederick Street in Landport when he was mobilised from the Royal Fleet Reserve and rated as a petty officer stoker in August 1914. He was 53

when he died of influenza whilst serving on HMS *Magnet* on 14 October 1918. He is buried in Kingston cemetery. HMS *Magnet* was employed in minesweeping and salvage tasks.[30] Petty Officer 2nd Class Samuel Greenway was aged 52 when he was killed serving onboard HM Yacht *Sanda* on 25 September 1915. He is remembered on the Portsmouth naval memorial and was living at 286 Lake Road. The presence of so many older sailors suggests that Landport was very much a naval community.

Older servicemen also served in the army. The demand for manpower, particularly towards the end of the war, meant that older men filled many roles that released younger soldiers for active duty overseas. Many of them had also seen much more of the world than we might imagine. One Portsmouth soldier, Alfred Hurst, was born in Plumstead, London, and enlisted in the Royal Artillery on 13 December 1879 at the age of 18. After learning to ride and spending some time as an ordnance storeman, Hurst was sent to Egypt in 1882, where he subsequently fought in the Mahdist Wars in the Sudan, including at the Battles of Tofrek and Suakin shortly after the fall of Khartoum in 1885. After leaving Egypt in 1887, Hurst re-enlisted for a further term of service and finally retired from the army as a battery sergeant major in 1894, settling in Upper Arundel Street. In 1899 he enlisted in the Hampshire and Isle of Wight Royal Artillery Volunteers as a gunner, and in 1911 he was working as an iron and brass trimmer.[31] Hurst served again during the First World War and was promoted to his old rank of sergeant major, but died whilst serving with 112th Howitzer Brigade of the Royal Field Artillery on 2 June 1915. The 112th Brigade was attached to the 25th Division,

E. W. WINTER
STOKER PETTY OFFICER, R.N.
127468
H. M. S. "MAGNET"
14TH OCTOBER 1918 AGE 53

UNTIL THE DAY BREAKS
AND THE SHADOWS FLEE AWAY
FROM HIS SORROWING WIFE

which eventually went to the Western Front in August 1915. Hurst was 53 at the time of his death and is buried in Kingston cemetery.

Some older men with no previous military service also volunteered to serve. Private Thomas Albert Pike, aged 60, died whilst serving with the 16th Battalion of the Hampshire Regiment on 19 January 1918. He is buried in Kingston cemetery. Pike, of Charlton Street, does not seem to have had a previous military career – in 1891 he was working as a rent collector and in 1911 as a carter.[32] He was well over the age for conscription or for active service and was

The grave of Leading Stoker Edward Winter. Mobilised from the Royal Fleet Reserve, Winter was 53 when he died of influenza in October 1918. (Author)

The grave of Sergeant Major Alfred Hurst, who died whilst serving in the Royal Field Artillery at the age of 53. (Author)

presumably serving in a training or administrative role on home service only. The 16th Hampshires provided reinforcements for the two Portsmouth Battalions on the Western Front.

One Landport soldier distinguished himself soon after the start of the war. Oliver Poulton was born in Portsmouth in 1888, the son of a builder. He joined the Royal Engineers as a bricklayer – something that he may well have had experience of in civilian life – and in 1911 was based at Gibraltar Barracks in Farnham in Surrey.[33] He was serving in Gibraltar when war broke out, but was sent to the Western Front in October 1914. Poulton, 30 years old and of Longs Road, was a qualified musketry instructor and the best shot in his company, a significant honour in an army that prided itself on its marksmanship.[34] Poulton put this skill to good effect when he was awarded the Distinguished Conduct Medal for bravery:

> For conspicuous gallantry on the 18th December 1914, when engaged with a party of men cutting the enemy's wires, he lay on the parapet of a German trench for one hour shooting at every head that appeared. Corporal Poulton subsequently assisted in rescuing a wounded comrade under fire.[35]

Poulton went on to serve on the Western Front for almost three years. He was killed on 28 June 1917 serving with the 5th Field Company, and is buried in Belgian Battery Corner cemetery in Belgium.

Other soldiers died of the effects of their war service years after they left the army. Driver W. Robson from Railway View served in the Boer War. After leaving the army, he re-enlisted in October 1914, joining the Army Service Corps. He was wounded and badly gassed at Arras. Although he was invalided home, he died on 16 April 1919 of tuberculosis caused by gas poisoning. He was 36, and at the time of his death was serving with the 432nd Horse Transport Company. He is buried in St Mary's cemetery in Southampton.[36]

Not all casualties were caused by enemy action. Accidents were far from rare in the early twentieth-century Royal Navy, even in peacetime. Stoker 1st Class Walter Sully was born in Portsmouth in 1888 and joined the Royal Navy in 1908.

Only a week after the Armistice, Sully was repairing a boiler on HMS *Boxer* in the dockyard on 18 November 1918 when it accidentally exploded, killing him. Sully, of Duke Street, is buried in Kingston cemetery. He was 26.[37] Able Seaman Reginald Light also suffered a tragic accident. Light was born in Salisbury in 1890. During the war he served onboard HMS *Emperor of India*, and then ashore at HMS *Excellent* on Whale Island, before joining HMS *Renown* in May 1917. Light survived the war, and was on *Renown* when she took the Prince of Wales, the future King Edward VIII, on a tour of the West Indies in 1919. On 10 November 1919, near Trinidad, Reginald Light attempted to rescue a man who had fallen overboard; Light was lost at sea, and presumed drowned. A resident of St Stephen's Road, Light is remembered on the Portsmouth naval memorial.[38]

The First World War was perhaps the first 'total war', in which many civilians were as involved as servicemen. A number of civilians from Landport were killed in action. Among them were merchant seamen, dockyard workers and naval canteen workers. Henry Kinshott was a waiter onboard the 30,396 liner SS *Lusitania* when she was sunk by *U-20* off Kinsale, Ireland, on 7 May 1915. Kinshott, who was born in Fareham and lived in Hampshire Street, is remembered on the Tower Hill memorial in London. A total of 1,198 people were killed when the *Lusitania* was sunk, and the deaths of so many civilians, in particular American citizens at a time when the United States was still neutral, caused a significant outcry; the sinking was a spectacular 'own goal' for Germany. Henry Vaughan, aged

28, was a shipwright in the dockyard at Gibraltar. Vaughan was born in Portsmouth, and his father was also a dockyard shipwright. On 26 September 1918 he was returning to Britain from Gibraltar onboard the US Coastguard Vessel *Tampa* when she was sunk in the Bristol Channel while escorting a convoy of merchant vessels. Vaughan has no known grave and is remembered on the Portsmouth naval memorial. A resident of Herbert Street, Vaughan had attended the Southern Grammar School.[39] During the First World War many naval canteen staff were civilians

The grave of Thomas Pike, who was 60 when he died serving with the Portsmouth Pals training battalion. (Author)

The grave of Stoker Walter Sully, who was killed by a boiler explosion in the dockyard after the Armistice. (Author)

W. J. SULLY
STOKER 1ST CLASS, RN,
K/3733
H.M.S. "BOXER"
18TH NOVEMBER 1914 AGE 26

DEAR TO OUR MEMORY
DEAR TO OUR HEARTS
LOVE FOR OUR LOVED ONE
WILL NEVER DEPART

employed by the Admiralty. Canteen assistant Andrew Gibbs was killed when HMS *Monmouth* was sunk during the Battle of the Coronel on 1 November 1914. Gibbs, aged 36 and of Lower Church Path, is remembered on the Portsmouth naval memorial.

Modern Landport is very different from the Landport of 1914–18. During the Second World War, bombing destroyed much of the area around St Agatha's, although the church itself survives. Post-war slum clearance reshaped the area dramatically. Gone are the multitudes of pubs, and the poor housing west of Commercial Road was demolished and replaced with car parks, the Tricorn shopping centre and extensions to the dockyard. Commercial Road was remodelled, and in the 1970s Guildhall Square was redesigned, with the construction of the civic offices.[40] As a result, Landport is perhaps the most changed neighbourhood of Portsmouth since the First World War.

Although historians have written of a 'lost generation' of privileged, well-educated young officers, the rate of losses among the working-class young men of Landport suggests that the area, and other similar neighbourhoods, experienced even more devastating casualty rates. The hundreds of young men from Landport who died in the First World War have largely been forgotten by history, but they represent a lost generation all of their own.

Henry Vaughan, a dockyard shipwright killed when the USS *Tampa* was sunk in the Bristol Channel. (SGS)

13

1 July 1916: The First Day on the Somme

Almost a century after it was fought, the Battle of the Somme remains possibly the most notorious and controversial battle in the history of the British Army.[1] Never before had Britain fielded such a vast army on the European mainland, and never before had such a large offensive been fought by the British Army, or indeed by any European army for that matter, with men who were overwhelmingly volunteers. Controversy has shrouded the Battle of the Somme right from its first day. Much of this has focussed on the command and leadership of the generals concerned, and whether the battle was worthwhile, or indeed a success or a failure. On paper, such horrific losses for so little territory gained have led to history seeing the Somme as a costly failure.

It had taken almost eighteen months for Kitchener's 'New Armies', consisting of men who had volunteered since the start of the war, to reach the Western Front. With his forces suitably reinforced by this influx of men, the commander-in-chief of the British Expeditionary Force, General Sir Douglas Haig, planned for a major offensive in the summer of 1916. He would have preferred to attack in Flanders, around Ypres, but was persuaded to attack further south near the River Somme, at the junction of the British and French armies. What was planned to be an allied offensive became increasingly British in nature, after the French Army suffered horrendous losses at the Battle of Verdun. Although Haig would have preferred to take more time, he was persuaded to bring the attack forward to 1 July to relieve the pressure on the French at Verdun.[2]

Whilst Haig hoped for a significant breakthrough, the army commander in charge of the offensive, General Sir Henry Rawlinson, was more cautious and had little faith in the inexperienced volunteers. Rawlinson hoped to capture each line of the German trenches in turn, with what has been referred to as 'bite and hold' tactics.[3] No less than fourteen divisions would attack on the first day, and 60 per cent of them were formed of New Army men.[4] These plans, it would transpire, were highly ambitious.[5]

The Germans had been able to choose the line of their defences on the Somme, and not only had they been able to use the lie of the land to make any attack a formidable prospect, but they had had several years to construct sophisticated defences, many of them of reinforced concrete up to 40ft underground.[6] A five-day preliminary bombardment by the Royal Artillery, it was hoped, would destroy the Germans' defences and cut their barbed wire, and a remarkable 1,058,622 shells were fired.[7]

Although the Battle of the Somme lasted from July until November 1916, the first day of the battle – 1 July – in particular has gone down in infamy as the most costly day in the history of the British Army. Twenty-five men from Portsmouth are known to have been killed on 1 July 1916 on the Somme – fourteen were killed while serving with the 1st Battalion of the Hampshire Regiment, the rest with various other units, all infantry battalions.

The 1st Battalion of the Hampshire Regiment had landed in France in August 1914 and fought as part of the 4th Division at Le Cateau, on the Marne, and at the First and Second Battles of Ypres. Although nominally a regular battalion, by July 1916 the 1st Hampshires had lost virtually all of its original pre-war soldiers, and in common with most units of the British Army in 1916 its men were mostly volunteers who had joined up early in the war and been sent to the Western Front as reinforcements.[8] However the battalion had not seen any serious fighting for several months. As a result, it was close to its pre-war strength and was described by the regimental history as being 'fighting fit'.[9]

Most historians have emphasised the prominent role that the Kitchener volunteer battalions from the industrial north and the midlands played during the first day of the Somme. Whilst these Pals Battalions did indeed form the majority of troops who fought on 1 July and did suffer heavy losses, as a result of this emphasis the role of many regular battalions has been overlooked, to the extent that the 1st Hampshires – one of relatively few regular units to go into action on 1 July 1916 – have received very little coverage in general histories of the Somme.[10] Of the 158 British battalions in action on 1 July, eighty-eight were of the New Armies, forty-three were regulars, and twenty-seven were from the Territorial Force.[11]

Although a large proportion of First World War army service records were lost in the blitz during the Second World War, some records do survive for some men who joined up as pre-war regulars. One such man was Reginald Buckland. Born in Gosport in 1889, he was the son of bricklayer.[12] However, in 1893 his father died, leaving his widow with a number of young children.[13] Although Reginald was working as a bricklayer's labourer, on 19 September 1905, at the age of 17, he joined the 3rd Militia Battalion of the Hampshire Regiment.[14] He only served with the militia for forty-nine days, for on 3 November 1905 he joined the regular Hampshire Regiment. Six years later, he was serving with the 2nd Hampshires in South Africa, at Harrismith in the Orange Free State.[15] By 1914 he was serving

with the 1st Hampshires, and was living at Milton Road in Copnor. Buckland first landed in France with the rest of the battalion on 23 August 1914.[16]

The 1st Hampshires spent much of May and June 1916 away from the front line, training hard for the upcoming operations. The plan was rehearsed again and again. The battalion took up their assembly positions on 30 June 1916, north-west of Beaumont Hamel and south of Serre. The men were ordered to advance in a calm and orderly fashion at walking pace across no-man's-land, so as to keep the advance organised – the generals having little faith that the New Army volunteers would be able to remain cohesive if they ran. They were burdened with much excess equipment, such as spades, sandbags and wire cutters. It became light at 4.00 a.m., and the men were issued with a tot of rum.[17]

At 7.30 a.m., the whole line attacked on a front of 18 miles. The Hampshires were in the second wave in their brigade's sector, advancing at 7.40 a.m., following closely behind the East Lancashires. As soon as the men of the battalion left their trenches, heavy machine-gun fire was brought to bear on them. The massive bombardment had been ineffective and the German barbed wire had not been cut, leaving the men trapped and at the mercy of the German machine gunners. Virtually every officer was killed or wounded, and losses were also grievous among other ranks. The loss of so many officers crippled what remained of the battalion, and the survivors hid in shell holes in no-man's-land for hours before crawling back after dark.[18]

In the 1st Hampshires, eleven officers and 310 men were killed or went missing on 1 July 1916, as well as fifteen officers and 250 men being wounded, adding up to total casualties of 585.[19] Many men died of their wounds in no-man's-land, where they could not be reached by medics or stretcher-bearers.[20] Survivors were few and far between, and the losses were so catastrophic that the war diary contains only brief details of the day's actions, most officers having been killed. Among the dead was the commanding officer, Lieutenant Colonel the Honourable Lawrence Palk. Although the battalion did not succeed and its losses were serious, it had, as

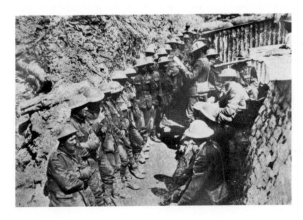

British Infantry in an assembly trench on the Somme. (GWPDA)

the regimental history points out, been given a task that 'proved to be more than any infantry could have accomplished' – a phrase that could be applied to the opening day of the Battle of the Somme in general.[21]

Fourteen of the dead were from Portsmouth. Among the dead was Private Reginald Buckland, who was 27 and is buried in Serre Road cemetery. He was entitled to the British War and Victory Medals and the 1914 Star.[22] Another pre-war soldier who had been with the battalion from August 1914 and was entitled to the same medals was Sergeant Norman Blissett, aged 23 and from Hunter Road in Southsea, who is buried in Beaumont Hamel cemetery.[23] Also lost were Private A.E. Ward, 19 and from Providence Place, Mile End; Lance Corporal Bertram Rogers, aged 29, a Portsmouth policeman from Hayling Island; and Sergeant Alfred New, aged 22 and from Westfield Road in Eastney. New had gone to France as a Lance Corporal in August 1914 and was awarded the Military Medal. They are buried in Redan Ridge No. 2 cemetery. Private Frank Goldring; Corporal Phillip Brymer, who went to France as a Private in April 1915, probably as a reinforcement;[24] Private Henry Bushnell;[25] Private William Symons; Private Walter Humphreys, of Ivy Street; Lance Corporal Timothy Nolan, aged 22 and from Britain Street, Portsea; Private Herbert Parkinson; and Private William Macey, aged 19 and from Riga Terrace, Landport, are all remembered on the Thiepval memorial. Also remembered on the Thiepval memorial is Colour Sergeant Major Charles Wood, another pre-war soldier who had gone to France in 1914 as a sergeant.

The losses would have been even more catastrophic had the British Army not instituted the practice of leaving around 10 per cent of each battalion out of the attack, so that in the event of heavy losses such as these there would at least be a basis upon which to rebuild the battalions.[26] The 1st Hampshires had been decimated and were withdrawn from the front line to recover and receive reinforcements. Sent to 'recuperate' in the Ypres Salient, the battalion would not be in action on the Somme again until 23 October, during the Battle of Transloy Ridge.

As the two Portsmouth Pals Battalions did not fight in the early phases of the Somme, Portsmouth escaped the massive losses that were experienced on 1 July by some of the towns and cities that had raised similar units – the Portsmouth Pals would receive their baptism of fire on the Somme several months later, in September. Many Portsmouth men had, however, joined units from other regions, and were also killed fighting on 1 July 1914.

Lance Corporal Bertie Bedford, of Hertford Street in Landport, was killed serving with the 1st Battalion of the Rifle Brigade. Having volunteered in August 1914, he was drafted to the front as reinforcement for what was a regular battalion, landing in France on 10 February 1915. He fought at Ypres and Loos, being promoted from private to lance corporal before being killed on 1 July 1914. The 1st Rifles were also part of the 4th Division, and fought alongside the 1st Hampshires. He was entitled to the British War and Victory Medals and the 1915 Star.[27]

Lance Corporal Edward Hatcher was killed serving with the 1/9th (Queen Victoria's Rifles) Battalion of the London Regiment. Hatcher attended Southern Grammar School between 1899 and 1901 and on deciding to pursue a career in teaching became a pupil-teacher in a Portsmouth school. He then progressed on to Winchester College, where he became a member of the cadet force. Hatcher was also a keen swimmer and a holder of the Royal Humane Society's lifesaving certificate. After leaving Winchester College in 1908, he was appointed an assistant master at a school in Pimlico, London. Although he was on holiday in Switzerland in August 1914, he returned to Britain and volunteered, enlisting in November 1914. Hatcher went to France in March 1915, and by 1916 he was a lance corporal. The 1/9th Londons made a diversionary attack along with the 56th (London) Division on 1 July at Gommecourt, to the north of the Somme battlefield. Although they took three lines of German trenches, the Londons were heavily shelled and counter-attacked. Heavy casualties forced them to withdraw, and by the next morning only around 100 men were left. Hatcher was last seen in no-man's-land, lying still and wounded in the back. He has no known grave, and is remembered on the Thiepval memorial.[28]

Another ex-pupil of Southern Grammar School was killed on the first day of the battle. Private Leslie Overton, who was at the school between 1907 and 1908 and later worked as an ironmonger, was serving with the 16th Battalion of the Middlesex Regiment, better known as the Public Schools Battalion. Overton first went to France on 17 November 1915. Going over the top near Beaumont Hamel with the 29th Division on 1 July 1916, Overton was reported missing after the battalion came under heavy machine-gun and shellfire. He was 21, and was entitled to the British War and Victory Medals and the 1915 Star.[29] Overton is

Left: Lance Corporal Ernest Hatcher, killed in the diversionary attack at Gommecourt on 1 July 1916. (SGS)

Right: Private Leslie Overton, who was killed at Beaumont Hamel on the first day. (SGS)

remembered on the Thiepval memorial, and his platoon sergeant later wrote about him glowingly: 'I was very fond and proud of him, he was so great out there, always cheerful and happy. Anything that required nerve and tact I always fell back on him for, and he never failed me.'[30]

Another Portsmouth man had been decorated only days before. Private William Curtis came from Chatham Row in North Street, Portsea. He joined the army shortly after the start of the war, and was posted to the 1st Battalion of the Dorsetshire Regiment, part of the 32nd Division. Curtis was awarded the Distinguished Conduct Medal, announced in the *London Gazette* on 21 June: 'For conspicuous gallantry in picking up and throwing over the parapet a live bomb thus saving casualties. On several occasions he has done fine work on patrol.'[31]

The 1st Dorsets attacked on the first day of the Somme, further south near Beaumont Hamel. Given the task of attacking Hawthorn Ridge, they suffered significant casualties. William Curtis was killed in action. He has no known grave and is remembered on the Thiepval memorial. He was 21.

Lance Sergeant Ian Paton, aged 35 and from Methuen Road in Eastney, was with the 7th Battalion of the Bedfordshire Regiment, a Kitchener battalion in the 18th (Eastern) Division. He is remembered on the Thiepval memorial. Paton first went to France on 6 October 1914 as a sergeant, but was reduced to the rank of corporal due to misconduct. He was entitled to the British War and Victory Medals and the 1914 Star.[32] Sergeant Frederick Buchanan was killed serving with the 15th Battalion of the Durham Light Infantry, a Newcastle-recruited battalion of Kitchener's New Armies in the 21st Division. Buchanan is remembered on the Thiepval memorial.

Several Portsmouth men were killed serving with the 2nd Battalion of the Lincolnshire Fusiliers on 1 July. Company Sergeant Major Tom Beal, aged 33 and from Connaught Road, North End, and Private Joseph Rowland, aged 28 and from Seymour Street, North End, are both remembered on the Thiepval memorial. Part of the 8th Division, Beal went to France on 5 November 1914 as a sergeant, and was entitled to the British War and Victory Medals and the 1914 Star.[33] Rowland first went to France on 13 August 1914, among the first British troops going to the Western Front. He was entitled to the British War and Victory Medals and the 1914 Star.[34]

Private John McDermott, 18 and from Trafalgar Street in Landport, was killed serving with the 20th Battalion of the Manchester Regiment, the 5th Manchester Pals. Part of the 7th Division, the 20th Manchesters captured their objective at Mametz. McDermott is buried in Dantzig Alley cemetery. McDermott arrived on the Western Front on 9 November 1915, and was entitled to the British War and Victory Medals and the 1915 Star.[35]

Sergeant George Ivamy was fighting with the 4th Battalion of the Worcestershire Regiment when he was killed on 1 July. Aged 34 and from

Reginald Road in Eastney, he is also remembered on the Thiepval memorial. Ivamy first went overseas as a lance sergeant on 18 August 1915, landing at Gallipoli. After the evacuation of the Gallipoli peninsula, he went to the Western Front. He was entitled to the British War and Victory Medals and the 1915 Star.[36]

The deaths of so many pre-regular soldiers with the 1st Hampshires on 1 July 1916 suggests that a significant number of men had survived almost two years of fighting on the Western Front – of the fourteen men from Portsmouth killed with the battalion on that day, four – more than a third – were regular soldiers. It is commonly thought that most pre-war regulars had become casualties well before 1916. Although the Somme has become known as the baptism of fire for many Kitchener battalions of the New Armies, it was also perhaps the final death knell for most of the few surviving pre-war soldiers.

Reaction to the losses on the Somme was mixed, particularly on the home front. Initially the *Evening News* reported a 'great allied advance', stating that 'casualties were not heavy' and that British troops had occupied the German front line. Coverage reached a more sober level when it was reported that wounded from the Somme began to arrive in Portsmouth on 4 July and were admitted to the hospital in Fawcett Road. A detailed report on 7 July revealed that the Hampshire Regiment had been in the thick of the fighting, and had 'suffered fearfully'.[37]

The Battle of the Somme raged on until November, before finally being 'closed down'. In total 382 men from Portsmouth were killed on the Somme. The spectre of the Somme loomed large over British society and haunted generals and politicians for many years. Future commanders would be more conscious of casualties, as shown by Field Marshal Montgomery's careful husbanding of his men during his campaigns in the Second World War.[38]

Early reports from the Somme underplayed the losses experienced and overplayed the results. (*EN*)

14

A Lost Generation? Portsmouth's First World War Army Officers

One of the most enduring popular conceptions of the First World War is of thousands of young men being cut down in their prime. In particular, the deaths of public schoolboys and poets have weighed heavily in collective memory, with the phrase 'lost generation' being frequently used. During the First World War, 246 officers from Portsmouth were killed – one colonel, five lieutenant colonels, twenty-one majors, fifty-five captains, seventy-seven lieutenants and eighty-four second lieutenants. Although this is of course a tragic number, it represents, at just under 8 per cent of all casualties, a minority of the 3,243 soldiers from Portsmouth who died.

The backgrounds of officers paint a vivid picture regarding society and class in early twentieth-century Portsmouth. Ten officers are known to have had university degrees, at a time when attendance at university was rare and army officers were not expected to have any kind of further or higher education.[1] However, attendance at public school certainly seems to have enhanced one's chances of becoming an officer, and thirty-nine of the Portsmouth officers killed attended Portsmouth Grammar School, while fourteen were old boys of Southern Grammar School. Military service was a tradition in many families, and twenty-four officers are known to have had fathers who were officers in either the army or the Royal Navy.

Unsurprisingly a large number of the officers killed – ninety-one – came from Southsea. In 1914 Southsea was still Portsmouth's most middle-class neighbourhood, a legacy of Thomas Ellis Owen's elegant streets and villas built in the mid-nineteenth century.[2] Southsea was a popular residence for professionals, naval and military officers and wealthy individuals during the Victorian period, and this trend seems to have persevered up to the time of the First World War. Second Lieutenant Robert Vernon-Inkpen lived at Branston Lodge in Waverley Road, Second Lieutenant John Wellesley-Miller at Gladstone House on Clarence Parade, and Second Lieutenant Tom Jeffrey at Elphinstone Mansions. By contrast, only one officer came from Landport,[3] two from Portsea,[4] and three from Buckland.[5]

That so few officers came from these neighbourhoods was almost certainly a result of their residents' more basic education, modest wealth and lower social class in a time when such things counted for much, particularly when compared to the inhabitants of an area such as Southsea.

The experience of one young gentleman from Portsmouth provides a striking example of not only how young men became officers, but also tells us much about contemporary Portsmouth society. For a town that boasted more pubs than any other comparable area, it is perhaps fitting that one of Portsmouth's most prominent citizens – and visibly recognisable names to this day – was Sir John Brickwood. Brickwood's Brewery had been founded in 1705. John Brickwood inherited a small but growing business in 1874 and, under his leadership, by 1914 it had become one of the largest breweries in the south.[6] With the large number of soldiers and sailors in the town, Brickwood's flourished in Portsmouth. In a city with a remarkable 742 licensed premises in 1910, 245 of them were owned by the company.[7] The relationship between the town and its most prominent brewer was not always an easy one – in 1899, for example, Brickwood's pubs were placed out of bounds to soldiers after a landlord asked two sergeants to leave his pub.[8] Aside from business, Sir John also became a pillar of Portsmouth society, as the founding chairman of Portsmouth Football Club in 1898,[9] and also a friend of Sir Arthur Conan Doyle. The Brickwoods had an impressive home, at Branksmere in the heart of Thomas Ellis Owen's Southsea.[10] The brewery, meanwhile, had an imposing presence near Queen Street in Portsea, fittingly just outside the dockyard gates.

Arthur, the eldest son of Sir John and Lady Brickwood, was born on 1 November 1896. As befitted the son of a wealthy local businessman and a knight of the realm, Arthur Brickwood entered Portsmouth Grammar School at

the age of 10, and stayed there until 1906. Arthur does not seem to have excelled at the grammar school, finishing bottom in arithmetic – when he was absent for the test – and in the bottom four for class work. He then went to Twyford Prep School, before going to Charter House School in the autumn of 1910. As at the grammar school, Arthur Brickwood does not seem to have distinguished himself

Sir John Brickwood, the owner of Brickwood's Brewery and founding chairman of Portsmouth Football Club. (Gates)

Second Lieutenant Arthur Brickwood, whilst a pupil at Charter House School. (Charter House School)

academically at Charter House and did not progress beyond what was then called the Remove Form, the equivalent of the modern Year 10. Brickwood left Charter House in the summer of 1913. Crucially, however, he had been a member of the school's Rifle Corps.[11]

Having not succeeded academically, a military career must have appealed to the young Arthur, a public school education – and not necessarily a successful one - being one of the prerequisites for admission to Sandhurst.[12] It was certainly not a career that could be entertained by most poor people, as considerable private income was required to fund the purchase of uniforms, equipment and other sundry costs that officers were expected to bear out of their own pocket.[13] Public school also prepared boys for officer status by instilling an ethos that aligned closely with that expected by the army; it taught them to see themselves as leaders and to exist within hierarchies, and fostered a sense of belonging.[14] The 'old school tie' could also be something of a social passport, in a way that men who had attended their local state school could never enjoy. That Arthur Brickwood was able to contemplate becoming an officer despite his poor academic record suggests how far influence and means could reach in what was still a very class-based society. In the context of the times, it was still relatively new for public schoolboys to pursue a career as an officer – the military historian Richard Holmes suggested that most pre-war officers came from the peerage or gentry, the clergy, or were the sons of military officers, and that the sons of traders and businessmen such as Brickwood made up a minority of the officer intake.[15]

Arthur Brickwood originally applied to join the army in December 1913, but was turned down, his chest being 1½in under the minimum size. Otherwise he was found to be healthy. Undeterred, Sir John wrote to the War Office pleading for his son to be accepted. A second medical board on 30 January 1914 found that whilst his chest was under the size limit he was of good physical condition, and in due course Arthur entered Sandhurst in February 1914. Tellingly, the medical board stated that the Secretary of State for War had accepted Brickwood on the recommendation of the Director General of Army Medical Services. Sir John Brickwood must have used his influence and appealed to the highest levels of authority in order to have his son accepted. This intercession certainly

demonstrates how a career as an officer was much more viable to the sons of the wealthy and the influential.[16]

Cadets usually spent eighteen months at Sandhurst, divided into three terms.[17] With the coming of war in August 1914, however, a severe shortage of officers meant that senior cadets at Sandhurst were instantly commissioned,[18] and Arthur Brickwood was gazetted as a Second Lieutenant in the York and Lancaster Regiment in September 1914.[19] It was certainly not unusual for cadets to join units with which they had no apparent connections, particularly in peacetime. Although social connections and influence could gain a young man a commission, positions in the more fashionable regiments, such as the Guards or the Rifle Brigade, were the preserve of the wealthier still. Hence many young men of the middle classes chose to join county infantry regiments.

The 1st Yorks and Lancasters had been in India on the outbreak of war, but were ordered back to Britain in October 1914 and only arrived on the front line on 1 February 1915.[20] Thus, on 2 February when Brickwood finally went to France, taking a draft of fifty men, he was not far behind. Brickwood joined the 1st Battalion of the Yorks and Lancasters and served seven tours of duty in the front line near Ypres. Less time was spent in the front line than popular wisdom suggests – one officer estimated that in 1916 he spent sixty-five days in the front line, plus another thirty-six days in the support trenches.[21]

Commanding men in the front line was a demanding responsibility, especially for an 18-year-old such as Arthur Brickwood – many of the men under his command will have been considerably older and will have come from much different backgrounds from his own. In the front line, junior officers such as Brickwood did largely share the discomforts of their men and were expected to show paternalism towards them, although they did have the advantage of a batman – a personal servant.[22] On the whole, however, front-line service on the Western Front has come to be seen as a great social leveller.

On 4 February Brickwood was admitted to the Red Cross Hospital in Rouen, suffering with influenza. Just over a week later he rejoined his battalion. Illness on active duty has constantly been a problem for armies, and even during the twentieth century it was by no means unusual for men to die of illness whilst on active service – indeed, Richard Holmes has estimated that 1.3 men were admitted to hospital sick for every one man who was wounded in action.[23] A total of 91,000 men died of non-military causes, such as accidents or disease, on the Western Front – slightly more than the capacity of the modern Wembley Stadium.[24] On 11 April Arthur Brickwood was transferred to the military hospital in Boulogne, suffering with what appears to have been tonsillitis. An abscess developed on his tonsils, but although a tracheotomy was performed, sadly his condition did not improve, and he died on 15 April 1915. He was 18. On 19 April 1915 the *Guardian* reported that:

Lieutenant A. C. Brickwood, York and Lancaster Regiment, son of Sir John
Brickwood of Portsmouth, died in hospital at Boulogne on Thursday night.
He was taken ill a few days ago at the front, where he had been fighting in the
trenches for some time.[25]

On 16 April Arthur Brickwood's parents received a telegram from the Secretary
of State for War, Lord Kitchener, expressing his sympathy. The next of kin of
officers received a telegram; the relatives of other ranks, meanwhile, could expect
a more formal and less personal army form. Brickwood was entitled to the
Victory Medal, the British War Medal and the 1915 Star.[26]

Brickwood's personal effects were shipped back to his family. The list gives an
insight into the rather spartan lifestyle of junior officers on the Western Front:
six pipes, one square torch and refill, one road torch and refill, first field dressing,
silver flash jack knife, mirror and case, stationery, a bullet struck penny, one small
Webley Pistol, a pocket knife and case, a metal cigarette case, a pouch, two keys,
an identity disc, a watch and straps (broken), safety razor and cover, notebook,
correspondence, devotional book, pocket book and notes, three postal orders,
10 francs, a tin box and three pencils.[27] Such possessions could not be considered
luxurious by modern standards, but are extravagant compared to the belongings
of soldiers of most other ranks on the Western Front.

For most of the war, the government's policy was that men would be buried
near to where they were killed, due to the logistical problems of transporting
remains home to Britain. Early in the war, however, there was no firm policy
and no official organisations were responsible for burying war dead, the Imperial
War Graves Commission only being formed in March 1915.[28] In some cases,
wealthy individuals were able to arrange for their sons' bodies to be brought
home for burial, something that poorer people could not have contemplated.
Sir John Brickwood must have arranged for his son's burial at Grayshott, near
to the Brickwood's home at Hazelgrove, near Hindhead in Surrey. He erected
a memorial on his son's grave, consisting of a cross surmounted with an officer's
Sam Browne belt, scabbard and service dress cap. This elaborate memorial also
circumvented the government's later policy of uniformity among gravestones.[29]
Brickwood was one of very few British soldiers who were killed on the Western
Front to be brought back for burial at home. Later in 1915 the War Office banned
the repatriation of fallen soldiers, the sheer number of casualties making it
impossible to bring them all home.[30]

Arthur Brickwood's former schools also remembered him. Public schools in
particular published lists of their old boys who were serving with the armed
forces, and also of those who were killed. Although the concept of the 'lost
generation' of young gentlemen has been challenged by some historians, it is
certainly true that a large percentage of public schoolboys who became junior

officers were killed in action.[31] Viewing them as a whole marginalises the impact of their loss – had they lived, men such as Arthur Brickwood may have developed into key figures within society.

Arthur Brickwood was not the only son of a prominent Portsmouth businessman to be killed. Harold Pink was the son of Sir Harold Pink, a wine and spirit merchant and grocer and also mayor in 1916 and 1917. The younger Harold Pink attended Salisbury School and the Southampton Institute, graduating in 1906. Pink worked as a civil engineer and was working in Argentina when war was declared. After returning to Britain he volunteered for the army and was commissioned as a second lieutenant in the 1/7th (Hants) Company of the Royal Engineers. On 3 October Harold Pink was wounded at Orijak, near Struma, and died of his wounds on 7 October 1916. Harold Pink is buried in Lahana cemetery, Greece. He is also remembered on the St Jude's parish church war memorial in Southsea. His commanding officer wrote that 'the whole of the officers and men respected him and much deplored his loss, stating that it would be difficult to find a good engineer to replace him.'[32]

Although prominent local men seem to have been able to secure their sons a commission, many more young officers came from a military or naval background. Children who grew up in a military environment would have been well inculcated with the military culture, and it was only natural that many followed their fathers into the armed forces. Senior officers also had the necessary contacts to obtain a commission for their sons. Major Ernest Hayes of the 2nd Cameronians was the son of Vice-Admiral John Hayes, Captain Hubert Daniell the son of a Royal Marines major general, Second Lieutenant John Shand of the Royal Garrison Artillery was the son of an engineer rear admiral and Lieutenant Robert Slade-Baker of the Royal Berkshire Regiment was the son of the brigadier general commanding at Gunwharf in 1914 and 1915. Some officers came from decorated military families. Captain William Temple of the 1st Battalion of the Gloucestershire Regiment was the son of an Irish medical officer who had won the Victoria Cross in 1863 during the New Zealand Wars, serving with the Royal Artillery. William Temple was commissioned in 1893 and served during the Boer War.[33]

Although commissioning from the ranks was extremely rare pre-war, shortages of manpower, and of suitable officers in particular, led the army to look to the ranks to find officer candidates. Nine Portsmouth officers killed are known to have been commissioned from the ranks, though the true figure is probably much higher. Many second lieutenants who were killed were in their thirties or even forties, suggesting that they may have been commissioned from the ranks. Second Lieutenant Eric Vickers of the Rifle Brigade was the son of Rev. Nathaniel Vickers of St Simon's church. He enlisted as a private before being commissioned in the field.[34] Second Lieutenant Henry Cecil Hall, a former pupil of the Southern Grammar School, served in the ranks of the Hampshire Regiment before being commissioned.

Alderman Sir Harold Pink, mayor of Portsmouth
from 1916 to 1918. (Gates)

Men who won medals whilst serving in
the ranks seem to have had a good chance of
being commissioned, and many went on to
win further decorations as officers. Lieutenant
Edward Fuller won a Military Medal serving
in the ranks of the Royal Garrison Artillery,
before being commissioned. He went on to
add a Military Cross and bar to his Military
Medal. Captain William West served in the
ranks of the 12th Lancers during the Boer
War. He won a Military Medal as a ranker
before adding a Military Cross as an officer
in the Hampshire Regiment, and was also awarded a Russian Cross of St George.
Captain George Wallis and Second Lieutenant Henry Russell were both holders
of the Distinguished Conduct Medal, and Second Lieutenant Cyril Buck had won
the Military Medal. Second Lieutenant Walter Morgan was a pupil at the Southern
Grammar School in 1904 and 1905, and after studying at Bristol University College
went on to become a teacher at the Royal Hospital School. He volunteered for
the 6th Battalion of the Hampshire Regiment in October 1914, before being
commissioned in 1915. Lieutenant Joseph Starkey was an old boy of Portsmouth
Grammar School, and enlisted into the Hampshire Regiment in September
1914. However, his potential as an officer was obviously recognised, for he was
commissioned in January 1915 and posted to the Highland Light Infantry.[35]

Several local doctors joined up, in the medical services and in other regiments.
Captain Ernest Robertson was the son of a doctor and a pupil at Portsmouth
Grammar School. He went on to become a doctor himself, training at Guy's
Hospital in London. Upon the outbreak of war he joined the Royal Army Medical
Corps. He died aged 33 on 28 October 1918, and is buried in St Peter and St Paul's
churchyard in Wymering. Second Lieutenant Percy King was also a doctor who
trained at Guy's Hospital, as well as a member of the Royal College of Surgeons.
Surprisingly, however, he joined the East Surrey Regiment and was killed on
5 August 1917. He was 28 years old and is buried in Duisans, France.

Although relatively few men from Portsmouth served as officers, those who
did reflected the nature of Portsmouth's middle-class society of the time. Very few
men seem to have been promoted from the ranks, but those who were fortunate
enough to be commissioned were early standard bearers for greater social mobility
in the army.

15

Recruitment, Conscription and the Portsmouth Military Service Tribunal

The popular image of the First World War is of millions of young men joining up in August 1914, sailing off to France, and marching up to the front line singing 'It's a Long Way to Tipperary', before sitting in a muddy hole in the trenches until 1918. Of course, as with many widely held conceptions in military history, the experience of many of Portsmouth's First World War servicemen was remarkably different and much more complex. The first total war in British history called for the full mobilisation of the British population, using a complex machinery that eventually had to resort to varying degrees of coercion.

First World War soldiers joined the army in a variety of ways. Firstly, the British Army initially consisted of a relatively small number of regular soldiers who had enlisted before the start of the war. As a garrison town Portsmouth was home to many soldiers – an infantry brigade and other assorted units in 1914 – and as units moved after several years, thousands of regular troops will have passed through Portsmouth in the years prior to the war.[1] The regular British Expeditionary Force was tiny, however, and nowhere near large enough to fight a sustained continental war. Although Kaiser Wilhelm's comment regarding it as a 'contemptible little army' is now thought to be fictional, it certainly was a small army compared to the vast armies of France and Germany. Secondly, the Territorial Force was formed in 1908. The Territorials were intended for home defence and could not be compelled to embark on foreign service, although many did volunteer to serve overseas.

The initial rush of volunteers overwhelmed the recruiting offices: 1,186,357 men joined the army between August and the end of 1914, with a record high of 462,901 enlistments in September alone.[2] Although 1.5 million men had answered Lord Kitchener's call and joined up by September 1915, the monthly rate of volunteering fell drastically, to a low of 55,152 in December 1915.[3] The casualty rates on the Western Front made it clear that if Britain relied on

Recruits queuing to enlist in Town Hall Square early in the war. (Gates)

volunteering alone, she would eventually run out of men.[4] It was soon recognised that Britain's manpower would have to be planned and managed in the same way that its finances and military equipment were – a new development in British society that signified total war more than any other.[5] The term 'manpower budget' demonstrated just how millions of lives had become ancillary to a war effort on an industrial scale.[6]

In a last-ditch attempt to gain more recruits and to delay such a serious political step as the introduction of conscription, a scheme was unveiled by Lord Derby under which men could attest their willingness to enlist and then be called up in due course.[7] Several Portsmouth men attested under the Derby Scheme and were subsequently killed in action. Private John Glanville, of Cardigan Road in Landport, attested and was called up in June 1916. He was sent to India where he joined the 2/5th Battalion of the Hampshire Regiment, which then served in Iraq and Palestine. Glanville was killed on 10 April 1918, and is buried in Ramleh war cemetery in Israel. Private Albert Haskett of Widley Road in Stamshaw also attested and was called to the colours in January 1917. He joined the 2nd Battalion of the Wiltshire Regiment and was awarded the Military Medal before he was killed near Honelle in Belgium on 6 November 1918, only five days before the Armistice during the final battles of the war leading up to the capture of Mons. He is buried in Roisin communal cemetery in Belgium.

However, the Derby Scheme was not considered a success; only 37 per cent of men who were eligible to attest did so nationally.[8] Conscription was by now inevitable, and was formally introduced on 2 March 1916.[9] The first conscripts arrived with the British Expeditionary Force on the Western Front

as reinforcements during the Battle of the Somme.[10] Under the National Registration Act a survey of the population was taken on 15 July 1915, providing a basis for compiling a list of potential recruits who had not yet joined up. The register eventually showed more than 5 million men of military age who had not, up to that point, volunteered for military service.[11] Of those, 1,433,827 men were in reserved occupations, and a further 748,587 men were exempt from military service.[12] Men who worked on the railways, in coalmines, in agriculture, munitions factories and in shipbuilding were among those reserved.[13] Between January and June 1916 alone, some 750,000 men applied for exemption.[14]

British public opinion had traditionally frowned upon conscription, preferring a more *laissez-faire* approach from the government, and as a result Britain had a smaller, volunteer army compared to the mass conscript forces of France and Germany. Although public opinion on the prospect of conscription became more mixed after the outbreak of the war, once the flow of volunteers began to ebb, popular consensus in Britain swung in favour of conscription.[15] Certainly the correspondence columns of the *Evening News* contained no dissenting opinions even when conscription was a hot topic in the rest of the country, and the editorials soberly acknowledged that conscription was necessary.[16] This was perhaps due to the prominence of the military in the town and the fact that so many local people were familiar with military service compared to other parts of the country.

Clearly, conscripting such a large number of men into the armed forces was not going to be a simple matter. Men who had not joined up so far were divided into

A demonstration in favour of national service in Town Hall Square. (Gates)

Alderman Sir William Dupree, a three-time former mayor of Portsmouth who felt strongly that women should not be allowed to sit on the tribunal. (Gates)

classes, by age and by marital status, and called up successively.[17] The logic employed appears to have been that younger men were more suitable for military service, and that calling up married men before unmarried men would be insensitive. Some men had various reasons for not wishing to join up, and military service tribunals were set up around the country to consider their cases. Although the first tribunals were formed on 19 November 1915, Portsmouth's was founded several months later, on 8 February 1916.[18] At the town council meeting that night there was a heated debate over the composition of the tribunal. It was left to individual towns to decide the membership, which need not be limited to members of the council, and could consist of as many as twenty-five members. Sir William Dupree was vehement that women should be not be permitted to join the tribunal, as in his opinion they were not able to serve in the front line, so they should not be in the position of sending men there.[19] The mayor was a member, along with other local political and business figures. The No Conscription Fellowship, the Trades & Labour Council and the Portsea Island Mutual Co-operative Society also sought representation on the tribunal, although only the request of the Trades & Labour Council was granted.[20]

The tribunal met twice-weekly, and the sessions often lasted for several hours. During its existence it met 199 times, and heard 7,785 cases – more than the total number of men from Portsmouth killed in the war. The advisory committee, which passed recommendations to the tribunal,

Sir John Corke, mayor of Portsmouth from 1912 until 1915 and the first chairman of the Portsmouth Tribunal. (Gates)

met three times a week, for between five and six hours, and examined up to seventy cases at each meeting.[21] Perhaps due to its sensitive nature, little of the tribunal's work was made public, and considering the number of cases that the tribunal heard, relatively few were reported in the local newspapers. On 6 March it was reported that a harpist had applied for exemption. Upon examination the applicant argued that he was needed to clean for a dependant, and the tribunal replied tartly that it was 'hardly a man's work at this time'.[22]

Popular history has emphasised the conscientious objector as prominent amongst those who appealed against serving in the armed forces. In fact, the vast majority of men who appeared before the tribunals had very practical reasons for wishing to stay at home. Men might have applied for exemption from military service for a number of reasons. A man might have been self-employed and being sent to serve overseas might damage his livelihood. A man might also have other personal reasons for not wishing to join up, such as being the only breadwinner in a large family. Finally, a small number of men did claim exception as conscientious objectors.[23] It has been estimated that there were around 16,000 conscientious objectors in Britain during the First World War – a tiny figure given the size of the population at the time. A total of 6,000 men were imprisoned in Britain for refusing to serve, and a number of them were held in Kingston Prison in Portsmouth.[24] Portsmouth seems to have had a particularly low rate of conscientious objection, perhaps due to its heritage as a naval and military town, with only forty-five Portsmouth men applying for exemption on the grounds of conscience.[25]

The flood of recruits in the late summer and autumn of 1914 had actually done great harm to vital war industries, and it was soon realised that a skilled man operating machinery in a munitions factory was playing as much a part in the war effort as a rifleman on the front line. As a result, certain vital industries had been

The Portsmouth Military Service Tribunal in session. (Gates)

given the status of 'reserved occupation' in an attempt to prevent unorganised recruiting from harming war industries.[26] Part of the process of maximising manpower was to 'comb out' reserved occupations, by reclassifying certain jobs.[27] Dockyard workers were regarded as reserved occupations for much of the war, until the later years when losses on the Western Front were becoming acute and some 'dockies' were called up. Much correspondence ensued between the tribunal and the dockyard authorities, enquiring as to the status and importance of individuals known to be working in the yard.[28]

The tribunal was initially chaired by the mayor, Alderman Corke, and the membership comprised aldermen, councillors and prominent local men, including businessmen. The tribunal also had military representatives to act as advisors, but in practice they were de facto members of the tribunal. The tribunal began by hearing appeals from men who attested before conscription was introduced, and presumably were willing to serve. After conscription was introduced the tribunal also began hearing appeals from men who had not attested and were apparently more hesitant about enlisting. Each case was heard by a court of three tribunal members, along with one of the military representatives.[29] With such a huge number of cases the tribunal members were hard pressed, and one historian has argued that the lack of time to consider such a number of applications meant the vast majority were rejected as a result.[30]

Very few men in Portsmouth appealed for exemption on the grounds of conscience. Most appealed for personal, business or employment reasons, on the grounds of disability or because their occupation was exempt. Men could appeal themselves, or in some cases employers appealed on their behalf in order to keep their employee. The tribunal granted very few unconditional exemptions. Most men were granted either temporary exemptions, in order to get their personal or business affairs in order, or conditional exemptions. Conditional exemptions could also be granted on the proviso that men provide some other contribution to the war effort.

As conscription began to take effect and the military service tribunals worked through the thousands of applications, the rate of enlistments into the armed forces did rise slightly, peaking at 156,386 in June 1916. The grievous losses on the Somme seem to have inspired the authorities to be stricter with the granting of exemptions, and enlistments rose from 52,005 in December 1916 to 119,539 in March 1917.[31] Notably, many men who appealed were in their thirties, forties or even in their fifties. As the war progressed and manpower shortages began to take effect, many older men who had not initially volunteered were called up – men who were more likely to have family and business commitments that made war service difficult. Although the introduction of conscription, the national register compiled under the 1915 National Registration Act and the military service tribunals did cause stress and trepidation for many, there were benefits.

The enlistment of underage boys declined drastically and vital war industries were protected.[32] Nationally, a total of 779,936 exemptions were granted by military service tribunals. Only 40,146 of these exemptions were total and 160,620 of them were temporary and usually required a man to reappear before the tribunal.[33] The rest were conditional, usually on the basis that a man would serve on the home front in some kind of capacity, for example in a home service military unit, the Red Cross or as a special constable.

Of the men who appeared before the tribunal and subsequently joined the armed forces, very few seem to have been killed. One was Gunner Frederick Frankham. A resident of Guildford Road in Kingston, Frankham worked as a wages clerk for Timothy White & Company of Chandos Street in Landport. Prior to the war White's were listed in local directories as 'chemists, dry salters, ironmongers, oil and colour merchants, stationers and printers', and had depots throughout Portsmouth. During the war however they described themselves as manufacturers of chemicals and hazardous materials, possibly because this sounded more important to the war effort. Frankham had been awarded a certificate of exemption in 1916, presumably because his employers were producing munitions. However, as part of the efforts to secure more men for the army, on 15 June 1917 a group of nine employees from White's, including the proprietor, appeared before the tribunal to have their exemptions reviewed at the request of the local recruiting officer. All had their certificates withdrawn, and were given short exemptions in order to attend to personal business before joining the army. Frankham was given a temporary exemption until 1 August 1917, when he joined the army. It was made clear that this exemption could not be extended. Conscripted into the Royal Field Artillery, he underwent basic training in Britain before going to the Western Front in March 1918, where he joined B Battery of the 275th Brigade Royal Field Artillery, which was operating in support of the 55th (West Lancashire) Division. Frankham was only in France for a month before he was killed on 18 April 1918. The 55th Division had been in the forefront of the fighting during the Germans' Operation Georgette on the River Lys between 12 and 15 April. He has no known grave and is remembered on the Loos memorial. He was 37.[34]

Of the eighty-nine men from Portsmouth who are known to have been conscripted – the National Roll of the First World War referred to them as 'joining' rather than 'volunteering' – only twenty-two served in the Hampshire Regiment. Particularly after the introduction of conscription, the army was less concerned about sending men to their local regiment, and preferred to send them to any regiment as quickly as possible, especially if a particular battalion was in need of reinforcements. Although men underwent their basic training with a particular regiment in Britain, as soon as they were sent to the Western Front they passed through base depots, where they were liable to be sent to completely different

regiments. In some cases men who were sent to fight wearing strange cap badges were deeply unhappy about it. Indeed, one of the advantages of volunteering rather than being conscripted was the ability to choose which regiment to enter. By contrast, 215 Portsmouth men are known to have volunteered. Of these, 109 did so between August and December 1914, and just over half – 129 – served in the Hampshire Regiment.

The Portsmouth Military Service Tribunal was a unique experience in Portsmouth's history, when citizens of the town sat in judgement of their fellow townspeople's ability to serve their country. That men were conscripted into the army and did not volunteer should not be seen as any indication of their bravery. The work of the Military Service Tribunal showed that men had a wide and diverse range of reasons for wishing to avoid or delay serving. The casual observer could be excused for thinking that all men who served in the First World War volunteered together in August 1914, but the recruitment of millions of men into the armed forces between 1914 and 1918 was a much more complex process than commonly thought. The government had learnt a valuable lesson, and the organisation of manpower during the Second World War was much more thorough, without the need to resort to tribunals.

16

Boy Soldiers and Sailors: Portsmouth's Underage Servicemen

One of the enduring popular images of the First World War is the collective memory of the not insignificant number of boys who joined up to fight. To this day, stories of boys who lied about their age are well known and graves of underage soldiers killed on the Western Front are well visited by school groups. By contrast, boys had been joining the Royal Navy at a young age for hundreds of years, and the practice was so well entrenched in British society that the deaths of boy seamen caused little or no consternation either during the war or since.

It is important, however, to place in context the phenomenon of so many young men joining up and being killed underage. Children – in particular the poor – routinely left school at the age of 14.[1] Although improvements in health had improved mortality rates since the mid-nineteenth century, it was still by no means certain that children would survive into adulthood. Life was hard, and death caused by illness or accident was more common than in the present day. In Portsmouth, it was estimated that one in seven newborn babies did not survive their first year.[2] Particularly in poorer working-class areas, malnutrition and a lack of medical care meant that children and younger people dying prematurely was not as unusual as it seems to us in the twenty-first century.

Technically, volunteers had to be aged 18 or over to join the army. However, many recruiting staff appear to have turned a blind eye to willing volunteers who were below this age, some of them significantly younger. In the patriotic fervour and the desire to recruit as many men as possible, no thought was given to the potential downside of recruiting so many boys to serve in a man's world. On the contrary, recruiting sergeants were paid a bonus of 2s 6d for each recruit that they were able to secure, and hence many were inclined to unscrupulousness.[3] Young boys certainly had a strong sense of adventure and were more susceptible to propaganda than older, wiser men might have been. They also may have had less comprehension of danger or of their own mortality.[4] Many boys had also served

in organisations such as the Boy Scouts or the Boys Brigade, which although ostensibly non-military must have encouraged many a boy to enlist. That Scouts were conspicuous at many recruiting rallies is also notable.

Thirty-one boys under the age of 18 from Portsmouth died serving with the British Army between August 1914 and 1921. Although several had joined legitimately as boy soldiers, the majority of them seem to have volunteered underage and had been enlisted as such. Of those who volunteered, we know exactly when seven joined up. Of those seven, five volunteered in those frantic days of August 1914 at the start of the war, when checks on age were extremely cursory. The vast majority joined the Hampshire Regiment. Popular destinations were the Portsmouth Pals Battalions and the 1/4th Battalion of the Territorial Force. Both of these units had to begin recruiting in an extremely ad hoc fashion, and it was potentially easier for an underage boy to slip through the net than through the sterner eye of a regular army recruiting office.

It is noticeable that of the underage soldiers who managed to reach the front line – some were indeed discovered and sent home – the vast majority were killed in action in 1915 and 1916, twenty-six of them in fact. Recruitment in 1914 was chaotic, with few if any recruiting sergeants being particular about checking birth certificates. One of the youngest boys reported to have enlisted did so at the age of 12 and served on the Somme for six weeks before his age was discovered.[5] However, with the introduction of National Registration and conscription in 1916, it was clearly much harder to lie about one's age. After 10 November 1915 no recruits were supposed to be accepted without showing their National Registration Card. Families, in particular concerned parents, may also have been more reluctant to let their children join up once lengthy casualty lists began to come back from the front. The cause of underage soldiers was also pressed vigorously in Parliament by Sir Arthur Markham MP, who uncovered a degree of indifference from ministers and the War Office regarding the issue. Gradually, it became much harder for underage boys to reach the front line, and by 1917 the casualty rates among under-18s fell by 80 per cent.[6]

Researching the civilian lives of underage First World War soldiers is by no means easy. As they were so young, the 1911 census rarely gives as much information as it would for a man who was, say, ten years older, as most boys who were 17 in 1914 were still at school in 1911. Several, however, were working at a very young age in 1911. William Bowyer, who would die at Gallipoli in 1915 serving with the 2nd Hampshires, was a newsboy as well as a school pupil. Joseph Long, who died in Britain in August 1916 serving with the Hampshire Fortress Royal Engineers, gave his occupation as 'chopping wood'. His father, a stoker in the Royal Navy, was away from home when the 1911 census was taken.

The youngest Portsmouth soldier to die whilst serving with the army was Henry Rampton, who was only 16. The son of a Royal Marine Light Infantry

private, in 1911 Henry Rampton was living with his family at Merry Row in Landport. He died on 28 April 1916 whilst serving with the 16th Battalion of the Hampshire Regiment, and is buried in Kingston cemetery. The 16th Battalion was the Depot Battalion for the other two Portsmouth Pals Battalions, and accepted and trained recruits before sending them to the Western Front. Although Henry Rampton did not leave Britain, nevertheless he was Portsmouth's youngest soldier to die in service during the First World War.[7]

It was also quite possible for underage soldiers who went undetected to do well and rise up the ranks in the army. The son of an accountant clerk in the Dockyard and from Fawcett Road, Clarence Tanner had attended Southern Grammar School between 1911 and 1913. He showed great promise in his studies and in the choir before leaving to work as a laboratory attendant at the Municipal College, whilst also studying part time. He volunteered for the 2nd Portsmouth Pals in August 1915, and presumably because he had a good education, he was quickly promoted to corporal and then sergeant. He was seriously wounded at the Battle of Flers on the Somme on 15 September 1916, and died two days later. He was aged just 17 and is buried in Dartmoor cemetery in France. His photo shows an extremely boyish-looking young man, and his colleagues must clearly have been aware of or at least had suspicions about his true age. That he not only survived but prospered in such a tough situation speaks volumes of his character.[8]

The reader could be excused for thinking that it would be harder to enlist underage as an officer, but remarkably two young men from Portsmouth managed to deceive the authorities and gain commissions whilst underage. Ernest Lancaster was the son of an auctioneer and surveyor. Born in Kingston-upon-Thames in 1900, in 1911 he was still at school.[9] He enlisted as a private in the Hampshire Regiment and was then able to apply for a commission thanks to the influence of a family friend who was a retired colonel, who may well have been aware of his real age. That he was the son of a surveyor may account for how he was able to obtain a commission – the

The grave of Private Henry Rampton, who joined the Portsmouth Pals underage and died before he could go overseas. (Author)

Sergeant Clarence Tanner, who died of wounds on
the Somme in 1916. He was only 17. (SGS)

sons of professionals and businessmen seem
to have been in demand to serve as officers,
and influence and nepotism could go a long
way.[10] His application was endorsed by a
character reference from a Portsmouth Justice
of the Peace. He was commissioned into the
7th Dorsets, before transferring to the Machine
Gun Corps. Serving as a second lieutenant in
the 16th Battalion of the Machine Gun Corps,
he was killed in action on 12 October 1916.
He has no known grave and is remembered on the Thiepval memorial to the
missing of the Somme.

The sons of former officers were also prime candidates for commissions.
James Hodding, born in Southsea, was the son of retired major of the Madras
Infantry of the Indian Army, who had immigrated to Canada sometime after
1911.[11] The Hodding family were living in Vancouver in Canada when war was
declared, and James returned to Britain to enlist. He served as a second lieutenant
in the 15th Battalion of the Royal Fusiliers, a reserve battalion that did not leave
Britain, before going to the Western Front with the 10th Battalion sometime in
1916.[12] The 10th Battalion was a Kitchener unit that had the unofficial name of
'the stockbrokers' and was made up mainly of recruits from London's financial
district. To enable Hodding to join what was a relatively exclusive unit may
well have involved some intervention from his father. Hodding died of wounds
on 10 July 1916. The 'stockbrokers' were involved in the diversionary attack on
Gommecourt on the first day of the Somme, and it was probably there that
Hodding was wounded. He is buried in Heilly Station cemetery, near Albert
on the Somme. In 1919 James Hodding's father applied to the War Office for his
campaign medals. He had been recalled to service and was based at a prisoner of
war camp near the Western Front after the armistice.[13]

Families of underage boys who enlisted reacted in a variety of ways. Some
encouraged their sons, motivated by the patriotism of the time. As the war
progressed and lengthy casualty lists exposed the horror of the war, anxious parents
applied to the army to have their sons discharged as being underage.[14] Earlier in
the war some requests for discharge could be refused, either by the army, officers
or the boy in question himself. Several men initially joined up underage, but were
discovered and discharged, only to subsequently re-enlist once they reached the
proper age. Francis Gibbons, from Canal Walk in Fratton, first volunteered for the

Hampshire Regiment in May 1915, when he was just 16. Once his true age was discovered he was discharged, but re-enlisted once he turned 18. He went to the front with the 10th Battalion of the Royal Warwickshire Regiment, only to be captured on 10 April 1918 during the Germans' spring offensive. Held as a prisoner of war, he died on 11 October 1918 – only a month before the armistice – and is buried in Terlinchtun in France. He was 19.

The background of many of the boy soldiers tells us much about the nature of Portsmouth's communities at the time. Many of them were the sons of manual workers or labourers, often connected with the dockyard. Others were the sons of sailors or royal marines. Most had at least one parent who had been born elsewhere and settled in Portsmouth later in life – evidence of Portsmouth's incredibly mobile society. Several were born abroad, at a time when many people in Britain never travelled further than the local town or perhaps to the local seaside resort. Frederick Rudd had been born in Malta in 1899, where his father was serving in the Royal Artillery. The Rudd family were living in Portsmouth in 1911, in Grosvenor Street in Southsea. Rudd joined the 14th Hampshires, and was killed in action on 30 June 1916. He was 17, and is remembered on the Loos memorial in France.[15]

Although most underage soldiers seem to have joined the Hampshire Regiment, others joined different units for a range of reasons. Thomas McCormac was born in Sandown on the Isle of Wight in 1900. In 1911 the McCormac family were living at 1 Frogmore Road in Milton, near Fratton Park. McCormac's father, Thomas, was an electrical fitter who had been born in Dublin in Ireland. Perhaps because of his Irish heritage, Thomas McCormac, although he was underage, enlisted in Portsmouth but volunteered for the Royal Munster Fusiliers. At some point he was transferred to the Royal Dublin Fusiliers – even more fitting, perhaps, given his father's place of birth – and went to the Western Front with the 9th Battalion. He died of wounds on 8 June 1917, and is buried in Bailleul cemetery in France. He was 17, and is remembered on St John's Roman Catholic Cathedral's war memorial.

As with all servicemen, underage soldiers were also vulnerable to wounds and illness. Alfred Downer was born in Portsmouth in 1899. The son of a master mariner who worked on boats sailing to Ryde on the Isle of Wight, Alfred is a rare example of a Portsmouth serviceman both of whose parents were born in Portsmouth. He volunteered for the army in August 1914 when he was just 15, joining the 2/4th Battalion of the Hampshire Regiment. The 2/4th Battalion had been sent to India to replace regular units which had returned to Britain for service on the Western Front, and hence Alfred Downer was drafted to India. He went to Mesopotamia with the battalion on 25 October 1915, and was captured at Kut.[16] Held by the Turks, he was eventually released but died in hospital of meningitis on 5 June 1916. He was 17. His original grave was lost, and he is now remembered on the Kirkee memorial.

Compared to Alfred Downer, Charles Brown's family were significantly more mobile. Downer was born in Freshwater on the Isle of Wight in 1900. His father was an 'agent', and his work obviously entailed travel as, according to the 1911 census, all four of his children had been born in different places – Bombay in India, the Isle of Wight, Donegal in Ireland and Brighton. He volunteered for the army in June 1915 when he would have been just 15. He joined the 15th Hampshires and was soon posted to the Western Front. He was seriously wounded on the Somme, and evacuated home to Britain. He died of his wounds in Hospital on 5 November 1916, and is buried in Kirkdale cemetery in Liverpool. He was just 17.

Whilst officially 14,108 underage boys died during the First World War, given that only around 50 per cent of entries on the Commonwealth War Graves Commission have an age recorded, the true figure could be nearer 30,000. The exact number of boys who served underage will never be known, but has been estimated by one historian as being in excess of 250,000.[17]

By contrast, boys had been serving at sea with the Royal Navy since at least the eighteenth century, and probably before as well. Unless they managed to lie about their age, boys had to obtain parental admission to join the Royal Navy, and as a result they were serving in an official capacity, unlike their counterparts who volunteered for the army. Young ratings who joined the Royal Navy spent several years in training vessels before joining their first ship. Among the training vessels was HMS *St Vincent*, moored in Portsmouth harbour. Until reforms in the early years of the twentieth century, training for boys was still very much sail orientated. With the introduction of the dreadnoughts, however, Admiral Sir 'Jacky' Fisher made training more relevant to the twentieth-century navy, as well as beginning to transfer training from floating hulks to more sanitary barracks ashore.[18]

Once they had completed their basic training, boys were then transferred to ships of the training squadron to gain sea-going experience. From there, they were sent to their first ship. Most naval ships carried a complement of boy ratings – up to fifty in larger ships – who were usually messed together away from the rest of the crew.[19] Most boys served as seamen, but others were telegraphists, and Leslie Goodwin, who died aged 17 on 2 February 1917, was a boy servant. Stokers normally joined the navy at a later age, due to the physical demands of their trade, and boys who were training to be artificers spent their initial training ashore in dockyard schools. Boy seamen were indeed an integral part of Portsmouth society, and many older sailors had first enlisted as boys. Rev. Robert Dolling of St Agatha's Church made special efforts to work with the boys who were living on training ships, and identified that they were particularly vulnerable, being away from home at such a young and impressionable age.[20]

Although boys played an integral part of life onboard ship, there were never any illusions as to their importance. They were never mollycoddled and were

regarded as the lowliest of the crew.[21] The navy made full use of boys, however. During the rapid expansion in naval manpower in the early twentieth century it was recognised that an increased intake of boys would be valuable for training future sailors. Even during the war the Admiralty made up for a shortage of able seamen by drafting extra boy seamen onto ship, varying from fifty extra boys on battlecruisers to almost 100 on battleships.[22]

Seventeen boy seamen from Portsmouth are known to have died during the First World War. The youngest Portsmouth sailors to be killed were only 15, but both died whilst at shore establishments. Eight boys from Portsmouth were killed at the age of 16, and seven at the age of 17. The tradition of young boys serving at sea seems to have been so ingrained in a naval society such as Portsmouth that little attention was given to the deaths of boy seamen compared to the shock of young boys being killed on the Western Front.

Two boy artificers were killed whilst serving at HMS *Fisgard*, an apprentice training establishment. Boy artificers Arthur Phelps and Albert Chandler were 15 and 16 respectively when they both died of illness on 5 October 1918. Arthur Phelps was living in Adair Road, Eastney, and is buried in Highland Road cemetery. Albert Chandler was living in Heidelberg Road and is buried in Haslar Royal Naval cemetery in Gosport. Midshipman Macnamara Marchant, the son of a Royal Marines Light Infantry major, was killed whilst serving on HMS *Vanguard* on 9 July 1917. He is remembered on the Chatham naval memorial, and at the time of his death was living in Southsea Terrace, Southsea.

It is telling that, whilst the death of so many young soldiers during the First World War has resonated throughout history and has become a part of the collective memory of the conflict, 16-year-old boy seaman Jack Cornwell was fêted for winning a Victoria Cross at the Battle of Jutland and the fact that he was there at all was not considered remarkable.[23] Whilst only one underage soldier from Portsmouth would die during the Second World War,[24] boys continued to serve at sea in the Royal Navy for many years.

17

'Damned Un-English': Portsmouth's First World War Submariners

As the first major European conflict since the Industrial Revolution, it is not surprising that during the First World War several key new technological innovations came to the fore. In terms of the land war, tanks, the machine gun and barbed wire rose to prominence, as did the aeroplane in the air. But on the waves – or, rather, under them – the submarine was perhaps the single development that visibly transformed naval warfare.

Proposals for submersible boats were nothing new, and had been advanced as far back as 1620 by Cornelius Drebbel, a Dutchman who demonstrated his prototype submarine on the Thames. Embryonic submarines were used during the American Civil War, but it was not until the late nineteenth century that advancing technology – in particular regarding propulsion – made the submarine a viable proposition.

The Royal Navy took possession of its first submarines in 1901. These early submarines, ordered very much as prototypes, were based in Portsmouth along with their depot ship, HMS *Hazard*.[1] In 1904 the submarines were based permanently at Fort Blockhouse in Gosport and many submariners found themselves living in Portsmouth, where they became a part of the social fabric of the area.[2] Early submarines were intended for use in harbour defences, but as they increased in size, so their role expanded to a more proactive level.[3] Admiral Sir John Fisher - the famous 'Jacky' Fisher – was commander-in-chief of Portsmouth from 1903, and took a keen interest in the submarines under his command.[4] Accordingly, the submarines proved their worth in the 1904 fleet manoeuvres – an exercise – 'sinking' two battleships and greatly restricting the fleet's ability to move.[5]

However, the development of the new weapon had not been an easy one. Many of what one historian has referred to as the 'saltwater admirals' were not keen on the submarine, feeling it to be an underhand form of warfare in the

rigid constrictions of the post-Victorian Royal Navy.[6] Whilst the influential Fisher was a keen advocate of the submarine, another senior admiral had gone as far as to argue that submariners captured in war should be treated as pirates and hanged.[7] Unsurprisingly, men who volunteered for service in submarines quickly developed their own unique brand of *esprit de corps*.[8] Submariners were all volunteers from within the Royal Navy, and the informality that became a hallmark of the submarine service was tempered by the presence of a high proportion of skilled ratings among the crew and the hard life that they experienced.[9]

Submarine service was not for the faint of heart. As a result of the pervading smell of diesel fuel, unwashed bodies and primitive toilets, submariners quickly became de-sensitised to smells. Early classes of submarines did not even possess toilets, instead providing a bucket. With so many men living together in a confined, airtight space for prolonged periods – not to mention the smell of stale breath and tobacco – submarines could not have been described as a pleasant environment. There was a complete lack of creature comforts, food was rudimentary and there was no doctor onboard. There were few bunks, so ratings had to 'hotbunk'. Not surprisingly, submariners received extra pay, which doubled an able seaman's salary.[10]

As well as swimming against the cultural tide, submarines were a relatively new concept and they held a number of physical dangers for the sailors who fought in them. Firstly, in many respects the technology had not been mastered, and accidents were far from rare. Secondly, submarine warfare was such a new concept that it took time for senior officers to work out how to deploy them.[11] Inevitably, errors were made. And as can be seen from the statistics of losses on submarines, it was comparatively much more difficult to survive the sinking of a submarine than a surface vessel. On the other side of the balance sheet,

HMS *Dolphin*, the submarine base at Fort Blockhouse in Gosport. (Author)

British submariners taking a break on deck. (GWPDA)

submariners were richly rewarded, many receiving decorations. All the same, all submariners must have been well aware of the long odds of survival, and it must have taken a particular kind of bravery to keep going on patrols. Unlike those onboard surface vessels, lower-deck ratings were much less aware of what was going on around them, with only the captain being able to 'see'.[12]

Just thirteen years after taking delivery of its first submarine, the Royal Navy fought the First World War at sea with an increasing fleet of boats.[13] In August 1914 the Royal Navy began the war with seventy-four submarines in commission. The majority of these were in home waters, but three were at Gibraltar, three at Malta, three at Hong Kong and two in Australia.[14] Britain had not been alone in developing submarines, however. The German Navy identified a role for submarines in attacking Britain's large surface fleet and strangling her vital maritime trade routes. One of the first major demonstrations of how deadly submarines could be came on 22 September 1914, when the German *U-9* sank three elderly cruisers, HMS *Aboukir,* HMS *Cressy* and HMS *Hogue* off the Dutch coast, with the loss of twenty Portsmouth sailors. It was a startling lesson that even large warships could not operate anywhere near as freely as they had done in Nelson's time, thanks to the submarine.[15] After this incident the Royal Navy maintained a much more distant blockade of the German coast, for fear of losing more ships to submarines.

Ironically, the first submarine with Portsmouth connections was lost about as far from the Solent as geographically possible – in the South Pacific. HM Submarine *AE1* had been loaned to the Australian Navy. Covering the occupation of German possessions in the Pacific, *AE1* failed to surface on 19 September 1914 and was never seen again. All of her crew of thirty were lost, and it was assumed that she had grounded on a coral reef. She was crewed entirely by British sailors who had been transferred to the Australian Navy and sailed her from Britain to the other side of the world. Among her crew were five Portsmouth sailors: Petty Officer Henry Hodge, aged 34 of Landport; Chief Engine Room Artificer Joseph Wilson, aged 34 of Landport; Petty Officer William Tribe, aged 33 of North End;

Able Seaman Arthur Fisher, of Landport; and Petty Officer Thomas Guilbert, aged 32 of Buckland.

Portsmouth's biggest submarine losses came early in the war. On 18 October 1914 HM Submarine *E3* was sunk by the German submarine *U27* off the Ems Estuary, on the German North Sea coast. There were no survivors. Eight men from Portsmouth were lost – Able Seaman Robert Jones, aged 28 of Landport; Able Seaman Peter Querotret, aged 28 of Fratton; Leading Seaman George Taylor, aged 28 of Mile End; Engine Room Artificer Charley Blake, aged 28; Sub Lieutenant John Scott of Emsworth; Chief Petty Officer George Macfarlane, aged 39 from the Isle of Wight; Leading Seaman John Westrope, of Gosport; and Engine Room Artificer Richard Hellon, aged 35 of Southsea. They are all remembered on the Portsmouth naval memorial.

Thirty-two Portsmouth-crewed submarines were lost in the North Sea, which became a key battleground. However British submarines did venture further afield, into the North Atlantic, the English Channel, the Irish Sea, the Baltic and the Mediterranean. With the beginning of the Gallipoli campaign in early 1915, it was decided to send seven E class boats to operate in the Dardanelles. These sailed via Gibraltar and Malta to Mudros, an island in the Aegean Sea. The Dardanelles were heavily mined, and in 1915 minesweeping was still in its infancy. Any submarine attempting to transit the narrow straits would have to dodge nets and tethered mines.[16] Of the submarine commanders, only *E15*'s captain, Lieutenant C.S. Brodie, was keen to try and penetrate the defences of the Dardanelles. Therefore *E15* was selected as the first British submarine to attempt to force the straits to disrupt Turkish shipping during the Gallipoli campaign. *E15* sailed at dawn on 17 April but became caught in fierce eddies off Kephez Point. Run aground, she came under fierce fire from Fort Dardanos onshore. Seawater rushed in through the torn hull, creating deadly chlorine gas from the submarine's batteries. The crew abandoned ship, but Lieutenant Brodie was killed by gunfire exiting the conning tower. The rest of the men were taken prisoner. Engine Room Artificer Ernest Hindman, aged 31 and born in Portsea, died the next day, possibly of wounds or of the effects of chlorine gas. He is buried in Chanak Consular cemetery in Turkey. Several of *E15*'s crew later died of illness in Turkish captivity.

A rather controversial submarine loss occurred later in 1915 in the Dardanelles. *E20* had just arrived in the Mediterranean, fresh from the builder's yard, when she was sent on a patrol into the Sea of Marmara. On 6 November she was due to rendezvous with the French submarine *Turquoise*. Unbeknown to the men on *E20*, *Turquoise* had been abandoned by her crew and the Turks and Germans had captured all of her charts, documents and orders. Hence, on 6 November when *E20* arrived at the rendezvous point, *UB14* was waiting for her. *E20* was swiftly sunk, and out of a crew of thirty-six, only nine men survived. Among the dead were Engine Room Artificer Arthur Lonergan and Stoker Percival Rodgers of

Kingston. The *Turquoise's* captain, Lieutenant Ravenel, was court-martialled for his negligence after the war but was found not guilty.

Another controversial loss took place on 18 August 1915 when *E13* was on her way to the Baltic. After leaving Harwich on 14 August, at 11.00 p.m. on 17 August she ran aground off the island of Saltholme, between Copenhagen and Malmo and in Danish territorial waters, due to a faulty gyro compass. Quite properly, the neutral Danes gave *E13* twenty-four hours to leave their waters. However, three German torpedo boats arrived and proceeded to attack the stricken submarine. The crew began to jump over the side, only to be machine-gunned by the Germans. A Danish patrol boat, however, shielded the crew, and rescued the survivors. Although they were interned in neutral Denmark for the rest of the war, the gallant actions of the Danes had saved the lives of twenty-three crew members, and only fifteen men were lost. Among them was Chief Stoker Benjamin Pink, a Portsmouth man who had been born in Canning Town, London, in 1876. His body was evidently returned to Britain, as he is buried in Haslar Royal Naval cemetery in Gosport.

Given the infancy of the technology and the conditions in which the boats operated, submarine accidents were not uncommon, and a sizeable proportion of submariners were lost through reasons other than enemy action. Often these accidents took place close to shore, as when *C16* sank on 16 April 1917. *C16* was carrying out an exercise in the North Sea, 7 miles east of Harwich, along with *C25* and the Destroyer *Melampus*. *C16* was accidentally rammed by *Melampus*. When the wreck was located and raised, it was found that the crew had survived the collision and had attempted to escape. Initially they had tried to escape through the torpedo tubes, and then through the conning tower hatch. Unfortunately the submarine flooded, drowning the crew. Sixteen men were killed and there were no survivors. Among the dead was Petty Officer John Gaunt, aged 30 and from Unicorn Terrace in Portsea. He had been born in Staffordshire, and is buried in Shotley cemetery in Suffolk.

An even more unfortunate loss occurred on 6 March 1918 in the Irish Sea. The steamer *Rutherglen* encountered what it suspected to be a German U-boat. The *Rutherglen's* captain promptly rammed the U-boat, but it was later found that the *Rutherglen* had sunk *H5* with the loss of all twenty-five of her crew. Among the dead were boy telegraphist James Thompson – at 17 the youngest Portsmouth submariner to be killed and a former pupil at the Royal Hospital School in Greenwich – and Petty Officer John Rowe. Also onboard *H5* was Lieutenant Sir John Anson, 5th Baronet, the son of a rear admiral. The Admiralty kept the incident secret and even awarded the captain of the *Rutherglen* the Distinguished Service Cross – it had, after all, exhorted merchant captains to ram U-boats on sight.

One Portsmouth submariner experienced a remarkable journey during the First World War, demonstrating how well-travelled some Portsmouth sailors were.

Percy John Kempster was born in Portsmouth in 1884. After joining the Royal Navy in 1901 as a boy seaman, he served onboard the Cruiser HMS *St George*. He married his wife Beatrice in Portsmouth in 1907 and in 1911 they were living in Longs Road, Landport with their son Percy. In 1913 Kempster was transferred to the Australian Navy and was part of the crew that sailed *AE2* to Australia, arriving in Sydney in May 1914. Although many of the submariners remained in Australia, Kempster returned to Britain in early 1915. Upon his return he technically remained an Australian seaman, but served in *G8*. He was awarded the Distinguished Service Medal for services in action against enemy submarines on 23 July 1917. He qualified as a submarine coxswain in August 1917. Kempster drowned when *G8* was lost in the North Sea on 15 January 1918. At the time of his death his family were living in Fratton Road.

Once war broke out the Admiralty embarked upon a massive expansion programme, ordering more submarines and new classes.[17] The K class in particular had a chequered history during the First World War. At 1,210 tons surfaced they were around twice the size of the E class boats, which weighed in at 660 tons, but they were felt to be technically inferior, and of the seventeen that entered service before 1919 five were lost in accidents.[18] Given the perilous nature of submarine service and the added pressures of wartime conditions, accidents were perhaps inevitable, but the K Class had more than their fair share of tragedies. One such tragic incident took place on 31 January 1918 and became known as the 'Battle of May Island'. That night, elements of the Grand Fleet left the Firth of Forth for an exercise, accompanied by several flotillas of submarines. *K17* was accidentally rammed by the cruiser HMS *Fearless*, and sank eight minutes later. Eighteen of her crew managed to escape out of the engine room, but only nine of them survived. Fifty of her crew were killed. In the confusion as ships and submarines circled the area attempting to rescue survivors, *K4* was rammed by *K6*, slicing her in half. All of her crew of fifty-nine were lost. In a matter of minutes two submarines had been sunk with the loss of a total of 103 submariners, ten of them coming from Portsmouth. On *K17* were Engine Room Artificer Dominick Myott, aged 29; Petty Officer William Cooley, aged 30; Leading Seaman Robert Gill, aged 33 of Kingston; and Petty Officer Stoker Charles Savage, aged 30 of Eastney. On *K4* were Chief Engine Room Artificer Leonard Adams DSM, aged 32 of Copnor; Petty Officer Stoker William Wyatt; Petty Officer Stoker Harry Sheath, aged 38 of Fratton; Able Seaman William Dangerfield, aged 20; Electrical Artificer Ralph Hill, aged 41 of Southsea; and Engine Room Artificer George Woods, aged 31 of Southsea. *K4* was a well-decorated boat, with Adams, Wyatt and Sheath all having been awarded the Distinguished Service Medal.

After the war against the Central Powers had ended in November 1918, British submarines continued to fight a little-known war in the Baltic against the fledgling Soviet Union. *L55* was lost on 4 June 1919 in the Gulf of Finland. It is not known

whether she was sunk by a mine or by Soviet destroyers. Forty-two men were killed and there were no survivors. In August 1928 the hull was raised and the men's bodies were returned to Britain onboard the Cruiser HMS *Champion* to be buried in a joint grave in Haslar Royal Naval cemetery. Four Portsmouth men were among the dead: Petty Officer Thomas Taylor, aged 24 of Stamshaw; Stoker Harry Butler, of Buckland; Petty Officer Telegraphist Charles Dagg, aged 26 of Mile End; and Engine Room Artificer William Shaw, aged 29 of Southsea. Shaw was awarded the Distinguished Service Medal on 28 September 1917 for service with the Royal Naval Air Service, ironically on anti-submarine patrols.

The impact of Royal Navy submarines was never likely to be as significant as those of the enemy: whereas Britain depended on the sea and its trade routes were vulnerable to being harassed by U-boats, the same could not be said for Germany.[19] When the Germans launched their unrestricted submarine campaign in 1917, more and more British submarines were tasked with anti-U-boat work.[20] Despite technical problems that caused their torpedoes to track much lower than the running depth set and undoubtedly hampered their effectiveness, British submarines managed to sink seventeen U-boats during the First World War.[21]

The Royal Navy's submarines had more than proved their worth in war, despite the myriad of problems facing them. The submariners had, however, suffered heavy losses in return. Between August 1914 and January 1921, 141 submariners from Portsmouth died from a staggering fifty-four different submarines. If ever one statistic demonstrates the bleak prospects of serving on board a First World War submarine it is that, of the forty-three submarines lost with Portsmouth men onboard, there were no survivors from thirty-two of them. To keep boarding a submarine knowing that such short odds existed must have called for a particular kind of bravery.

18

Portsmouth's Early Tank Men

War so often encourages technological innovations that lack impetus during the more stringent budgetary considerations of peacetime. The First World War occurred at a time when the British armed forces had not fought a major war on the mainland of Europe for almost a century, but also when more than a century of industrial development had revolutionised society. One of the most prominent technological advances of the First World War was probably that of the tank. Strangely – and ironically, given Portsmouth's naval heritage – the early development of these land weapons was largely prompted by the Admiralty.

As the Western Front bogged down into siege warfare conditions, movement was severely restricted by trenches, barbed wire and machine guns. The minds of more forward-thinking officers began to consider ways of breaking this deadlock. As a result the Admiralty Landships Committee first met on 22 February 1915.[1] The First Lord of the Admiralty at the start of the war, Winston Churchill, was an early supporter of the concept of 'landships'. However, as often occurs with military technology, many officers were initially sceptical of such a radical idea. Many early experiments bordered on the farcical.

Other regiments and corps were developing their own interpretation of the tank. The Royal Artillery experimented with the use of tractors to pull guns, to make use of caterpillar tracks over the muddy terrain of the Western Front. The Royal Naval Air Service also went to war with a motley collection of vehicles and privately assembled a section of armoured cars, and the Royal Naval Brigade that fought at Antwerp had taken London buses in order to enhance their mobility.

How to organise these new weapons in the army's hierarchy puzzled the War Office. As a *ruse de guerre*, it seemed logical to place the early tank crews under the banner of the Heavy Section of the Machine Gun Corps in May 1916. The majority of the early members came from the Machine Gun Corps, with a few men also coming from the Army Service Corps.[2] Six companies were formed, lettered from A to F.

Contrary to popular belief, Field Marshal Sir Douglas Haig was relatively open-minded towards new developments such as the tank, despite some of his staff officers being less enthusiastic.[3] Although only a small number of tanks had

arrived in France and the crews had had little training, they were used in action for the first time during the Battle of Flers on 15 September 1916.[4] The Heavy Branch's commanders advised Haig to wait until they were available in sufficient numbers to attack in strength and to make best use of the element of surprise, but the hard fighting on the Somme prompted Haig to use them as soon as possible. Incidentally, a number of tanks accompanied the 15th Hampshires in their attack from Delville Wood that day. Of the eighteen tanks scheduled to attack from Delville Wood only fourteen managed to get moving, and even fewer reached the objective.[5]

Although the results of the use of tanks at Flers was mixed, they had given the initial attack impetus and had been useful in helping to overcome resistance. Haig was impressed enough to order more tanks. An order for 1,000 new tanks was placed, and with each tank requiring a crew of eight men, this would entail a substantial increase in manpower. In May 1916 the Tank Corps had a humble establishment of 133 officers and 1,089 men; by November 1918 this had mushroomed to 2,801 officers and 25,498 men – a remarkable expansion for a corps that did not even exist in 1914.[6] Men from Portsmouth who fought and died in tanks seem to have joined from this period onwards. In October 1916 the existing companies were enlarged to the size of battalions. As a completely new unit, the Heavy Branch recruited men from all sections of the Army. As with all new units formed in wartime, men volunteered to serve in tanks for a variety of reasons including the extra pay or adventure. The Tank Corps might not have been as glamorous as the Royal Flying Corps, for example, but it did attract men who were fed up of the trenches and were willing to try a different way of going to war. The expansion of the corps also called for infrastructure such as workshops, schools and gunnery ranges, all of which had to be manned.

Tanks were used again at Vimy Ridge in April 1917, during the Battle of Arras.[7] This time, sixty tanks were available, and although many became stuck in mud, the attack proceeded well. Sergeant Charles McNamee had previously been a corporal in the Royal Fusiliers, landing in France on 30 July 1915, before transferring to the Heavy Branch. An old boy of Portsmouth Grammar School, McNamee was the son of a greengrocer and lived in Somers Road, Southsea; he was 21 when he was killed on 9 April 1917 fighting with D Battalion. He has no known grave and is remembered on the Arras memorial. He was entitled to the British War and Victory Medals and the 1915 Star.[8]

Although the limitations of the tanks had again been exposed, Haig was still impressed with their performance. Seeing them as a manpower-effective weapon, able to exert a decisive effect on the battlefield using few men, he ordered the Heavy Branch once more to double in size. As with most units that were formed from volunteers, once the initial intake of enthusiastic men had run out, some of the later men who found themselves serving in tanks were, in the words of

A British tank crossing no-man's-land. (GWPDA)

one author, 'less than keen'. As the Heavy Branch continued to expand, the Tank Corps was established as a separate entity by royal warrant on 28 July 1917.[9]

Tanks were also used in the third Battle of Ypres, although the muddy conditions were far from ideal for them. The ground at Ypres was more often than not a morass, and many tanks ditched. Lance Corporal Wilfred Over, of B Battalion of the Tank Corps, died of wounds on 2 August 1917 and is buried in Lijssenthoek in Belgium. He was 28 and lived in Laburnum Grove, North End. A parishioner of St Matthew's church, he had previously served with the Hampshire Regiment, arriving on the Western Front in 1916, and had been awarded the Military Medal. Over was born in Chichester in 1890 and was the son of a fishmonger and poultry man.[10]

Corporal George Blanchard was born in Portsea in 1880, the son of a naval pensioner. He had had a varied career, having previously served in the Canadian Navy before joining the 15th Hampshires in October 1915. He was later transferred to the Machine Gun Corps and then to the Tank Corps. He was wounded in action and died in the 12th Stationary Hospital at St Pol, near the Tank Corps headquarters, on 6 November 1917. He was 37 and is buried in St Pol. At the time of his death he was living at Wymering Road, North End.[11]

No Portsmouth men were killed in the Battle of Cambrai in November 1917. Although Cambrai is often erroneously thought to be the first tank battle, it was the first time that they had been used significantly and en masse. The tanks at Flers in September in 1916 were relatively few in number and were an addition to an existing battle plan. At Cambria, however, the use of tanks was central to the plan, and all nine Tank Battalions then in France took part.

Tank men were caught up in the Germans' Kaiser Offensive in the spring of 1918. Tanks were not particularly useful in defence, due to their slow speed and the time taken to deploy them to the battlefield. Some men may not have been manning tanks when they were killed, as the urgency of the situation and the danger of a German breakthrough led to men going into the front lines without

their tanks. Private Edmond Sutton, aged 34, lived in Bonchurch Road in Milton. He was serving at the Tank Corps Reinforcement Depot when he died of wounds on 1 April 1918, and is buried in Doullens communal cemetery. A former Sapper in the Hampshire Fortress Company of the Royal Engineers, Sutton was born in Gosport and was an upholsterer before joining up.[12]

After the Germans' spring offensive ground to a halt, the allied armies began to drive the Germans back on the Western Front. By mid-May 1918 there were 600 British tanks on the Western Front, with more arriving at the rate of fifty a week.[13] Significant numbers of Portsmouth men were killed fighting in tanks during the allied offensive in the late summer and autumn of 1918. The offensive began on 8 August near Amiens, when 580 tanks were employed. Two men from Portsmouth were killed on the first day. Private Arthur Kerrison came from Andover Road in Southsea. Serving with C Company of the 8th Battalion, he was killed on 8 August 1918. He was 26. Kerrison is buried at Heath in France, but was originally buried elsewhere and was reinterred at Heath after the end of the war. Kerrison had been born in Umbulla in India in 1892 when his father was serving with the Royal Artillery, and had previously served with the Hampshire Fortress Royal Engineers.[14] Private Hugh Cull also died on the same day. He was serving with B Company of the 2nd Battalion. Cull had originally served with the Army Service Corps, suggesting that he may have been a tank driver, and is buried at Villers-Brettoneux in France. Cull was also reinterred after being originally buried elsewhere. Cull was born in Kensington, London, and enlisted in Acton, also in London, so it is unclear why he appears on the Portsmouth war memorial.[15]

Private Sydney Wills was killed several days later. Aged 27, from Powerscourt Road in North End and a parishioner of All Saints' church, Wills was serving with the 8th Battalion when he was killed on 11 August 1918. He is buried at Heath cemetery.

Sergeant Charles McNamee, pictured whilst an army cadet. (PGS)

He had formerly served with the Hampshire Fortress Royal Engineers. Sydney Wills was born in 1892, and took after his father in working as a hairdresser.[16]

The heavy losses continued throughout August 1918, as tanks were used to break through the German defences. Private Arthur Bailey was serving with the 12th Battalion when he was killed on 20 August 1918. He was 24. Bailey is buried at Berles new military cemetery in France. A parishioner of St Matthew's church, Bailey came from Stansted Road in Southsea. A former sapper in the Royal Engineers, prior to enlisting Bailey worked as a pawnbroker's assistant.[17]

Corporal Alfred Blackler was serving with 20th Battalion when he died on 21 August 1918. He has no known grave and is remembered on the Vis-en-Artois memorial. He was 36 and lived in Trevor Road, Southsea. It is interesting that Corporal Blackler was killed in France, as the 20th Battalion does not seem to have gone to France, having only been formed later in 1918, and did not leave the depot at Bovington. Blacker had also previously served in the Royal Engineers and prior to the war had worked as a joiner and carpenter.[18]

Several of the tank battalions formed later in the war received drafts of men from a range of units. One of those men was Sergeant Ernest Ritchie. Born in Umata, South Africa, Ritchie had served in the Boer War with the King Edward's Horse, a unit made up mainly of Britons who had settled in the colonies, and also in Gorringe's Flying Column, a mounted unit formed to combat Boer Kommando troops. King Edward's Horse was a Special Reserve Unit based in London in August 1914, and its individual squadrons served on the Western Front. According to one historian, the 11th Battalion received a large draft of men from King Edward's Horse when it was formed, and these men proved to be somewhat unruly. Ritchie died of wounds on 2 September 1918 and is buried at Ligny-Saint-Flochel British cemetery in France. He was 40 and gave his address at the time of his death as Cornwall Road, Fratton.[19]

Large parts of the army remained on the Western Front for some time after the end of the war, including the Tank Corps, and men died of illness even months after the Armistice. Sergeant Reginald Rourke was born in Ireland in 1889, the son of a company sergeant major in the Royal Engineers, and worked as a joiner prior to enlisting. He was serving in the Stores Department at the Tank Corps Headquarters in France when he died on 25 February 1919, and is buried in St Pol. He was 29 and came from Tredegar Road in Southsea. Rourke had been awarded the Meritious Service Medal as a corporal in June 1918 for valuable service in France during the war.[20]

Lieutenant Arthur Whitfield had a rather interesting service record. Born in Portsmouth in 1890, he was the son of a hosier's assistant from the Isle of Wight. Originally serving in the ranks of the Royal Army Service Corps, he was commissioned as a second lieutenant in the King's Shropshire Light Infantry, before transferring to the 12th Battalion of the Tank Corps. He died in South

The grave of Lieutenant Arthur Whitfield. (Author)

Stoneham near Southampton on 14 January 1921 and is buried in Milton cemetery in Portsmouth. He was 31 and lived in Marmion Road, Southsea.[21]

By the end of 1918 there were over 2,000 tanks in service on the Western Front, a remarkable achievement not only for their designers and builders but also for the men who fought in these early armoured vehicles.[22] By the time of the Armistice the Tank Corps consisted of 561 officers and 2,627 men.[23] In the twenty-first century, tanks are a central part of warfare, but when the First World War began the concept had not even been invented. That so many young men volunteered to fight in such little-known and dangerous weapons is testament to their bravery.

After the end of the war, redundant tanks were presented to many cities and towns as a 'thank you' for their fundraising efforts. One tank was presented to Portsmouth and stood on Southsea Common for many years until it was sold for scrap in 1940. Another tank was presented to HMS *Excellent* on Whale Island on 1 May 1919 to commemorate the navy's assistance in providing gunnery training for tank crews. After many years on display it was presented to the Tank Museum in Bovington in 1975, where it can still be seen today – a fitting tribute to Portsmouth's tank men.[24]

19

Guest of the Kaiser: Portsmouth's Prisoners of War

During the First World War 173,575 British servicemen were captured.[1] Their stories, however, have been largely overshadowed by those of their successors who were captured during the Second World War. Whilst we know much about the Great Escape and Colditz, by comparison we know very little about the men who were held prisoner by the Germans and the Turks during the First World War.

In part this is due to the dearth of information about them – there are very few records available to researchers that shed any light on their experiences. However, it is still possible to reconstruct their stories and gain some kind of perspective on how lives were affected by captivity. A total of 16,402 servicemen died in captivity during the First World War, representing a death rate of around 9.4 per cent. Compared to the Second World War, escaping from captivity does not seem to have been a priority for many prisoners – only 405 officers and men managed to escape from prisoner of war camps and make their way back to Britain.[2]

Most soldiers never expected to be captured alive by the enemy. Foremost in the minds of many was the possibility of being killed or perhaps seriously wounded.

British prisoners of war being marched into captivity. (GWPDA)

Surrender was on the minds of very few soldiers. Most were not trained in terms of how to approach surrender, and in any case most other ranks were merely at the mercy of events and the decisions of those further up the chain of command.[3] When a situation arose in which men were captured or forced to surrender, most men were completely in the dark as to what would happen to them.

Naturally, many men were captured in France and Flanders by the Germans, as not only was the Western Front the most active theatre throughout the war, but it was also where the bulk of the British Army fought. The majority of British soldiers captured during the First World War were taken prisoner on the Western Front – 6,106 officers and 155,181 men.[4] Although the Germans were unprepared to receive prisoners early in the war, soldiers captured by the enemy were protected by the Geneva Convention, to which both Britain and Germany were signatories.[5] Despite horror stories propagated in the British media regarding German ill-treatment of Allied prisoners, in general captured troops were treated relatively well.[6] Although for much of the war the Western Front was relatively stationary, mobile warfare during the opening and closing phases of the war in 1914 and 1918, and to an extent during offensives such as the Somme and Ypres, led to conditions in which men could become captured by the enemy. Prisoners could also be taken during raids, when either side would seek to capture prisoners in order to identify the units facing them and to interrogate for intelligence purposes.

Prisoners were captured almost as soon as the British Army began fighting on the Western Front. Private Arthur Cooper was aged 28 and serving with the 1st Battalion of the Lincolnshire Regiment, which had been stationed in Portsmouth before embarking for France in August 1914. He lived in Stanley Road in Stamshaw. Cooper was probably wounded and captured during the retreat from Mons or at the First Battle of Ypres. Sadly he died on 22 January 1915, and is buried in Berlin South-Western cemetery.

A senior officer from Portsmouth was captured during the retreat from Mons. Lieutenant Colonel Alexander Abercrombie, aged 50, was commanding the 2nd Battalion of the Connaught Rangers when he was captured on 10 September 1914. Abercrombie lived at Crescent Lodge, Southsea. The capture of a lieutenant colonel must have been a great coup for the Germans. Officer prisoners were usually held separately, and Abercrombie died in a prison camp at Magdeburg on 5 November 1915. His body was later exhumed and reinterred in Berlin South-Western cemetery.[7] Abercrombie was born in Bengal, India, and entered Sandhurst as a cadet in 1884. Leaving Sandhurst in 1885, he joined the Yorkshire Regiment. By 1901 he had transferred to the Connaught Rangers, and during the Boer War he served on the staff of the deputy assistant adjutant general, including during the Siege of Ladysmith. In 1911 he was serving with the headquarters staff at the Gibraltar Garrison.

Sailors were also captured by the enemy, often when their ships were sunk and they were rescued. Engine Room Artificer David Garrett lived in Percy Road in Southsea. He was part of the crew onboard HMS *Maori*, a torpedo boat destroyer, when she was sunk by a mine off Zeebrugge on 7 May 1915. Although rescued, Garrett died as a result of an accident in captivity on 4 May 1916. He was 34. Originally buried in Soltau, Garrett was later reinterred in Hamburg war cemetery. Born in Islington, North London, in 1880, by 1911 Garrett was living in Portsmouth, having been married for three years.

Men from the Portsmouth Pals were also captured in action. Corporal Francis Ennis, of the 14th Battalion of the Hampshire Regiment, died of wounds in captivity on 15 December 1916, and is buried Niederzwehren cemetery. The son of a seafarer, Ennis was born in Jersey in 1889, and although he lived in Gosport, he joined the Hampshire Militia in December 1906 prior to joining the regular forces in 1907. In 1911 he was serving as a private with the 2nd Battalion of Hampshire Regiment at Wynberg, near the Cape of Good Hope in South Africa. As a regular soldier, Ennis was probably one of the regular non-commissioned officers transferred to the Pal Battalions to provide experience. Another Portsmouth Pals man captured was Lance Corporal George Avis, also serving with the 14th Battalion of the Hampshire Regiment. Avis died of wounds on 5 May 1917, and is buried in Niederzwehren. Avis was born in 1888 in Greenwich, but enlisted in Portsmouth. At the time of the 1911 census he was living with his sister and brother-in-law in Lion Terrace in Portsea and working as a butcher's assistant.

Many prisoners were captured during the Germans' Spring Offensive in early 1918. Ten men from Portsmouth are known to have been captured during that period and subsequently died in captivity; the true figure is likely to have been higher. Sapper E.G. Barham, aged 20, came from Balfour Road in North End. Serving with the 50th (Northumbrian) Signal Company of the Royal Engineers, Barham was captured and died on 13 September 1918. He is buried in Niederzwehren. Barham was awarded a posthumous Military Medal, announced in the *London Gazette* on 7 October 1918. Although Barham was born in Portsmouth, he had enlisted in Petersfield.

Chaos reigned behind the German lines; due to years of allied naval blockade the German authorities could not feed the civilian population, let alone thousands of prisoners.[8] Private George Atkins, aged 28 and from Tennyson Road, Copnor, was serving with the 1/8th Battalion of the Durham Light Infantry. He was captured during the German offensive and died in captivity on 6 October 1918. He is buried in Niederzwehren. As a former soldier in the Royal Army Service Corps, Atkins was mobilised in August 1914 and served at Mons, on the Somme and at Ypres before he was captured in 1918. He was born in Portsmouth in 1890 and had originally enlisted in the army in his home town. In 1911 Atkins was

living in Jersey Road in Portsmouth and working as a central improver. His father was an army pensioner and had been born in Canada.

Prisoners were still dying even after the Armistice on 11 November 1918. Private William Morey, from Vivash Road, Southsea, served with the 6th Battalion of the West Yorkshire Regiment. Morey was taken prisoner on the Somme in 1916 and subsequently died in a prisoner-of-war camp at Langensatz on 27 November 1918. He is buried in Niederzwehren. Morey had volunteered for the army in October 1915.

By the end of the war, food shortages in Germany were acute and prisoners were largely surviving on starvation rations of black coffee and black bread. In such a desparate situation, Red Cross food parcels kept many men alive, along with parcels sent by a myriad of other organisations and committees.[9]

Inevitably, with many men being wounded in action before they were captured, and with medical care being rudimentary at best, many wounded prisoners died before they could be transported to Germany. Some men were too seriously wounded to be moved to Germany, and died in hospitals near the front line. In addition, many prisoners were kept in the front-line area to work.[10] The authorities had much difficulty in keeping track of these men, as they often moved from place to place and were kept in makeshift camps that were not inspected by representatives of the Red Cross or neutral countries.

Several Portsmouth men died whilst prisoners near the front line. Private Albert Corben was a member of the 14th Battalion Hampshire Regiment. A

Packing boxes for the Portsmouth Prisoners of War Appeal Committee. (Gates)

resident of Newcomen Road in Stamshaw, Corben volunteered for the army early in the war in September 1914. He served on the Somme and at Hollebeke, Arras and Ypres in 1917. He was wounded in 1918 and died in captivity on 2 May 1918, and is buried in Premont in France. Corben was born and enlisted in Portsmouth. In 1911 Corben was working as a butcher's assistant, his father being a journeyman butcher.

Private George Foot was serving with the 2/4th Battalion of the Yorkshire Regiment. Aged 20, he was a resident of Toronto Road in Buckland. Foot originally joined the army in September 1916 upon turning 18. He served at Ypres, Cambrai, and on the Somme before he was captured on 18 April 1918 on the Lys. He died on 5 September 1918 and was buried in Glageon in France. Although Foot was born in Portsmouth, he had enlisted in Taunton. The 1911 census shows Foot living in Gamble Road. He was a scholar, and his father was a shipwright. In 1901 the family were living at Sheerness in Kent.

In 1911, Francis Gibbons was living with his parents in Guildford Street, Landport; his father was a barman and licensed victualler. Gibbons had volunteered in May 1915 when he was 17 and joined the Hampshire Regiment, but was discharged due to being underage. At the age of 19, while living at Canal Walk, Fratton, he enlisted in the Hampshire Regiment before being transferred to the 10th Royal Warwickshire Regiment. Taken prisoner on 10 April 1918, Private Gibbons died in captivity on 11 October 1918 – some time after he had been captured – and is buried in Terlinchtun in France.

Some men were not technically 'prisoners', but were interned in Holland. Whilst Holland was a neutral country in the First World War, any servicemen of either side who found themselves in Holland – for whatever reason – were held in internment for the duration of the war. Sadly, one naval officer from Portsmouth died by his own hand in 1917 whilst being held in Holland. He had been interned after entering Holland while fighting with the Royal Naval Division at Antwerp in 1914.[11]

A large number of men were captured by Turkish forces during the campaigns in theatres such as Gallipoli, Mesopotamia and Palestine. Men captured by the Turks were held in particularly harsh conditions and suffered a horrific casualty rate. The British Government was well aware of the plight of many of the prisoners in Turkish captivity. In October 1917 the Secretary of State for War, Lord Derby, circulated a memo describing the situation. The Turkish government, it was reported, was being less than honest – even to the point of claiming that no British prisoners in Turkish hands were sick or wounded, a claim that was 'plainly absurd' according to Lord Derby. In addition, there had been practically no independent inspections of Turkish camps by the representatives of neutral countries.[12] The memo was forwarded to colonial governments, and a letter from the Prime Minister's Office to the Governor-General of New Zealand stated that

'the condition of many of these prisoners is extremely bad and the outlook for the winter is grave'.[13]

One of the men held by the Turks was Sapper Percy Fox. Aged 23 and from Coburg Street in Fratton, Fox was an engineer in civilian life with an engineering degree. As a territorial soldier he was mobilised in August 1914, and served with 506th Field Company of the Royal Engineers. He was captured at Kut and taken to Turkey. He died of malaria in hospital on 20 November 1918 and is buried in Chanak cemetery.

A large contingent of men was captured at the fall of Kut in Mesopotamia in 1915. Although they had endured serious privations from the climate, tropical diseases and siege conditions, their suffering had only just begun. Many of them were territorial soldiers from Portsmouth serving with the 1/4th Battalion of the Hampshire Regiment. Private Leonard Fry came from Plymouth Street in Southsea, and was a parishioner of St Luke's. Born in Poole, he enlisted in the army in January 1905, and in 1911 he was serving in Poona in India. After going to Mesopotamia with the 2nd Battalion of the Dorsetshire Regiment, he was wounded twice at Kut before being taken prisoner. On 6 June 1916 during the march from Kut to Tikrit he fell out of the march suffering with dysentery and was left at the side of the road to die. He was never seen again and is remembered on the Basra memorial. William Crosby, aged 45 and from Cleveland Road in Southsea, was a company quartermaster sergeant with the 1/4th Battalion of the Hampshire Regiment. William Crosby had an interesting civilian career as a town postman and assistant inspector of telegram messengers. Volunteering for the army in August 1914, Crosby's senior role in civilian life obviously made him a prime candidate to be promoted to senior non-commissioned officer. Crosby went with the 1/4th Hampshires to India and then Iraq. Captured by the Turks, he died in captivity on 1 September 1916. He has no known grave and is remembered on the Basra memorial. Crosby received a Military Medal. Private James Bath, 19 years old and from Radnor Street in Southsea, was also serving with the 1/4th Battalion of the Hampshire Regiment. The son of a naval pensioner, Bath volunteered for the army in Portsmouth in October 1914. He died in Turkish captivity on 12 September 1916 and is buried in Baghdad North Gate war cemetery. Private Frederick Bell, of Jervis Road in Stamshaw, was also serving with the 1/4th Hampshires. Bell died on 21 April 1917 and is buried in Baghdad North Gate war cemetery. As a territorial soldier he was mobilised in August 1914. Bell was actually born in 1895 in Karachi, India (now Pakistan). His two older brothers were born in Poona and Quetta – both army garrisons, suggesting that Bell's father was a soldier.

Several Portsmouth submariners were captured by the Turks in dramatic circumstances after their submarine *E15* ran aground in the Dardanelles. Petty Officer Stoker Ernest Mitchell lived in Netley Street, Fratton. The son of a

railway porter, Mitchell was born in Somerset in 1877. He died of disease on 26 November 1916 and is buried in Baghdad North Gate war cemetery. He was 39. Petty Officer George Williams was also onboard *E15* when she ran aground. Living in Sutherland Road in Southsea, Williams was born in Holt in Wiltshire. He died of disease at the age of 37 on 4 December 1916 and is buried in Baghdad North Gate war cemetery. His original grave has been lost and he is remembered by a special memorial in the cemetery. Another *E15* crew member was Leading Stoker James Bond, a 33-year-old from Chatham Row, Portsea. Born in Gosport, Bond joined the Royal Navy in January 1905. He died on 2 February 1917, and is buried in Baghdad North Gate. The cause of Bond's death is not recorded.

Prisoners of war were very much in the minds of people on the home front, with many towns launching appeals to provide for prisoners.[14] Almost as soon as war broke out, the people of Portsmouth began to think of their menfolk in captivity. In Portsmouth a prisoners' fund was launched, raising funds to provide men with food parcels and basic comforts.[15] Parcels cost 9 shillings each, and the committee had a monthly expenditure of £600. In June 1916 the mayor took over as chairman of the fund and various activities were organised to raise money, including concerts, festivals, whist drives and flag days. Over the course of the war, 16,842 parcels were sent. According to Gates, many liberated prisoners of war called in at the town hall to thank the committee in person.[16]

20

Portsmouth's War Horses

The cost of the First World War was not limited to human life. Michael Morpurgo's novel *War Horse,* which tells the fictional story of a young Devon boy and his horse, has recently shed new light on another, non-human dimension of the First World War – the experience of horses in action. Although twenty-first century Portsmouth is almost completely urban, in 1914 horses were central to life in the town. At the beginning of the nineteenth century, settlements in Portsmouth had been contained in the south-west corner of the island, while the majority of the land was still overwhelmingly rural. In 1853, for example, 74 per cent of Portsea Island was being farmed in some way.[1] Despite unprecedented growth and urbanisation in the preceding century, Portsmouth in 1914 still contained a significant number of farms.[2] Large areas of Portsea Island were still farmland, in particular around Hilsea, while other areas such as Milton and Copnor were still very much villages.[3] On the mainland, Cosham was little more than a village and Paulsgrove was inhabited by a mere handful of human beings. When Portsmouth Football Club was founded in 1898, its future home of Fratton Park was 5 acres of farmland, complete with cows grazing.[4] Despite the introduction of farm machinery in the late nineteenth century and the obvious benefits that it offered in cutting labour costs, most farms still made use of horsepower.[5] At the turn of the century there were an estimated 1 million horses in Britain, compared to only 10,000 cars.[6]

Horses were a common sight in early twentieth-century Portsmouth. The corporation employed about seventy horses in 1915. (EN)

TENDERS.

BOROUGH OF PORTSMOUTH.

TENDERS are invited, to be delivered not later than 9.30 a.m. on Monday, the Third day of May, 1915, for SIX MONTHS FORAGE for about 70 horses at the Corporation Stables and six at the Asylum, Milton.

Specification and form of tender may be obtained at the Town Hall, Portsmouth.

G. HAMMOND ETHERTON,
Town Clerk.

The Town Hall,
20th April, 1915.

The names of public houses are often an indication of the nature of local society, and several Portsmouth pubs give an indication of the town's forgotten rural roots. Many of them were in locations that today seem far from rural. The Coach and Horses in Hilsea was built on the main road from Portsmouth to London and was named after the stagecoaches that used the road. Nearby, the Green Farm – now a carvery restaurant – was the last working farm in Portsmouth. The Cabman's Rest in Somers Town was opened by Brickwood's as recently as 1922, and to this day its sign depicts a horse-drawn cab. The Yorkshire Grey stood in Guildhall Walk for many years and is believed to have been named after the grey horses used by the Royal Artillery, whose barracks were nearby. The horses would have been a common sight in the town.[7]

Many local businesses made use of horses, most notably breweries such as Brickwood's, which employed many dray horses to deliver beer. Horses also provided the main means of transportation. Although the motor car had become a more frequent sight on British streets, it was still very much the preserve of the rich and wealthy. Horse trams had only been replaced by electric-powered vehicles in Portsmouth as recently as 1901.[8] Railways also made extensive use of horses to transport goods and parcels on from stations, particularly to outlying areas.[9]

There were also road accidents involving horses. On 17 August 1914 George May Clue was killed when his horse was panicked – ironically by a motor car – and threw the trap that it was riding into the air, killing Clue instantly.[10]

Advertisements in the *Evening News* just after the outbreak of war suggest how pivotal horses were to local society, even in areas that might not immediately be considered rural. On 5 August an ex-laundry van horse was advertised for sale in Cosham and a fishmonger's pony and cart in Eastney.[11] On 8 August a greengrocer's pony and a light trolley were for sale in Raglan Street, and a carthorse in Railway View – both in Landport, an area that we would not generally consider to be horse country in the twentieth century.[12] The number of horses advertised for sale or for hire in the local press increased substantially throughout August 1914. The reasons for this are unclear, although it may have been due to owners wishing to secure a better price for their animals than through them being requisitioned. Alternatively, perhaps men who were joining up were disposing of animals that they no longer needed. The rising cost and possible shortages of fodder might also have been a consideration.

The British Army had to expand exponentially from 1914 onwards, both in terms of manpower and horsepower. The War Office knew that in the event of war the army would not have enough horses and so instigated a scheme whereby horse owners could register their animals for service in the army in return for a guaranteed price. Even after these horses had been 'called up' there were still not enough, however. Although the government could not countenance conscription of the human population until 1916, horses that had not been volunteered by

With many men being enlisting in the forces, businesses such as Brickwood's were soon short of experienced horsemen. (*EN*)

DRAYMEN REQUIRED AT ONCE,
Brewery experience unnecessary, but must understand horses.
Apply—BRICKWOOD & Co., Ltd,, Portsea.

their owners were conscripted into the army immediately upon the outbreak of war under the Army Act of 1881, which entitled the War Office to requisition horses in a national emergency.[13] The War Office also purchased many horses from abroad. As a result of this shortage, many horses that were not ideally suited to active service were requisitioned or purchased and sent overseas.

Many local horses were commandeered for the war effort in Portsmouth, and it was reported that the loss of horses led to difficulties for several local businesses.[14] During the first twelve days of the war the War Office requisitioned many horses, after which it relied on purchasing animals on the open market.[15] Not only was there a shortage of horses, but also of men that were used to working with horses. On 30 April 1915 Brickwood's advertised for draymen, having allowed many of their employees to join up. Applicants did not need to have brewery experience, but 'must understand horses'.[16] With a lack of men to work the remaining horses in the town, many women took to driving horses and carts.[17]

From early on it was feared that demand for horses would far outstrip supply. In 1914, the British Army had a total of 25,000 horses, compared to only eighty motor vehicles.[18] Immediately upon the outbreak of war, the army's capacity for horses was increased to 165,000.[19] With a view to further expansion and replacing losses, however, the Army Remount Service assessed a need for 245,000 horses. Of these, 68,000 came from Britain, while 75,000 were obtained from Australia, and 70,000 mules were also imported from the United States.[20] The training of horses was by no means a simple task, and many thousands of animals used to a relatively quiet life in the countryside had to be trained to work in the heat and noise of battle.[21]

Sadly, horses that served with the British Army during the First World War did not have service records in the same manner as soldiers and no sources survive that allow us to trace the stories of individual horses from Portsmouth. Nor do we know exactly how many horses from Portsmouth served, but the total must surely have numbered in the hundreds, if not more. Thus we can only imagine what happened to them once they left the town.

Cavalry units were certainly among the most fashionable in the army and the horse was a major status symbol in society. It has frequently been thought that the majority of horses sent to the Western Front served in cavalry units, waiting behind the lines for years on end for a cavalry charge that never materialised, while eating tons of expensive fodder.[22] Horses did indeed demand huge amounts of

fodder – 5.8 million tons of fodder were shipped to the Western Front, compared to 5.2 million tons of ammunition.[23] However, most of that fodder was probably consumed by horses serving in decidedly less glamorous roles than in the cavalry, for example pulling guns with the Royal Artillery (the largest artillery pieces required twenty draught horses) supply wagons with the Army Service Corps or providing transport for infantry units. In 1914 the cavalry possessed 34.4 per cent of all horses in the British Army; by 1918 this figure had fallen to 6 per cent.[24] Senior officers in infantry battalions were allotted horses, which represented the most reliable form of transport.[25] Each field ambulance alone used 78 draught horses.[26] Soldiers frequently developed close bonds with their horses, and inter-unit horse shows, gymkhanas for officers and even race meetings were popular events.[27]

Many Portsmouth soldiers would have had experience of working with horses in their civilian lives and also during their war service. The use of horses by the British Army was reflected by the ranks of some soldiers. Many servicemen in the artillery and the Service Corps in particular held the rank of driver – equivalent to an infantry private – in connection with their role in driving horses.

Working with horses could frequently be dangerous. Driver Arthur Marshman, of Rivers Street in Southsea, was serving with the Royal Field Artillery when he was accidentally killed by his horse on 12 January 1915.

Other ranks reflected the support that horses needed. Farriers served with horse units, combining blacksmithing skills with basic veterinary care. Farrier Sergeant J.A. Derrick, of the 325th Field Company of the Royal Engineers, died on 17 April 1918 and is buried in Chocques in France. Farrier Corporal William Price, of Sultan Road in Mile End, was a regular soldier who had originally enlisted into the Army Service Corps in 1909. After serving in French ports, he died on 16 August 1916. Price does not appear on the Commonwealth War Graves Commission's register, suggesting that he was demobilised and died whilst a civilian. With so many horses being used on active service, the Army Veterinary Corps expanded significantly. Veterinary Corps personnel worked at remount depots on both sides of the channel, on attachment with mounted units, and also in veterinary hospitals.

Horses behind the lines at Gallipoli. (GWPDA)

The grave of Richard Levey, a reservist called up to be
a riding instructor. (GWPDA)

Five men from Portsmouth died whilst serving
with the Veterinary Corps. None were officers,
and therefore were presumably not qualified
veterinary surgeons.

Hundreds of thousands of raw recruits,
many of whom had to work with horses, also
required intensive training in horsemanship.
Lance Bombardier Richard Levey, 32 and from
Kilmiston Street in Fratton, had been called up as
a reservist in August 1914. After serving at Mons,
Ypres and on the Somme, he returned to Britain
in September 1916 as a riding instructor. He died
after the end of the war on 10 November 1919,
and is buried in Kingston cemetery.

Historians have paid very little attention to the role of British cavalry on
the Western Front during the First World War.[28] A relatively small number of
Portsmouth men fought and died serving in cavalry units. Those who did seem to
have died outside of major offensives or when serving in the front line as makeshift
infantry, often during times of crisis or manpower shortages. Only thirty-one men
from Portsmouth were killed whilst serving with cavalry units during the First
World War. Of these, most died whilst on the Western Front but several were killed
in other theatres where horses were more useful than in the static warfare of the
Western Front. Sergeant George Wilsher, of the Queen's Own Worcestershire
Yeomanry, died on 16 November 1916 and is buried in Baghdad North Gate War
cemetery in Iraq. He was 33 and was born in Southsea. Some specialist cavalry
units fought in far-flung areas of the British Empire. Private George Burnett was
serving with the 5th Mounted Rifles of the Imperial Light Horse when he died
on 21 January 1915 in Namibia, a German colony in Southern Africa. He was 26
and is buried in Swakopmund on the Namibian Coast.

One cavalry unit with particularly strong links with Portsmouth was the
Hampshire Yeomanry. A cavalry unit of the Territorial Force, the yeomanry
units were regarded as particularly horse-loving.[29] The yeomanry had their
headquarters in Bedhampton, and upon the start of the war they were mobilised
and became part of the Portsmouth Garrison defences, before leaving the town
in September 1914. Remaining in Britain to defend against a possible German
invasion, beginning in February 1915 the yeomanry were instructed in trench
warfare before going overseas in May 1916. The Hampshire Yeomanry served as
corps cavalry on the Western Front.

One of Portsmouth's watering carts, driven by a female driver in the absence of so many men. (Gates)

As the war progressed and manpower shortages loomed, the army disbanded some cavalry units and dispersed the men into infantry battalions. After the 15th Battalion of the Hampshire Regiment had suffered heavy losses at the Third Battle of Ypres, the survivors were amalgamated with the disbanded Hampshire Yeomanry. Many men from Portsmouth who had originally enlisted into the yeomanry and went overseas on horseback ended up fighting and dying on foot.

A shortage of horses from 1916 onwards caused a crisis on two fronts. Firstly, the War Office began to invest in motor vehicles for use in theatres overseas, and farmers in Britain began to make more use of machinery to compensate for the shortage of horsepower. The number of horses in the British Army peaked at 869,931 in August 1917.[30] The problems of obtaining horses had led to an increase in number of motor vehicles, and by the end of the war the army had 57,000 lorries and tractors, 23,000 light vehicles and 7,000 motor ambulances.[31]

Many horses did not return from active service; 376,201 horses were killed whilst serving with the British Army on the Western Front. Just to give an indication of how heavy losses could be in a short period, the Cavalry Corps lost 1,208 horses between 1 and 14 April 1917, with a further 690 wounded.[32] Of the few horses that did return from the war, a tiny fraction will have made it home to their original owners, if any at all. Only 132,649 returned to work in Britain. A total of 197,181 were sold in France and an estimated 46,885 ended up as horsemeat.[33] The loss of so many horses, in a society that depended on them, would have had a significant impact upon many local families and businesses. At a time when farmers were being exhorted to increase their output, the loss of horses must have proved to be problematic. This shortage of horsepower led many farmers to invest in machinery and helped to stimulate the mass appearance of the motor car on Britain's roads.[34]

Whilst we know very little about the experiences of individual horses from Portsmouth that served during the First World War, horses were central to local society in 1914, and the national context would suggest that the loss of so many animals altered life in the town significantly. The impact of war was by no means limited to humans alone.

21

Their Name Liveth For Ever More: Remembrance in Portsmouth

The First World War devastated Portsmouth's population, certainly more than any other conflict before or since. Across Great Britain 764,457 people were killed, with over 6,000 of them coming from Portsmouth.[1] Nationally, around 9 percent of all adult men under 45 were killed, and the proportion of younger men was higher still.[2] 2,085,952 men were wounded. If applied locally, the national ratio of killed to wounded would suggest that over 16,000 men from Portsmouth were wounded.[3] No event since the Black Death had so touched the lives of people in Britain – and indeed Europe – and a whole generation and society experienced grief on a collective scale.[4]

Whilst Portsmouth was no stranger to men going off to fight, the First World War was the first major war Britain had fought for a century, and its aftermath witnessed a new kind of mourning and remembrance. The Victorian cult of death and mourning endured into the Edwardian age, and whereas a soldier who died at Waterloo in 1815 might have been dumped in a mass grave and forgotten, his counterpart who fell on the Western Front was commemorated in a vastly different manner.[5]

Thoughts of remembrance began whilst the war was still in progress. Early in the war, the government decreed that men who died overseas were to be buried close to where they fell. Given the hundreds of thousands of war dead, it would have been impossible to repatriate them all. However, this meant that bereaved families did not have a grave to mourn over, and travel to visit overseas graves would have been impossible for all but the wealthiest of families. Many sailors were also lost at sea. As a result, war memorials assumed a deeply personal resonance for thousands of bereaved families and acted as surrogate graves.

The Armistice was a difficult event for many. War was all that many men – and indeed women and children – had known for years.[6] The tradition of observing a two minutes' silence on 11 November, Armistice Day, was not initially officially

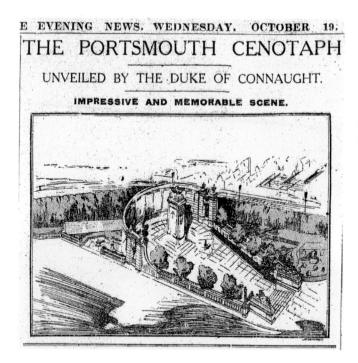

E EVENING NEWS, WEDNESDAY, OCTOBER 19.

THE PORTSMOUTH CENOTAPH

UNVEILED BY THE DUKE OF CONNAUGHT.

IMPRESSIVE AND MEMORABLE SCENE.

An artist's impression of the cenotaph, published in the *Evening News* the day after it was unveiled by the Duke of Connaught. (*EN*)

sanctioned, but grew out of a popular desire among normal people – the widowed, the orphaned and veterans – to attempt to give some kind of meaning to the deaths of so many.[7]

The end of war did not mean the end of suffering for many. The demobilisation of so many men led to mass unemployment and the annual mayoral banquet being cancelled in 1921 due to the distress and hardship being experienced in the town.[8] The sense of loss after the First World War did, however, lead to the founding of the Royal British Legion in 1921 and the first Poppy Appeal in the same year.

Even while the war was underway, the people of Portsmouth began to consider how to remember their fallen loved ones. On 20 October 1915, what became the Roll of Honour Committee first met, under the lengthy name of the 'special committee as to perpetuating the memory of Portsmouth's taking part in the war'. It was proposed at this early stage that a roll of honour should be kept of men from Portsmouth who had served, along with an additional roll of men who had performed distinguished service, had been wounded or killed. Much of the work for this was undertaken by W.G. Gates, the editor of the *Evening News*. It was decided that only men who had either been born in Portsmouth or whose parents were residing in the town throughout the war should be regarded as 'from Portsmouth'.[9]

The First World War was the first conflict which saw large numbers of memorials being erected in Britain.[10] Such losses had never been experienced

before, and society had been touched by war to an extent never felt before, in particular among civilian communities.[11] It was also the first major conflict since Victorian attitudes had ritualised death and mourning. Understandably, given the scale of losses and the difficulty of visiting graves overseas, the general public yearned for sites where they could pay homage to their lost menfolk. Even before the end of the war, local communities began to commemorate the sacrifice of local men. Parish churches, schools and businesses all erected their own memorials and published rolls of honour. A significant memorial was also built on Southsea Common to remember Portsmouth-based sailors who were lost and have no known grave other than the sea.

Plans for a civic memorial to Portsmouth's fallen were discussed soon after the close of hostilities but, as in many towns, discussions over what form the memorial should take delayed proceedings and it was not until 1920 that a formal appeal was made for donations.[12] Along with names that had already been compiled for the roll of honour, local people were asked to nominate service people whose names should appear on the memorial. The criteria were set that a man should either have been born in Portsmouth, lived in Portsmouth when the war began, or had his home in the city. Despite strenuous efforts to make sure that every name was included, research since has shown that hundreds of Portsmouth men were not included on the civic memorial.

A prominent site was chosen bordering the Guildhall, Victoria Park and Commercial Road. A competition was held to choose a design and received scores of entries. The entries were judged by Paul Waterhouse, an assessor appointed by the Institute of British Architects, who selected the design submitted by Messrs Gibson & Gordon of Old Bond Street, London. Prizes were awarded to three runners up. On 1 April 1921 it was reported that twelve tenders had been

The cenotaph
in Guildhall
Square.
(Author)

received to build the memorial, all of which were above the estimated cost. The tender of Samuel Salter, the lowest at £19,997, was accepted. The War Memorial Committee was still keen to reduce costs, however, and the architect and builder were instructed to meet to decide which items could be deleted. On 4 April it was reported that the cost had been reduced to £11,997 by deleting ironwork, the fountain, urns, statues, a wing wall, an arch connecting the memorial to the railway, and by reducing the balustrade. These amendments were accepted by the committee. It was also later decided to use stone for the circular wall instead of brick, and the cost of the statues was also debated. It was decided to have two groups of statues, one each of a military and naval nature. Work commended immediately and the foundation stone was laid by the mayoress on 25 May 1921.

Once work had begun on the cenotaph at the centre of the war memorial, attention turned to how to record the thousands of names. It was decided on 24 June that the names should be written in ⅜in block letters in bronze. Men who served in the army were to be listed on one side, and seamen on the other, with one panel set aside for the Royal Air Force. W.G. Gates was again delegated the task of investigating names submitted for inclusion on the memorial. On 20 June the Mayor stated that around 6,000 names were to be recorded. The committee considered the question of how exactly the names were to be incorporated into the memorial. It was felt that bronze panels would be the most appropriate, and that the names should be as large and well spaced as possible. Seven tenders were received for the bronze plaques on 28 August 1921, although it was considered unlikely that these would be complete by the time of the unveiling, scheduled for 12 October 1921. By 1 August 1921 it was observed that progress on constructing the memorial was slow. The cenotaph at the centre of the memorial was being constructed as a priority in time for the unveiling, followed by the wall surrounding it. Salter was employing nineteen stonemasons on the project and could not recruit any more.

The memorial was unveiled by Field Marshal the Duke of Connaught on 19 October 1921, in a ceremony attended by more than 30,000 people. The ceremony was described by the *Evening News* as 'religious-cum-civic and military in character', and was conducted by the Bishop of Southampton, with the mayor, John Timpson, making a speech. Representatives of all of the armed forces were formed up around the memorial and enclosures were provided for relatives of the fallen and subscribers to the memorial appeal. Music was provided by the band of the Royal Marines Artillery and the Portsmouth Philharmonic Society. The mayoress laid the first wreath, followed by Sergeant James Ockendon VC. However, it later emerged that the first floral tribute had been laid before the ceremony, clandestinely, by a young boy who evaded the police lines to place a bouquet on the memorial.[13] Throughout the ceremony, the muffled bells of St Mary's church tolled. The queue to place wreaths lasted well into the night,

One of the machine
gunners guarding
the entrance to the
cenotaph. (Author)

and had to be illuminated by an arc light. Dockyardmen even removed their pipes, which was interpreted as mark of respect. The event was described by the *Evening News* as 'one of the saddest yet one of the proudest days in Portsmouth's history'.[14]

The bronze plaques of names had not been completed before the unveiling. The tendering and construction process proved taxing and they took some time to complete. On 1 March 1922 it was decided that it would be unwise to proceed with ordering the bronze panels until more funds had been raised. It was eventually decided to seek tenders on 18 August 1922, when the War Memorial Committee became the Names Committee. On 30 November it was reported that the list of names stood at around 5,000. By 12 February 1923, sixteen tenders had been received, and the tender by Carlo Magnoni of London was accepted as the cheapest, at £1,500, with an estimated completion time of ten months. Magnoni proved to be a difficult contractor, however, for he failed to obtain sufficient sureties in Britain to guarantee the work. Problems were then experienced with the factory in Italy to which Magnoni sub-contracted the production of the panels, who refused to ship them without full payment in

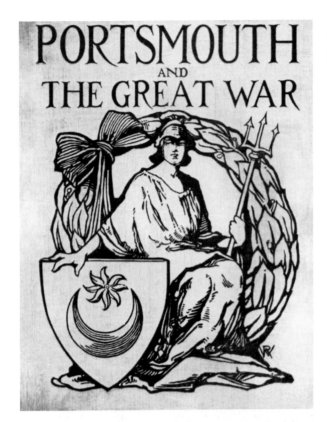

Portsmouth and the Great War by W.G. Gates. (Gates)

advance. This proved to be the last straw and Magnoni's tender was withdrawn. The work was eventually offered to D&W Castings of Portsmouth.

The problems with the bronze panels possibly inspired the architect to submit an alternative means of recording names on 28 February 1924. Gordon proposed that the list of names could be written in a book, to be housed in a small chapel on the memorial site. Designs were submitted and the idea developed as far as tenders being received before Sir William Dupree – a major benefactor of the memorial – declined to fund the chapel concept. On 30 June 1924 it was decided to go back to the original idea of bronze panels, which prompted Dupree to hand over a cheque for £500 immediately. The work for the bronze panels was awarded to the Tudor Art Metal Company, at a cost of £1,897. The panels were duly installed, and the committee's last meeting was on 19 January 1927 – over eight years after the war had ended.[15]

The memorial may have taken some time to complete, but the final result was a fitting tribute to the names that would be recorded on it. It consisted of a centrepiece cenotaph surmounted by a funerary casket and clad with relief images of ranks of soldiers, and was surrounded by bronze plaques listing thousands of names, each embellished in gold. The entrance to the memorial is guarded by

The Portsmouth naval memorial on Southsea Common. (Author)

two machine gunners, one a soldier and the other a rating of the Royal Naval Division, sculpted by Charles Sargeant Jagger, a prominent sculptor who was much in demand for work on war memorials in the 1920s.[16]

The war memorial became the centrepiece for Portsmouth's annual remembrance services. Even though the memorial was hidden and marginalised

by the construction of the civic offices and the City Arms pub in the mid-1970s –
and the entrance balustrade was significantly shortened – Portsmouth still boasts
perhaps one of the finest cenotaphs in the country. By comparison, Portsmouth's
dead from the Second World War went un-commemorated for over sixty years:
weariness after two devastating conflicts, destruction from bombing, and a
lessening of the Victorian cult of death altered the priorities of city folk.

The memorial fund eventually recorded a surplus of funds, which were given
to other suitable causes in the city. A lesser-known memorial to Portsmouth's war
dead consisted of new memorial gates to the Royal Portsmouth Hospital, along
with improvements made to the hospital itself.[17] Sadly these were demolished
along with the rest of the hospital in 1969, and a Sainsbury's supermarket now
occupies the site.[18]

Most parish churches in the town erected some kind of memorial, usually by
public subscription. Richer parishes built elaborate crosses or memorial windows,
whilst parishes with more modest means marked their lost menfolk with wooden
plaques or framed scrolls. Some chose more unconventional memorials – the
Church of the Ascension building a reredos (also known as an altar screen).
St Matthew's, in one of the poorer parts of Southsea, managed to raise enough
funds to build a fine wooden memorial outside the church, consisting of Christ
on the cross and listing the names of parishioners who were killed. Whilst public
schools such as Portsmouth Grammar School and St John's College erected fine
memorials to their old boys, little evidence remains of how or even if former state
school pupils were remembered by their old schools. That none of the local state
schools that existed in 1914 remain in the same form and that they had much
less *esprit de corps* than their wealthier counterparts indicates that the humble
former state-school pupil who was killed in the First World War is much less
likely to be remembered. A notable exception was Southern Grammar School,
which admittedly took in the more able and affluent of state-school pupils.
Other organisations erected memorials. Civic bodies such as the town police, the
gas company and the City of Portsmouth passenger transport depot all erected
memorials to employees who had fallen, as did Royal Mail. The only surviving
war memorial erected by a private business is that of Handley's, a Southsea
department store, which is now in Debenhams in Palmerston Road.

War memorials have long been a focal point on Armistice Day and
Remembrance Sunday, but it must be acknowledged that most are ignored to
varying degrees throughout the rest of the year. But once a memorial is read, and
a name acknowledged, it is transformed from a stone tribute into a gateway to
the past.

Not all memorials were carved in stone. Shortly after the end of the war the
prominent local historian and editor of the *Evening News*, W.G. Gates, published
Portsmouth and the First World War, a history of the city's involvement in the war.

The St Matthew's parish church war memorial. (Gates)

Included were a roll of honour of fallen local people and a list of men who won medals – both of which were probably compiled whilst the author was assembling identical lists for the Corporation Roll of Honour Committee. However, the First World War has been largely ignored in local history, and significant events such as the contribution of the two Portsmouth Pals Battalions and the deadly impact of the Battle of Jutland have been all but forgotten.

The loss of life and suffering in Portsmouth did not end with the Treaty of Versailles in 1919. Some men were still fighting – and dying – in the Russian Civil War. Ten men from Portsmouth died whilst fighting with British forces in northern Russia, and are mainly buried in Archangel and Murmansk. The influenza pandemic also claimed many lives, in the worst outbreak of illness in Portsmouth since the cholera in 1849.[19] The outbreak seemed to affect the young and the healthy worst, and with many thousands of men on the move, germs spread relatively easily.[20] The illness peaked in April and May 1918, and again in September. Many of the men who died in 1918 would have been as a result of influenza – between 12 October and the end of November 1918 the army on the Western Front suffered 45,000 cases of whom 1,883 died.[21] Particularly susceptible to influenza were prisoners of war, many of whom had spent years in captivity and were malnourished from surviving on basic rations.[22] The historian Richard Holmes has argued that the influenza pandemic was more destructive than war losses.[23]

Nationally, 6.3 per cent of men aged between 15 and 49 who served were killed.[24] In 1911 Portsmouth was home to 115,260 males. The deaths of 5,988

men from Portsmouth during the war represent a casualty rate of 5.19 per cent among the male population. The historian Gordon Corrigan has estimated that 1.53 per cent of Britain's total population was killed.[25] Although it has become routine to talk of a 'lost generation' killed in the trenches, and the loss of thousands of men certainly was traumatic, it is hard to argue that an entire generation was lost to war. The proportion of losses might have been higher among officers, in particular those who were public school educated, but Portsmouth was home to relatively few such officers.

However, although 12.91 per cent of soldiers who served were killed in action, 34.39 per cent were wounded, captured or reported missing, suggesting that almost three times as many men were substantially affected by their war service in some way than the number that were killed. If this national trend is applied to Portsmouth casualties, it would be realistic to estimate that around 18,000 men from Portsmouth would have been wounded, captured or reported missing. Nationally, it is estimated that 500,000 men were seriously maimed, 240,000 became amputees, 10,000 men were blinded, 13,000 became mentally ill as a result of their war service, and 60,000 suffered from neurasthenia, a nervous disorder.[26] Those who were disabled by war fared badly in the post-war economic slump, and in 1920 there were 100,000 unemployed disabled veterans in Britain.[27] 344,606 pensions were granted to children who had lost parents in the war and 192,678 to war widows.[28]

The psychological impact of war service has become better understood in recent years. In 1917 one out of every thousand civilians was admitted to a psychiatric hospital; for servicemen the ratio was four out of every thousand. Despite a War Office Inquiry into shell shock in 1922, the mental scarring suffered by many veterans had an enduring effect on society.[29]

Perhaps the most poignant – but often overlooked – reminders of Portsmouth's role in the First World War are the hundreds of war graves in Portsmouth cemeteries, cared for by the Commonwealth War Graves Commission. There are 221 First World War graves in Highland Road cemetery, 378 in Kingston and 194 in Milton cemetery. Many men died in Britain of wounds, illness or of natural causes, yet their sacrifice has often been overshadowed by better-known war cemeteries on the Western Front.

If the people of Portsmouth need a reminder of the cost and futility of war, they need look no further than the many hundreds of simple, white Portland gravestones scattered throughout the city's cemeteries.

Notes

1   Portsmouth Before the First World War

1   Quail, Sarah, 'The Origins of Portsmouth and the First Charter', *The Portsmouth Papers*, 65 (1994).

2   Washington, E.S., 'Local Battles in Fact and Fiction: The Portsmouth Election of 1895', *The Portsmouth Papers*, 43 (1985), p.5.

3   Stapleton, Barry and Thomas, James H. (eds), *The Portsmouth Region* (Stroud: Sutton, 1989), p.80.

4   *LG*, 23 April 1926; *LG*, 26 April 1927.

5   Riley, R.C. and Eley, Phillip, 'Public Houses and Beerhouses in Nineteenth-Century Portsmouth', *The Portsmouth Papers*, 38 (1983), p.26.

6   Riley and Eley, 'Public Houses and Beerhouses', p.3.

7   Riley and Eley, 'Public Houses and Beerhouses', p.3.

8   Yates, Nigel, 'The Anglican Revival in Victorian Portsmouth', *The Portsmouth Papers*, 37 (1983), p.7; Dolling, Rev. Robert, *Ten Years in a Portsmouth Slum* (1897), p.134.

9   Lavery, Brian, *Able Seamen: The Lower Deck of the Royal Navy, 1850 to 1939* (London: Conway Maritime Press, 2011), p.111; Weston, Agnes, *My Life Among the Bluejackets* (1909).

10   Webb, J., Quail, S., Haskell, P., Riley, R., *The Spirit of Portsmouth: A History* (Stroud: Phillimore, 1989), p.109.

11   Neasom, Mike, Cooper, Mick and Robinson, Doug, *Pompey: The History of Portsmouth Football Club* (Horndean: Milestone, 1984), p.9.

12   Bilton, David, *The Home Front in the Great War* (Barnsley: Leo Cooper, 2003), p.25.

13   Webb et al., *Spirit of Portsmouth*, p.28.

14   Beckett, Ian, 'A Nation in Arms 1914–1918' in Beckett, Ian and Simpson, Keith, *A Nation in Arms: A Social Study of the British Army in the First World War* (Manchester: Manchester University Press, 1985), p.18.

15   Riley and Eley, 'Public Houses and Beerhouses', p.7.

16   Hughes, Clive, 'The New Armies', in Beckett and Simpson, *A Nation in Arms*, p.106.

17   Neasom, Cooper and Robinson, *Pompey*, pp.234, 241.

18   Dolling, *Ten Years in a Portsmouth Slum*, pp.99, 108.

19   Lavery, *The Lower Deck of the Royal Navy*, p.134.

20   Sadden, John, *Portsmouth: In Defence of the Realm* (Stroud: Phillimore, 2010), p.7.

21   Neasom, Cooper and Robinson, *Pompey*, pp.7–9.

22   Washington, 'The Portsmouth Election of 1895', p.6; Stapleton and Thomas, *The Portsmouth Region*, p.76.

23   Massie, Robert K., *Dreadnought: Britain, Germany and the Coming of the Great War* (London: Vintage, 2007), pp. 479–82.

24   Webb et al., *The Spirit of Portsmouth*, p.45.

25   Stapleton and Thomas, *The Portsmouth Region*, p.76; Sadden, John, *Keep the Home Fires Burning: The Story of Portsmouth and Gosport in World War I* (Portsmouth: Evening News, 1990), p.115.

26   Webb et al., *The Spirit of Portsmouth*, p.45.

27   Sadden, *Keep the Home Fires Burning*, p.44.

28   Stapleton and Thomas, *The Portsmouth Region*, p.167.

29   Sadden, *Keep the Home Fires Burning*, p.114.

30   Massie, *Dreadnought*, p.479.

31   Sadden, *Keep the Home Fires Burning*, pp.18–9.

32   Stapleton and Thomas, *The Portsmouth Region*, p.184.

33   Sadden, *Keep the Home Fires Burning*, p.10. Reportedly the Kaiser fondly recalled his childhood visits to Portsmouth. Massie, Robert K., *Castles of Steel: Britain, Germany and the Winning of the Great War at Sea* (London: Vintage, 2007), p.6.

34   1911 census; Riley, R.C., 'The Industries of Portsmouth in the Nineteenth Century', *The Portsmouth Papers*, 25 (1976).

35   City of Portsmouth, *Records of the Corporation*, 1966–74 (1978).

36   Stapleton and Thomas, *The Portsmouth Region*, pp.79–80.

37   Stapleton and Thomas, *The Portsmouth Region*, p.167.

38   Winter, J.M., 'The Army and Society' in Beckett and Simpson, *A Nation in Arms*, pp.195, 203.

39   Winter, 'The Army and Society' in Beckett and Simpson, *A Nation in Arms*, p.195.

40   Sadden, *Keep the Home Fires Burning*, p.57–9; Sadden, *Defence of the Realm*, p.115; Lavery, *The Lower Deck of the Royal Navy*, p.111.

2   The Armed Forces: The Royal Navy

1   Massie, Robert K., *Castles of Steel: Britain, Germany and the Winning of the Great War at Sea* (London: Vintage, 2007), p.10.

2   Massie, Robert K., *Dreadnought: Britain, Germany and the Coming of the Great War* (London: Vintage, 2007), p.454.

3   Simkins, Peter, Jukes, Geoffrey and Hickey, Michael, *The First World War: The War to End All Wars* (Osprey, 2013), p.22.

4   Bourne, John, *Britain and the First World War 1914–1918* (London: Hodder and Stoughton, 1989), p.28.

5   Lavery, Brian, *Able Seamen: The Lower Deck of the Royal Navy, 1850 to 1939* (London: Conway Maritime Press, 2011), p.131.

6   TNA ADM 286/107-21: Mobilisation Returns, Complements of Ships, Royal Marines and Air Stations, July 1914–October 1918.

7   Lavery, *The Lower Deck of the Royal Navy*, p.190.

8   Lavery, *The Lower Deck of the Royal Navy*, p.117.

9   Webb, J., Quail, S., Haskell, P., Riley, R., *The Spirit of Portsmouth: A History* (Stroud: Phillimore, 1989), p.80.

10   Lavery, *The Lower Deck of the Royal Navy*, p.118.

11   Lavery, *The Lower Deck of the Royal Navy*, p.125.

12   Lavery, *The Lower Deck of the Royal Navy*, p.176.

13   Lavery, *The Lower Deck of the Royal Navy*, p.113.

14   Massie, *Dreadnought*, p.374.

15   www.naval-history.net.

16   Massie, *Dreadnought*, p.487.

17   Massie, *Castles of Steel*, p.571.

18   Lavery, *The Lower Deck of the Royal Navy*, p.191.

19   Riley, R.C., 'Railways and Portsmouth Society, 1847–1947', *The Portsmouth Papers*, 70 (2000), p.16.

20   Lavery, *The Lower Deck of the Royal Navy*, pp.104–5; Corrigan, Gordon, *Mud, Blood and Poppycock: Britain and the Great War* (Phoenix, 2004), p.54.

21   Lavery, *The Lower Deck of the Royal Navy*, pp.127–8.

22   Weston, Agnes, *My Life Among the Bluejackets* (1909).

23   Weston, *My Life Among the Bluejackets*.

24   Lavery, *The Lower Deck of the Royal Navy*, p.234.

25   TNA WO 161/82: Armies at home and abroad, 1914–1920: statistical abstract.

26   Sadden, John, *Portsmouth: In Defence of the Realm* (Stroud: Phillimore, 2010), pp.34–5.

27   TNA ADM 201/94: Abstract of weekly returns of strength of Royal Marine Corps, 1914–1917.

3 The Armed Forces: The British Army

1   Wilkinson, Roni, *Pals on the Somme: Kitchener's New Army Battalions Raised by Local Authorities During the Great War* (Barnsley: Pen and Sword, 2006), p.38.

2   Simkins, Peter, Jukes, Geoffrey and Hickey, Michael, *The First World War: The War to End All Wars* (Osprey, 2013), pp.27, 30.

3   Rawson, Andrew, *British Army Handbook 1914–1918* (Stroud: The History Press, 2006), p.3.

4   Mallinson, Allan, *The Making of the British Army: From the English Civil War to the War on Terror* (Bantam, 2011), p.272.

5   Winter, J.M., *The Great War and the British People* (Macmillan Education, 1986), p.9.

6   *Army List* (1914).

7   Winter, *The Great War*, p.6.

8   Winter, *The Great War*, p.46.

9   Beckett, Ian, 'A Nation in Arms 1914–1918', in Beckett, Ian and Simpson, Keith, *A Nation in Arms: A Social Study of the British Army in the First World War* (Manchester: Manchester University Press, 1985), p.1.

10 Corrigan, Gordon, *Mud, Blood and Poppycock: Britain and the Great War* (Phoenix, 2004), p.112.

11 Reed, Paul, *Great War Lives: A Guide for Family Historians* (Barnsley: Pen and Sword, 2010), p.61; Bridger, Geoff, *The Great War Handbook: A Guide for Family Historians and Students of the Conflict* (Barnsley: Pen and Sword, 2009), p.197.

12 Ashworth, Tony, *Trench Warfare 1914–18: The Live and Let Live System* (Pan, 2004), p.2.

13 Corrigan, *Mud, Blood and Poppycock*, pp.88–91.

14 Holmes, Richard, *Tommy: The British Soldier on the Western Front* (Harper Perrenial, 2005), p.275.

15 Ashworth, *Trench Warfare*, p.15.

16 Ashworth, *Trench Warfare*, pp.173–5.

17 Holmes, *Tommy*, p.483.

18 Bridger, *Great War Handbook*, p.81.

19 Bridger, *Great War Handbook*, p.82.

20 Simkins, Peter, *Kitchener's Army: The Raising of the New Armies 1914–1916* (Barnsley: Pen and Sword, 2007), p.203.

21 Moran, Lord, *The Anatomy of Courage* (London: Robinson, 2007).

22 Beckett, 'A Nation in Arms 1914–1918' in Beckett and Simpson, *A Nation in Arms*, p.43.

23 TNA WO 95/1495: 1st Battalion Hampshire Regiment War Diary.

24 Ashworth, *Trench Warfare*; Brown, Malcolm, *The Imperial War Museum Book of the Western Front* (Pan, 2004).

25   Holmes, Tommy, p.108.

26   Simkins, Kitchener's Army, p.199.

27   Holmes, Tommy, p.564.

28   Winter, J.M., The Great War and the British People (Macmillan Education, 1986),
      p.91.

29   Winter, The Great War, p.66.

30   Beckett, 'A Nation in Arms 1914–1918' in Beckett and Simpson, A Nation in
      Arms, p.18.

4   A Man of Three Armies: Lieutenant-Colonel Dick Worrall DSO and Bar MC and Bar

1   LAC RG150, 1992-3/166, 10581-44: Dick Worrall Canadian Army Attestation
      Papers.

2   TNA WO 96/1368/315: Dick Worrall Service Record.

3   Montreal Gazette, 18 April 1919.

4   Nicholson, G.W.L., Official History of the Canadian Army in the First World War:
      Candian Expeditionary Force 1914–1919 (1964), p.5.

5   LAC, RG150, 1992-3/166, Box 10581-44.

6   Nicholson, Canadian Expeditionary Force, pp.7, 17.

7   Montreal Gazette, 18 April 1919.

8   Nicholson, Canadian Expeditionary Force, p.20.

9   LAC RG9, Militia and Defence, III-D-3, 14th Battalion Canadian Infantry
      War Diary 1914–1919. All Battalion movements etc. are taken from the relevant
      section of 14th Battalion war diary, unless otherwise stated.

10   Nicholson, Canadian Expeditionary Force, p.51.

11   Nicholson, Canadian Expeditionary Force, p.62.

12   LG, 23 June 1915.

13   Nicholson, Canadian Expeditionary Force, p.92.

14   LAC: 14th Battalion War Diary.

15   Holmes, Richard, Tommy: The British Soldier on the Western Front (London:
      Harper, 2005), p.198.

16   Nicholson, Canadian Expeditionary Force, p.100.

17   LG, 24 August 1915.

18   Holmes, Tommy, p.588.

19   Montreal Gazette, 18 April 1919.

20   Nicholson, Canadian Expeditionary Force, p.151.

21   Nicholson, Canadian Expeditionary Force, p.154.

22   Ashworth, Tony, Trench Warfare 1914–1918: The Live and Let Live System
      (London: Pan, 2004), p.73.

23   Nicholson, *Canadian Expeditionary Force*, p.178.

24   *LG*, 1 January 1917.

25   Cave, Nigel, *Vimy Ridge: Arras* (Barnsley: Pen and Sword, 1995), p.112.

26   Nicholson, *Canadian Expeditionary Force*, pp.266–7; Holmes, *Tommy*, p.52.

27   *LG*, February 1918.

28   *LG*, 18 July 1918.

29   Corrigan, Gordon, *Mud, Blood and Poppycock: Britain and the Great War* (London: Phoenix, 2004), p.288.

30   Holmes, *Tommy*, p.182.

31   Brown, Malcolm, *Imperial War Museum Book of 1918: Year of Victory* (London: Pan, 1998), p.192.

32   *LG*, 10 January 1919.

33   *LG*, 17 September 1918.

34   *LG*, 31 January 1919.

35   Brown, *1918*, p.131.

36   *LG*, 31 December 1918.

37   *Montreal Gazette*, 18 April 1919.

38   *Montreal Gazette*, 18 April 1919.

39   *Toronto World*, 18 February 1920; www.canadiangreatwarproject.com.

5   The Portsmouth Pals Battalions

1   Holmes, Richard, *Tommy: The British Soldier on the Western Front* (Harper Perrenial, 2005), p.139.

2   Westlake, Ray, *Kitchener's Army* (Gloucestershire: Spellmount, 1998), p.23.

3   Rawson, Andrew, *British Army Handbook 1914–1918* (Stroud: The History Press, 2006), p.23.

4   Corrigan, Gordon, *Mud, Blood and Poppycock: Britain and the Great War* (Phoenix, 2004), p.66; Simkins, Peter, *Kitchener's Army: The Raising of the New Armies 1914–1916* (Barnsley: Pen and Sword, 2007), p.120.

5   Westlake, *Kitchener's Army*, p.9.

6   Simkins, *Kitchener's Army*, p.38.

7   Holmes, *Tommy*, p.135.

8   Wilkinson, Roni, *Pals on the Somme: Kitchener's New Army Battalions Raised by Local Authorities During the Great War* (Barnsley: Pen and Sword, 2006), p.16.

9   *EN*, 31 August 1914.

10   Wilkinson, *Pals on the Somme*, p.60.

11   Gates, W.G., *Portsmouth and the Great War* (Portsmouth: Evening News and Hampshire Telegraph Company, 1919), p.31.

12   *EN*, 1 September 1914.

13   *EN*, 2 September 1914.

14   TNA PRO 30/57/73: Horatio Herbert Kitchener, 1st Earl Kitchener of Khartoum: Papers; Admiral Lord Charles Beresford. His (B's) recruiting efforts for the Portsmouth battalion; Gates, *Portsmouth and the Great War*, p.31.

15   Keegan, John, *The Face of Battle: A Study of Agincourt, Waterloo and the Somme* (London: Pimlico, 1991), p.218.

16   *EN*, 3 September 1914.

17   *EN*, 4 September 1914.

18   *EN*, 5 September 1914.

19   *EN*, 7 September 1914, 9 September 1914, 11 September 1914.

20   *EN*, 8 September 1914, 12 September 1914.

21   *EN*, 30 September 1914.

22   *EN*, 10 September 1914.

23   Sadden, John, *Portsmouth: In Defence of the Realm* (Stroud: Phillimore, 2010), p.29.

24   Simkins, *Kitchener's Army*, p.82.

25   Corrigan, *Mud, Blood and Poppycock*, p.68.

26   Holmes, *Tommy*, pp.82–3.

27   Corrigan, *Mud, Blood and Poppycock*, p.109.

28   *EN*, 15 September 1914.

29   Simkins, *Kitchener's Army*, p.290.

30   Gates, *Portsmouth and the Great War*, p.31.

31   *EN*, 5 September 1914.

32   Rawson, *British Army Handbook*, p.26.

33   Gates, *Portsmouth and the Great War*, p.33.

34   *EN*, 7 February 1916.

35   Gates, *Portsmouth and the Great War*, p.33; *EN*, 24 April 1915.

36   *EN*, 20 October 1915.

37   *EN*, 20 November 1915.

38   Gates, *Portsmouth and the Great War*, p.35.

39   Atkinson, C.T., *The Royal Hampshire Regiment 1914–1918* (Naval and Military Press, 2009), p.138.

40   TNA WO 95/2583/6: 14th Battalion Hampshire Regiment War Diary February 1916–February 1918. Unless otherwise noted, information regarding the battalions' activities on active service are taken from their respective war diaries.

41   TNA WO 95/2634/5: 15th Battalion Hampshire Regiment War Diary May 1916–October 1917.

42   I have withheld this young man's name.

43   Most tours in the front line seem to have lasted an average of five to six days, depending on operations.

44   Atkinson, *The Hampshire Regiment*, p.180.

45   Atkinson, *The Hampshire Regiment*, p.182.

46   Atkinson, *The Hampshire Regiment*, p.183.

47   Brown, Malcolm, *The Imperial War Museum Book of the Western Front* (Pan, 2004), p.184.

48   Corrigan, *Mud, Blood and Poppycock*, pp.69, 71.

49   Wilkinson, *Pals on the Somme*, p.190.

50   Stedman, Michael, *Thiepval* (Barnsley: Leo Cooper, 1995), p.102.

51   Holmes, *Tommy*, p.75, 90.

52   McDonald, Lyn, *They Called it Passchendaele: The Story of the Battle of Ypres and of the Men Who Fought in it* (Penguin, 1993), p.104.

53   Although not a Portsmouth man, Moore was born in nearby Worthing.

54   Snelling, Stephen, *VCs of the First World War: Passchendaele 1917* (Stroud: The History Press, 2012), pp.140–8.

55   TNA WO 95/2634/5.

56   TNA WO 95/2583/6.

57   TNA WO 95/2634/6: 15th Bn Hampshire Regiment War Diary March 1918– March 1919.

58   Cooksley, Peter, *The Home Front: Civilian Life in World War One* (Stroud: Tempus, 2006), p.126; Mallinson, Allan, *The Making of the British Army: From the English Civil War to the War on Terror* (Bantam, 2011), pp.301–2.

59   Corrigan, *Mud, Blood and Poppycock*, p.69.

60   Keegan, John, *The Face of Battle*, p.217.

61   For example, Gilbert, Martin, *Somme: The Heroism and Horror of War* (John Murray, 2007), p.18; Messenger, Charles, *Call to Arms: The British Army 1914–18* (London: Weidenfeld Military, 2005), p.100.

62   Gates, *Portsmouth and the Great War*, p.35.

6   'Those Magnificent Men in their Flying Machines': Portsmouth's First World War Airmen

1   Steel, Nigel and Hart, Peter, *Tumult in the Clouds: the British Experience of War in the Air, 1914–1918* (London: Hodder and Stoughton, 1997), p.xi.

2   Barker, Ralph, *The Royal Flying Corps in France: From Mons to the Somme* (London: Constable, 1994), p.9.

3   Barker, *Royal Flying Corps*, p.9; Steel and Hart, *Tumult in the Clouds*, pp.12, 15.

4   Steel and Hart, *Tumult in the Clouds*, p.13.

5   Delve, Ken, *The Military Airfields of Britain: Southern England: Kent, Hampshire, Surrey, Sussex* (Ramsbury, Crowood Press, 2002), p.111.

6   Steel and Hart, *Tumult in the Clouds*, p.26.

7   Barker, *Royal Flying Corps*, p.51.

8   LAC RG150 1992-93/166, 1589-11 Stanley Caws Attestation Papers.

9   *De Ruvigny's Roll of Honour 1914–1924.*

10   LAC RG150 1992-93/166.

11   www.canadiangreatwarproject.com.

12   *Flight,* 12 March 1915, 2 April 1915.

13   *De Ruvigny's Roll of Honour.*

14   www.canadiangreatwarproject.com.

15   TNA AIR 76/80/155: Stanley Caws Service Record.

16   Barker, *Royal Flying Corps,* p.51.

17   Barker, *Royal Flying Corps,* pp.142, 157.

18   1911 census.

19   PGS.

20   *Flight,* 2 November 1916.

21   *De Ruvigny's Roll of Honour.*

22   PGS.

23   Barker, *Royal Flying Corps,* p.224.

24   Information received from Rugby School.

25   www.ceredigion-war-memorial.co.uk.

26   Barker, *Royal Flying Corps,* p.20.

27   Barker, *Royal Flying Corps,* p.21.

28   *Flight,* 28 September 1916; TNA WO 372/13/86319 Percy Main Medal Index
     Card.

29   Steel and Hart, *Tumult in the Clouds,* p.16.

30   Sadden, John, *Portsmouth: In Defence of the Realm* (Stroud: Phillimore, 2010),
     p.102; Delve, *Military Airfields,* p.159.

31   Lavery, Brian, *Able Seamen: The Lower Deck of the Royal Navy, 1850 to 1939*
     (London: Conway Maritime Press, 2011), p.227.

32   1911 census.

33   TNA ADM 171/89-93: Royal Naval Officers Medal Roll 1914–1920 (accessed
     via ww.findmypast.co.uk)

34   1901 census.

35   TNA AIR 76/152/1: Cyril Emmett Service Record

36   TNA ADM 171/89-93: *De Ruvigny's Roll of Honour.*

37   PGS.

38   GRO Consular Death Indices, vol. 9 p.534.

39   TNA AIR 76/394/227: John Paynter Service Record.

40   PGS.

41   *Flight,* 25 April 1918.

42   www.theaerodrome.com.

43   TNA AIR 76/394/227.

44   *Naval Casualties 1914–19* (accessed via www.findmypast.co.uk).

7   Comings and Goings: Portsmouth's First World War Emigrants and Immigrants

1   MacDougall, Phillip, 'Settlers, Visitors and Asylum Seekers: Diversity in Portsmouth Since the Late 18th Century', *The Portsmouth Papers*, 75 (2007), p.1.

2   TNA ADM 188: Royal Navy Registers of Seamen's Services.

3   NAA B2455: Australian Imperial Force Service Records.

4   1881 and 1891 census; TNA ADM 188/232/158891: Royal Navy Service Record; NAA B2455 8034850 James Rolls Australian Army Service Record.

5   LAC RG 150: Canadian Army First World War Service Records.

6   TNA WO 97: Royal Hospital Chelsea Service Records; LAC RG 150, Accession 1992-93/166, Box 10246–52.

7   TNA WO 97 Royal Hospital Chelsea Service Records; LAC RG 150, Accession 1992–93/166, Box 3840–18.

8   Sandhurst Registers (1889).

9   1901 census; Sandhurst Registers (1909).

10 1911 census; Sandhurst Registers (1912).

11 1901 census.

12 1891 census.

13 Southern Grammar School Roll of Honour.

14 MacDougall, 'Settlers, Visitors and Asylum Seekers', pp.6–7.

15 1911 census.

16 Surname research taken from Hans, Patrick and Hodges, Flavia, *A Dictionary of Surnames* (Oxford: University Press, 1988).

17 Sadden, John, *Keep the Home Fires Burning: The Story of Portsmouth and Gosport in World War I* (Portsmouth: Evening News, 1990), pp.28–9.

18 1891 census; TNA ADM 188/1069/25936 Bernard Koerner Royal Navy Service Record.

19 MacDougall, 'Settlers, Visitors and Asylum Seekers', p.5.

20 1901 and 1911 census.

21 MacDougall, 'Settlers, Visitors and Asylum Seekers', p.10.

22 FMP census; MacDougall, 'Settlers, Visitors and Asylum Seekers', p.10.

23 1911 census.

24 1891, 1901 and 1911 census.

25 TNA ADM 188/1029/5959: Arthur Mazonowicz Royal Navy Service Record; MacDougall, 'Settlers, Visitors and Asylum Seekers', pp.5, 9.

26 1901 census.

27 1911 census.

28 TNA ADM 188/298/179709: George Temple Royal Navy Service Record; 1911 census.

29 TNA ADM 340/146/44: George Walker-Williamson Royal Navy Service Record.

30   TNA ADM 188/1027/4659: William Opie Royal Navy Service Record; 1911 census.

31   TNA ADM 188/1032/7460: Frederick Shephard Royal Navy Service Record; TNA WO 97/5885/096: Harry Shephard Service Record.

32   TNA ADM 188/131/108269: Samuel Greenway Royal Navy Service Record.

33   TNA ADM188/696/24717: William Morrison Royal Navy Service Record; *National Roll of the Great War: Section X – Portsmouth.*

34   TNA ADM 188/651/2377: Edward Williams Royal Navy Service Record.

35   TNA ADM 188/432/269679: Stamper Wade Royal Navy Service Record; 1871 and 1881 census.

36   Betancourt, Romulo, *Venezuela, política y petróleo* (Monte Avila Editores Latinoamericana, 2001), accessed via Google Books.

8   Sea Soldiers: The Royal Naval Division and the Royal Marines

1   Lavery, Brian, *Able Seamen: The Lower Deck of the Royal Navy, 1850 to 1939* (London: Conway Maritime Press, 2011), p.142.

2   Sparrow, Geoffrey and Macbean-Ross, J.N., *On Four Fronts with the Royal Naval Division* (Hodder and Stoughton, 1918), pp.3–4.

3   Jerrold, Douglas, *The Royal Naval Division* (Hutchinson, 1923), p.xi.

4   Sellers, Leonard, *The Hood Battalion: Royal Naval Division: Antwerp, Gallipoli, France 1914–1918* (Barnsley: Leo Cooper, 1995), p.7.

5   Jerrold, *Royal Naval Division*, p.xi; Thompson, Julian, *History of the Royal Marines: From Sea Soldiers to a Special Force* (London: Sidgwick and Jackson, 2000), p.63.

6   Messenger, Charles, *Call to Arms: The British Army 1914–18* (London: Weidenfeld Military, 2005), p.108.

7   Lavery, *The Lower Deck of the Royal Navy*, pp.203, 234.

8   Sparrow and Macbean-Ross, *On Four Fronts*, p.5.

9   Jerrold, *Royal Naval Division*, p.xv.

10   Messenger, *Call to Arms*, p.108.

11   Brooks, Richard, *The Royal Marines: History of the Royal Marines 1664–2000* (London: Constable, 2002), p.244.

12   TNA ADM 137/3112: Capture of officers and men of Portsmouth Battalion, R.M. Brigade at Moerbeke, Belgium.

13   Moulton, J.L., *The Royal Marines* (Barnsley: Leo Cooper, 1972), p.68.

14   Sparrow and Macbean-Ross, *On Four Fronts*, p.55; Jerrold, *Royal Naval Division*, p.59.

15   TNA ADM 188/278/170030: Alfred Hutchings Service Record.

16   Jerrold, *Royal Naval Division*, p.166.

17 Thompson, *History of the Royal Marines*, p.145.

18 Messenger, *Call to Arms*, p.109.

19 Jerrold, *Royal Naval Division*, p.174.

20 Jerrold, *Royal Naval Division*, pp.194, 206.

21 The Jack Clegg Memorial Database of Royal Naval Division Casualties of The First World War, accessed via www.findmypast.co.uk.

22 Jerrold, *Royal Naval Division*, p.242.

23 Jerrold, *Royal Naval Division*, p.262.

24 Jerrold, *Royal Naval Division*, p.338.

25 Sellers, *The Hood Battalion*, p.227.

26 Oakley, Derek, *Royal Marines and Eastney* (Supplement to the Globe and Laurel, 1991), p.1.

27 Brooks, *The Royal Marines*, p.206; Blumberg, General Sir H.E., *Britain's Sea-Soldiers: A Record of the Royal Marines During the War 1914–1919* (Devonport: Naval and Military Printers and Publishers, 1927), p.4.

28 TNA ADM 159: Royal Marines Service Records.

29 Moulton, *The Royal Marines*, pp.64–5.

30 Oakley, *Eastney*, p.2.

31 TNA ADM 201/94: Abstract of weekly returns of strength of RM Corps, 1914–17.

32 TNA ADM 159/114/369: Archibald Bareham Service Record.

33 Thompson, *History of the Royal Marines*, p.140.

9 The Easterners: The War in the Middle East

1 Atkinson, C.T., *The Royal Hampshire Regiment 1914–1918* (Naval and Military Press, 2009), p.70.

2 Atkinson, *Hampshire Regiment*, p.71.

3 Rodge, Huw and Jill, *Gallipoli: The Landings at Helles* (Barnsley: Leo Cooper, 2003), pp.40, 130.

4 PGS. I am grateful to the school's archivist John Sadden for providing this information and to the former students of the school who carried out the research.

5 Atkinson, *Hampshire Regiment*, p.75.

6 Atkinson, *Hampshire Regiment*, p.79.

7 Chambers, Stephen, *Gallipoli: Gully Ravine* (Barnsley: Leo Cooper, 2003), p.37.

8 Atkinson, *Hampshire Regiment*, p.83.

9 Chambers, *Gully Ravine*, p.49, 55; Atkinson, *Hampshire Regiment*, p.86.

10 Bourne, John, *Britain and the Great War 1914–1918* (London: Hodder and Stoughton, 1989), p.149.

11   Crowley, Patrick, *Kut 1916: Courage and Failure in Iraq* (Stroud: The History
      Press, 2009), pp.14–5.

12   TNA WO 95/5146: 1/4th Battalion Hampshire Regiment War Diary (March–
      Oct 1915).

13   Crowley, *Kut*, pp.49, 64, 91.

14   Crowley, *Kut*, p.46.

15   Crowley, *Kut*, p.103.

16   TNA WO 95/5146: 1/4th Battalion Hampshire Regiment War Diary
      (December 1915–April 1916).

17   Crowley, *Kut*, p.169.

18   Southern Grammar School Roll of Honour.

19   Southern Grammar School Roll of Honour.

20   Commonwealth War Graves Commission, *Annual Report 2011–12* (2012).

21   Wakefield, Alan, and Moody, Simon, *Under the Devil's Eye: The British Military
      Experience in Macedonia 1915–18* (Barnsley: Pen and Sword, 2010), p.3.

22   TNA WO 161/82: Armies at home and abroad, 1914–1920: statistical abstract.

23   Wakefield and Moody, *Under the Devil's Eye*, p.182.

24   TNA WO 161/82.

25   Bourne, *Britain and the Great War*, p.149.

26   Southern Grammar School Roll of Honour.

10   Brothers in Arms: Portsmouth Families at War

1   1911 census.

2   TNA WO 372/21/939: George Ware Medal Index Card.

3   TNA WO 372/21/9582: Wynn Ware Medal Index Card.

4   TNA WO 372/21/9271: Jack Ware Medal Index Card.

5   TNA WO 372/21/9539: Walter Ware Medal Index Card.

6   www.1914-1918.net.

7   Terraine, John, *Mons: The Retreat to Victory* (Barnsley: Pen and Sword, 2010),
      p.160.

8   Murland, Jerry, *Retreat and Rearguard 1914: The BEF's Actions from Mons to the
      Marne* (Barnsley: Pen and Sword, 2011), p.93.

9   Murland, *Retreat and Rearguard 1914*, p.99.

10   *LG*, 16 October 1917.

11   TNA WO 372/19/4368: Albert Squires Medal Index Card; TNA WO
      372/19/4419: Charles Squires Medal Index Card; TNA WO 372/19/4731:
      Harry Squires Medal Index Card.

12   TNA WO 372/6/2843: John Dennis Medal Index Card.

13   TNA WO 372/6/2063: Arthur Dennis Medal Index Card.

14   TNA WO 372/10/142720: Robert Hyson Medal Index Card; TNA WO
      372/10/142713: Frederick Hyson Medal Index Card.

15   Grundy, Nigel J.H., 'W.L. Wyllie, The Portsmouth Years', *The Portsmouth Papers*,
      68 (1996), pp.10–6; TNA WO 372/22/104302: Robert Wyllie Medal Index
      Card.

16   TNA WO 372/22/104343: William Wyllie Medal Index Card.

11   Portsmouth's Bloodiest Day: The Battle of Jutland

1   Massie, Robert K., *Dreadnought: Britain, Germany and the Coming of the Great
      War* (London: Vintage, 2007), p.461.

2   Massie, *Dreadnought*, pp.492–3.

3   Massie, *Dreadnought*, p.494.

4   Hart, Peter and Steel, Nigel, *Jutland 1916: Death in the Grey Wastes* (London:
      Cassell Military, 2003), p.26.

5   Steel and Hart, *Jutland 1916*, p.44.

6   Steel and Hart, *Jutland 1916*, p.40.

7   *LG*, 3 November 1899.

8   *Navy List* (1907); GRO Portsmouth June 1904 Quarter Vol. 2b pg. 1141.

9   *The Times*, 25 June 1910. Dixon-Wright was also present at the confirmation of
      Prince Albert, the future King George VI in 1912.

10   *LG*, 8 September 1911; *The Times*, 26 October 1911.

11   1911 census.

12   *LG*, 13 February 1912.

13   *Navy List* (1915).

14   PGS.

15   Steel and Hart, *Jutland 1916*, p.46.

16   Massie, Robert K., *Castles of Steel: Britain, Germany and the Winning of the Great
      War at Sea* (London: Vintage, 2007), p.579.

17   Steel and Hart, *Jutland 1916*, p.60.

18   Massie, *Castles of Steel*, p.301.

19   Massie, *Castles of Steel*, p.567.

20   Massie, *Castles of Steel*, p.585.

21   Massie, *Castles of Steel*, p.592.

22   PGS.

23   Steel and Hart, *Jutland 1916*, p.113.

24   Steel and Hart, *Jutland 1916*, p.117.

25   Steel and Hart, *Jutland 1916*, p.123–5.

26   Massie, *Castles of Steel*, p.599.

27   TNA ADM 188/303/181814: Thomas Peters Service Record.

28   Massie, *Castles of Steel*, p.654.

29   Massie, *Castles of Steel*, p.657.

30   Dixon-Wright's son would die serving as a wing commander in the Royal Air Force during the Second World War. See Daly, James, *Portsmouth's World War Two Heroes* (Stroud: The History Press, 2012).

31   Steel and Hart, *Jutland 1916*, p.408.

32   Steel and Hart, *Jutland 1916*, appendix.

33   Gates, W.G., *Portsmouth and the Great War* (Portsmouth: Evening News, 1919), p.24.

34   Sadden, John, *Keep the Home Fires Burning: The Story of Portsmouth and Gosport in World War I* (Portsmouth: Evening News, 1990), p.63.

35   Sadden, John, *Portsmouth: In Defence of the Realm* (Stroud: Phillimore, 2010), p.116.

36   Gates, *Portsmouth and the Great War*, p.26.

37   Webb, J., Quail, S., Haskell, P., Riley, R., *The Spirit of Portsmouth: A History* (Stroud: Phillimore, 1989), p.80.

38   Webb et al., *Spirit of Portsmouth*, p.80. Roy Adkins suggests that 449 British sailors were killed at Trafalgar. Adkins, Roy, *Trafalgar: The Biography of a Battle* (London: Little Brown, 2004), p.290.

39   *EN*, 9 June 1916.

40   For example, an advertisement for Marshall's mourning department, *EN*, 9 June 1916.

41   See Daly, *Portsmouth's World War Two Heroes*.

42   Massie, *Castles of Steel*, p.565.

43   Gates, *Portsmouth and the Great War*, p.26.

12   A 'Sink of Iniquity'? Landport: A Portsmouth Community at War

1   Riley, R.C., 'Railways and Portsmouth Society, 1847–1947', *The Portsmouth Papers*, 70 (2000), p.24.

2   Webb, J., Quail, S., Haskell, P., Riley, R., *The Spirit of Portsmouth: A History* (Stroud: Phillimore, 1989), p.14.

3   1911 census.

4   Webb et al, *Spirit of Portsmouth*, p.88.

5   Sadden, John, *Keep the Home Fires Burning: The Story of Portsmouth and Gosport in World War I* (Portsmouth: Evening News, 1990), p.59.

6   Webb et al, *Spirit of Portsmouth*, p.88.

7   Riley, R.C. and Eley, Phillip, 'Public Houses and Beerhouses in Nineteenth-Century Portsmouth', *The Portsmouth Papers*, 38 (1983), p.25.

8   Weston, Agnes, *My Life Among the Bluejackets* (1909).

9   Marwick, Arthur, *The Deluge: British Society and the First World War* (Macmillan, 1991), p.64.

10   MacDougall, Phillip, 'Settlers, Visitors and Asylum Seekers: Diversity in Portsmouth since the late 18th Century', *The Portsmouth Papers*, 75 (2007), p.8.

11   Dolling, Rev. Robert, *Ten Years in a Portsmouth Slum* (1897).

12   Dolling, *Ten Years in a Portsmouth Slum*.

13   Dolling, *Ten Years in a Portsmouth Slum*.

14   Dolling, *Ten Years in a Portsmouth Slum*.

15   Washington, E.S,, 'Local Battles in Fact and Fiction: The Portsmouth Election of 1895', *The Portsmouth Papers*, 43 (1985), p.8.

16   Weston, *My Life Among the Bluejackets*.

17   Hubbuck, Rodney, 'Portsea Island Churches', *The Portsmouth Papers*, 8 (1969), p.22.

18   TNA WO 372/5/32349: William Corris Medal Index Card.

19   The National Roll of the Great War, Section X – Portsmouth.

20   *Kelly's Directory* (1914–15).

21   TNA WO 372/2/140470: Robert Billing Medal Index Card; TNA WO 372/2/140314: Albert Billing Medal Index Card.

22   *Southern Grammar School Roll of Honour.*

23   *Kelly's Directory* (1914–15).

24   *LG*, 3 August 1915.

25   1881 census.

26   1891 and 1911 census.

27   www.naval-history.net.

28   1901 census.

29   1911 census.

30   *The National Roll of the Great War, Section X – Portsmouth.*

31   TNA WO 97/3120/073: Alfred Hurst Service Record; 1911 census.

32   1891 and 1911 census.

33   1911 census.

34   *The National Roll of the Great War, Section X – Portsmouth.*

35   *LG*, 1 April 1915.

36   *The National Roll of the Great War, Section X – Portsmouth.*

37   *The National Roll of the Great War, Section X – Portsmouth.*

38   *The National Roll of the Great War, Section X – Portsmouth.*

39   *Southern Grammar School Roll of Honour.*

40   Stedman, John, 'Portsmouth Reborn: Destruction and Reconstruction 1939–1974', *The Portsmouth Papers*, 66 (1995), pp.20–2.

13 1 July 1916: The First Day on the Somme

1   Sheffield, Gary, *The Somme: A New History* (Phoenix, 2004), p.xii.

2   Gilbert, Martin, *Somme: The Heroism and Horror of War* (John Murray, 2007), pp.20–21.

3   Middlebrook, Martin, *The First Day on the Somme* (Barnsley: Leo Cooper, 2003), p.70.

4   Middlebrook, *First Day on the Somme*, p.79.

5   Sheffield, *The Somme*, p.21.

6   Middlbebrook, *First Day on the Somme*, pp.62, 65; Gilbert, *Somme*, p.62.

7   Middlebrook, *First Day on the Somme*, p.105.

8   TNA WO 95/1495: 1st Battalion Hampshire Regiment War Diary; Holmes, Richard, *Tommy: The British Soldier on the Western Front* (Harper Perrenial, 2005), p.89.

9   Atkinson, C.T., *The Royal Hampshire Regiment 1914–1918* (Naval and Military Press, 2009), p.170.

10 For example, Middlebrook, *First Day on the Somme*, p.6; Gilbert, *Somme*.

11 Gilbert, *Somme*, p.49.

12 1891 census.

13 GRO March Quarter 1893, vol. 2b p.325.

14 TNA WO 96/0642/277: Reginald Buckland Service Record.

15 1911 census.

16 TNA WO 372/3/153577: Reginald Buckland Medal Index Card.

17 Middlebrooke, *First Day on the Somme*, p.113.

18 TNA WO 95/1495: Atkinson, *Hampshire Regiment*, p.172.

19 Atkinson, *Hampshire Regiment*, p.172.

20 Keegan, John, *The Face of Battle: A Study of Agincourt, Waterloo and the Somme* (London: Pimlico, 1991), p.268.

21 Atkinson, *Hampshire Regiment*, p.170.

22 TNA WO 372/3/153577.

23 TNA WO 372/2/185572: Norman Blissett Medal Index Card.

24 TNA WO 372/14/199625: Alfred New Medal Index Card.

25 *De Ruvigny's Roll of Honour, 1914–1924.*

26 Middlebrook, *First Day on the Somme*, p.94.

27 *National Roll of the Great War: Section X – Portsmouth*; TNA WO 372/2/71099: Bertie Bedford Medal Index Card.

28 *Southern Grammar School Roll of Honour.*

29 TNA WO 372/15/74119: Leslie Overton Medal Index Card.

30 *Southern Grammar School Roll of Honour.*

31 *LG*, 21 June 1916.

32 TNA WO 372/15/147848: Ian Paton Medal Index Card.

33   TNA WO 372/2/55176: Tom Beal Medal Index Card.

34   TNA WO 372/17/107054: Joseph Rowland Medal Index Card.

35   TNA WO 372/12/207369: Joseph McDermott Meda Index Card.

36   TNA WO 372/10/166583: George Ivamy Medal Index Card.

37   *EN*, 7 July 1916.

38   Mallinson, Allan, *The Making of the British Army: From the English Civil War to the War on Terror* (Bantam, 2011), p. 310.

14   A Lost Generation? Portsmouth's First World War Army Officers

1   Moore-Bick, Christopher, *Playing the Game: The British Junior Infantry Officer on the Western Front 1914–1918* (Hellion, 2011), pp. 20–1.

2   Riley, R.C., 'The Growth of Southsea as a Naval Satellite and Victorian Resort', *The Portsmouth Papers*, 16 (1972); Riley, R.C., 'The Houses and Inhabitants of Thomas Ellis Owen's Southsea', *The Portsmouth Papers*, 32 (1980).

3   Captain William Corris.

4   Captain Laurence Lindsay Young and Captain Terence Brabazon.

5   Lieutenant Walter Russell and Lieutenant John Bowyer.

6   Riley, R.C., 'The Industries of Portsmouth in the Nineteenth Century', *The Portsmouth Papers*, 25 (1976), p. 20.

7   Eley, Phillip and Riley, R.C., 'The Demise of Demon Drink? Portsmouth Pubs 1900–1950', *The Portsmouth Papers*, 58 (1991), p. 3.

8   Eley and Riley, 'Portsmouth Pubs 1900–1950', p. 9.

9   Neasom, Mike; Cooper, Mick and Robinson, Doug, *Pompey: The History of Portsmouth Football Club* (Horndean: Milestone, 1984), p. 9.

10   Branksmere later became a girls' school, a police station, a social services office and is now an architect's office.

11   Much of the information on 2nd Lieutenant Brickwood was provided by Portsmouth Grammar School and Charter House School.

12   Moore-Bick, *Playing the Game*, p. 20.

13   Holmes, Richard, *Tommy: The British Soldier on the Western Front* (Harper Perrenial, 2005), pp. 120–1.

14   Moore-Bick, *Playing the Game*, pp. 107, 109, 143.

15   Holmes, *Tommy*, p. 120.

16   Moore-Bick, *Playing the Game*, p. 25.

17   Messenger, Charles, *Call to Arms: The British Army 1914–18* (London: Weidenfeld Military, 2005), pp. 288–9.

18   Moore-Bick, *Playing the Game*, p. 19.

19   Royal Military Academy Sandhurst: Admission Registers (1914).

20 www.1914-1918.net.

21 Clayton, Anthony, *The British Officer: Leading the Army from 1660 to the Present* (Longman, 2007), p.168.

22 Clayton, *The British Officer*, p.167; Holmes, *Tommy*, p.572.

23 Holmes, *Tommy*, p.483; Moore-Bick, *Playing the Game*, p.72.

24 Bridger, Geoff, *The Great War Handbook: A Guide for Family Historians and Students of the Conflict* (Barnsley: Pen and Sword, 2009), p.146.

25 *Guardian*, 19 April 1915.

26 TNA WO 372/3/62096: Arthur Brickwood Medal Index Card.

27 Portsmouth Grammar School and Charter House School.

28 Reed, Paul, *Great War Lives: A Guide for Family Historians* (Barnsley: Pen and Sword, 2010), p.21; Holmes, *Tommy*, p.628.

29 Bridger, *The Great War Handbook*, p.206.

30 Reed, *Great War Lives*, pp.23–4.

31 Corrigan, Gordon, *Mud, Blood and Poppycock: Britain and the Great War* (Phoenix, 2004), p.19.

32 De Ruvigny's Roll of Honour 1914–1918.

33 De Ruvigny's Roll of Honour 1914–1918; *LG*, 23 September 1864.

34 www.cwgc.org.

35 Southern Grammar School Roll of Honour.

15 Recruitment, Conscription and the Portsmouth Military Service Tribunal

1 Army List (1914).

2 TNA WO 161/82: Armies at home and abroad, 1914–1920: statistical abstract.

3 TNA WO 161/82.

4 Rawson, Andrew, *British Army Handbook 1914–1918* (Stroud: The History Press, 2006), p.24.

5 Winter, J.M., *The Great War and the British People* (Macmillan Education, 1986), p.25.

6 Winter, *The Great War*, p.43.

7 Marwick, Arthur, *The Deluge: British Society and the First World War* (Macmillan, 1991), pp.116–7; Simkins, Peter, *Kitchener's Army: The Raising of the New Armies 1914–1916* (Barnsley: Pen and Sword, 2007), p.152.

8 Winter, *The Great War*, p.39.

9 By the end of 1916 the army was 165,000 men below strength – the equivalent of several army corps. Rawson, *British Army Handbook*, p.35.

10 Messenger, Charles, *Call to Arms: The British Army 1914–18* (London: Weidenfeld Military, 2005), p.134.

11   Simkins, *Kitchener's Army*, p.148.

12   Rawson, *British Army Handbook*, p.34.

13   Bilton, David, *The Home Front in the Great War* (Barnsley: Leo Cooper, 2003), p.102.

14   Messenger, *Call to Arms*, p.136.

15   Marwick, *Deluge*, p.117.

16   *EN*, 27–29 January 1916.

17   Messenger, *Call to Arms*, p.132.

18   Marwick, *Deluge*, p.117; Sadden, John, *Keep the Home Fires Burning: The Story of Portsmouth and Gosport in World War I* (Portsmouth: Evening News, 1990), pp.91–2; PHC DC45: Portsmouth Military Service Tribunal papers.

19   *EN*, 9 February 1916.

20   PHC DC45.

21   *EN*, 6 March 1916.

22   *EN*, 6 March 1916.

23   Simkins, *Kitchener's Army*, p.170.

24   Bilton, *Home Front*, p.58; Sadden, *Keep the Home Fires Burning*, p.97.

25   Gates, *Portsmouth in the Great War* (Portsmouth: Evening News, 1919), p.100.

26   Marwick, *Deluge*, p.96.

27   Marwick, *Deluge*, p.97.

28   PHC DC45.

29   PHC DC45.

30   Messenger, *Call to Arms*, p.135.

31   TNA WO 161/82.

32   Van Emden, Richard, *Boy Soldiers of the Great War* (London: Headline, 2006), p.157.

33   TNA WO 161/82.

34   PHC DC45.

16   Boy Soldiers and Sailors: Portsmouth's Underage Servicemen

1   Marwick, Arthur, *The Deluge: British Society and the First World War* (Macmillan, 1991), p.323.

2   Sadden, John, *Keep the Home Fires Burning: The Story of Portsmouth and Gosport in World War I* (Portsmouth: Evening News, 1990), p.59.

3   Van Emden, Richard, *Boy Soldiers of the Great War* (London: Headline, 2006), pp.24, 48.

4   Van Emden, *Boy Soldiers*, p.4.

5   Messenger, Charles, *Call to Arms: The British Army 1914–18* (London: Weidenfeld Military, 2005), p.107.

6   Van Emden, *Boy Soldiers*, p.241.

7   1911 census; *Soldiers Died in the Great War 1914–1919* (London: HMSO, 1921).

8   Southern Grammar School Roll of Honour; *Soldiers Died in the Great War*.

9   *Soldiers Died in the Great War*; 1901 census; 1911 census.

10 Van Emden, *Boy Soldiers*, pp.105, 107.

11 1911 census.

12 TNA WO 372/9/221229: James Hodding Medal Index Card.

13 TNA WO 372/9/221229.

14 Van Emden, *Boy Soldiers*, p.96.

15 1911 census; *Soldiers Died in the Great War* (London: HMSO, 1921); GRO British Army Overseas Births: Malta 1898, vol. 1586 p.32.

16 TNA WO 372/6/79660 Alfred Downer Medal Index Card.

17 Van Emden, *Boy Soldiers*, pp.317, 321.

18 Phillipson, David, *Band of Brothers: Boy Seamen in the Royal Navy, 1800–1956* (Stroud: Sutton, 1996), pp.18, 26.

19 Phillipson, *Band of Brothers*, pp.44–5.

20 Dolling, Rev. Robert, *Ten Years in a Portsmouth Slum* (1897).

21 Phillipson, *Band of Brothers*, pp.47, 96.

22 TNA ADM 286/107-21: Mobilisation Returns, Complements of Ships, Royal Marines and Air Stations, July 1914–October 1918.

23 Phillipson, *Band of Brothers*, p.101.

24 Private Bobby Johns, who was 16 when he was killed in Normandy in 1944. See Daly, James, *Portsmouth's World War Two Heroes* (Stroud: The History Press, 2011).

17   'Damned Un-English': Portsmouth's First World War Submariners

1   Compton-Hall, Richard, *Submarines and the War at Sea, 1914–18* (London: Macmillan, 1991), p.119.

2   Compton-Hall, *Submarines*, p.7.

3   Lavery, Brian, *Able Seamen: The Lower Deck of the Royal Navy, 1850 to 1939* (London: Conway Maritime Press, 2011), p.174.

4   Massie, Robert K., *Dreadnought: Britain, Germany and the coming of the Great War* (London: Vintage, 2007), p.451.

5   Massie, Robert K., *Castles of Steel: Britain, Germany and the Winning of the Great War at Sea* (London: Vintage, 2007), p.124.

6   Gray, Edwyn, *British Submarines in the Great War: A Damned Un-English Weapon* (Barnsley: Leo Cooper, 2001), p.12.

7   Gray, *British Submarines*, p.14.

8   Compton-Hall, *Submarines*, p.119.

9   Lavery, *The Lower Deck of the Royal Navy*, pp.174–5.

10   Compton-Hall, *Submarines*, pp.22–26.

11   Gray, *British Submarines*, p.23.

12   Lavery, *The Lower Deck of the Royal Navy*, p.225.

13   Submarines have always been referred to as 'boats' rather than 'ships'.

14   Gray, *British Submarines*, p.25.

15   Massie, *Castles of Steel*, pp.135–9.

16   Crossley, Jim, *The Hidden Threat: Mines and Minesweeping in WW1* (Barnsley: Pen and Sword, 2011), p.97–99, 107.

17   Compton-Hall, *Submarines*, p.23.

18   Gray, *British Submarines*, pp.242, 247.

19   Lavery, *The Lower Deck of the Royal Navy*, p.225.

20   Lipscomb, Frank W., *British Submarine* (A.& C. Black, 1954), p.33.

21   Terraine, John, *Business in Great Waters: the U-Boat Wars 1916–1945* (Barnsley: Pen and Sword, 2009), p.34.

18   Portsmouth's Early Tank Men

1   Campbell, Christy, *Band of Brigands: The Extraordinary Story of the First Men in Tanks* (Harper Perennial, 2008), p.62.

2   Fletcher, David and Tait, Janice, *Tracing Your Tank Ancestors* (Barnsley: Pen and Sword, 2011), p.25.

3   Campbell, *Band of Brigands*, p.160.

4   Campbell, *Band of Brigands*, p.166.

5   Campbell, *Band of Brigands*, p.187.

6   TNA WO 161/82: Armies at home and abroad, 1914–1920: statistical abstract.

7   Fletcher and Tait, *Tank Ancestors*, p.42.

8   TNA WO 372/13/58890: Charles McNamee Medal Index Card; *Soldiers Died in the Great War 1914–1919* (London: HMSO, 1921); 1901 census.

9   Campbell, *Band of Brigands*, pp.278, 283, 298; Holmes, Richard, *Tommy: The British Soldier on the Western Front* (Harper Perrenial, 2005), p.427.

10   *Soldiers Died in the Great War, 1914–1919* (London: HMSO, 1921); 1891 and 1901 census; TNA WO 372/15/74931: Wilfred Over Medal Index Card.

11   *Soldiers Died in the Great War*, 1891 census; TNA WO 372/2/426455: George Blanchard Medal Index Card.

12   *Soldiers Died in the Great War*, 1911 census.

13   Campbell, *Band of Brigands*, p.384.

14   *Soldiers Died in the Great War*, GRO Army Birth indices, 1892 p.211.

15   *Soldiers Died in the Great War*, 1901 census.

16   *Soldiers Died in the Great War*, 1901 and 1911 census.

17   *Soldiers Died in the Great War*, 1911 census.

18   *Soldiers Died in the Great War*, 1911 and 1901 census.

19   *Soldiers Died in the Great War*; TNA WO 127/8 Boer War Nominal Roll; TNA WO 100/361: Boer War Campaign Medal Roll.

20   1891 and 1911 census.

21   1891 census; GRO 1921 March Quarter, Volume 2c p.99.

22   Holmes, *Tommy*, p.427.

23   Campbell, *Band of Brigands*, p.397.

24   Information about the Whale Island tank was accessed via www.memorialsinportsmouth.co.uk and www.tankmuseum.org.

19   Guest of the Kaiser: Portsmouth's Prisoners of War

1   Bridger, Geoff, *The Great War handbook: A Guide for Family Historians and Students of the Conflict* (Barnsley: Pen and Sword, 2009), p.115. This total includes officers and Royal Navy personnel.

2   TNA WO 161/82: Armies at home and abroad, 1914–1920: statistical abstract.

3   Van Emden, Richard, *Prisoners of the Kaiser: The Last POWs of the Great War* (Barnsley: Pen and Sword, 2009), pp.1–3.

4   TNA WO 161/82.

5   Jackson, Robert, *Prisoners, 1914–1918* (Routledge, 1989), p.4.

6   Jackson, *Prisoners*, pp.6–8.

7   Jackson, *Prisoners*, p.12.

8   Jackson, *Prisoners*, p.22.

9   Van Emden, *Prisoners of the Kaiser*, pp.106, 121.

10   Jackson, *Prisoners*, p.24.

11   I have withheld this young officer's name.

12   TNA FO 141/786: British Embassy in Egypt correspondence; TNA CO 537/1123: British prisoners of war in Turkey.

13   TNA FO 141/786; TNA CO 537/1123.

14   Bilton, David, *The Home Front in the Great War* (Barnsley: Leo Cooper, 2003), p.201.

15   Jackson, *Prisoners*, pp.64, 66.

16   Gates, W.G., *Portsmouth and the Great War* (Portsmouth: Evening News and Hampshire Telegraph Company, 1919), p.43.

20   Portsmouth's War Horses

1   Shuttleworth, Suzanne, 'Farms and Market Gardens on Portsea Island 1770–1880', *The Portsmouth Papers*, 61 (1993), p.20.

2   Webb, J., Quail, S., Haskell, P., Riley, R., *The Spirit of Portsmouth: A History* (Stroud: Phillimore, 1989), p.14.

3   Webb et al., *Spirit of Portsmouth*, p.34.

4   Neasom, Mike, Cooper, Cooper and Robinson, Doug, *Pompey: The History of Portsmouth Football Club* (Horndean: Milestone, 1984), p.9.

5   Butler, Simon, *The War Horses: The Tragic Fate of a Million Horses Sacrificed in the First World War* (Wellington: Halsgrove, 2001), p.20.

6   Butler, *War Horses*, p.23.

7   www.portsmouthpubs.org.uk.

8   Butler, *War Horses*, p.43; Webb et al, *Spirit of Portsmouth*, p.97.

9   Gittins, Sandra, *The Great Western Railway in the First World War* (Stroud: The History Press, 2010), p.17.

10   *EN*, 17 August 1914.

11   *EN*, 5 August 1914.

12   *EN*, 8 August 1914.

13   Butler, *War Horses*, p.42.

14   Sadden, John, *Keep the Home Fires Burning: The Story of Portsmouth and Gosport in World War I* (Portsmouth: Evening News, 1990), p.172.

15   TNA WO 161/82: Armies at home and abroad, 1914–1920: statistical abstract.

16   *EN*, 20 April 1915.

17   Gates, W.G., *Portsmouth and the Great War* (Portsmouth: Evening News and Hampshire Telegraph Company, 1919), pp.66, 68.

18   Butler, *War Horses*, p.48.

19   TNA WO 161/82.

20   Messenger, Charles, *Call to Arms: The British Army 1914–18* (London: Weidenfeld Military, 2005), p.120.

21   Butler, *War Horses*, p.57.

22   Kenyon, David, *Horsemen in No Man's Land: British Cavalry and Trench Warfare 1914–1918* (Barnsley: Pen and Sword, 2011), pp.2, 3.

23   Kenyon, *Horsemen in No Man's Land*, p.7.

24   Kenyon, *Horsemen in No Man's Land*, pp.7–8.

25   Van Emden, Richard, *Tommy's Ark: Soldiers and Their Animals in the First World War* (London: Bloomsbury, 2010), p.2.

26   Butler, *War Horses*, p.53.

27   Holmes, Richard, *Tommy: The British Soldier on the Western Front* (Harper Perrenial, 2005), p.603.

28   Kenyon, *Horsemen in No Man's Land*, p.1.

29 Holmes, *Tommy*, p.126.

30 TNA WO 161/82.

31 Butler, *War Horses*, p.138.

32 Kenyon, *Horsemen in No Man's Land*, p.249.

33 TNA WO 161/82.

34 Cooksley, Peter, *The Home Front: Civilian life in World War One* (Stroud: Tempus, 2006), p.65.

21 Their Name Liveth For Ever More: Remembrance in Portsmouth

1   TNA WO 161/82: Armies at home and abroad, 1914–1920: statistical abstract.

2   Marwick, Arthur, *The Deluge: British Society and the First World War* (Macmillan, 1991), p.330.

3   TNA WO 161/82.

4   Gregory, Adrian, *The Silence of Memory: Armistice Day, 1919–1946* (Oxford: Berg, 1994), p.1.

5   Oliver, Neil, *Not Forgotten* (Hodder and Stoughton, 2005), p.42.

6   Holmes, Richard, *Tommy: The British Soldier on the Western Front* (Harper Perrenial, 2005), p.613.

7   Gregory, *The Silence of Memory*, pp.8–10.

8   *EN*, 18 October 1921.

9   PHC CCM 10/3: Minutes of Roll of Honour Committee.

10 Rawson, Andrew, *British Army Handbook 1914–1918* (Stroud: The History Press, 2006), p.348.

11 Cooksley, Peter, *The Home Front: Civilian life in World War One* (Stroud: Tempus, 2006), p.123.

12 Rawson, *British Army Handbook*, p.349.

13 *EN*, 20 October 1921.

14 *EN*, 19 October 1921.

15 PHC XCM4: Minutes of Local Memorial Fund Committee, 1919–1927.

16 A half-sized Maquette of one of the sculptures is in the care of the City Museums Service.

17 *EN*, 21 October 1921.

18 Sadden, John, *Portsmouth: In Defence of the Realm* (Stroud: Phillimore, 2010), p.132.

19 Sadden, John, *Keep the Home Fires Burning: The Story of Portsmouth and Gosport in World War I* (Portsmouth: Evening News, 1990), p.181.

20 Bilton, David, *The Home Front in the Great War* (Barnsley: Leo Cooper, 2003), p.107.

21   Corrigan, Gordon, *Mud, Blood and Poppycock: Britain and the Great War*
      (London: Phoenix, 2004), p.59.

22   Jackson, Robert, *Prisoners, 1914–1918* (London: Routledge, 1989), p.110.

23   Holmes, *Tommy*, p.625.

24   Winter, J.M., *The Great War and the British people* (Oxford: Macmillan
      Education, 1986), p.63.

25   Corrigan, *Mud, Blood and Poppycock*, p.55.

26   Gregory, *The Silence of Memory*, p.52.

27   Gregory, *The Silence of Memory*, p.53.

28   Gregory, *The Silence of Memory*, p.44.

29   Holmes, *Tommy*, p.485.

Bibliography

Primary Archive Sources

The National Archives (TNA): Admiralty (ADM) 1, 137, 159, 161, 185, 188, 193, 171, 173, 201, 273, 286, 339, 340, 196; Air Ministry (AIR) 76; Cabinet (CAB) 12; Colonial Office (CO) 537; Foreign Office (FO) 141, 383; Ministry of National Service (NATS) 1; Public Record Office (PRO) 30; War Office (WO) 32, 95, 114, 161, 372.

Portsmouth History Centre (PHC): CCM10/3, DC45, XCM4.

Library and Archives Canada (LAC): Soldiers of the First World War Service Records; Canadian Expeditionary Force War Diaries; Canadian Navy Service Records.

National Archives of Australia (NAA): Australian Imperial Force Service Records; Royal Australian Navy Service Records.

Portsmouth Grammar School (PGS): Students' research into Old Portmuthians.

RMAS Sandhurst: Admission Registers.

Primary Printed Sources

De Ruvigny's Roll of Honour, 1914–1924.

Dolling, Revered Robert, *Ten Years in a Portsmouth Slum* (1897).

Gates, W.G., *Portsmouth and the Great War* (Portsmouth: Evening News and Hampshire Telegraph Company, 1919).

National Roll of the Great War: Section X – Portsmouth (National Publishing Company, n.d.).

Officers Died in the Great War 1914–1919 (London: HMSO, 1919).

Soldiers Died in the Great War 1914–1919 (London: HMSO, 1921).

Southern Grammar School Roll of Honour

Weston, Agnes, *My Life Among the Bluejackets* (1909).

Secondary Printed Sources

Ashworth, Tony, *Trench Warfare 1914–18: The Live and Let Live System*, (London: Pan, 2004).

Atkinson, C.T., *The Royal Hampshire Regiment 1914–1918*, (London: Conway Naval and Military Press, 2009).

Barker, Ralph, *The Royal Flying Corps in France: From Mons to the Somme*, (London: Constable, 1994).

Beckett, Ian and Simpson, Keith, *A Nation in Arms: A Social Study of the British Army in the First World War*, (Manchester: Manchester University Press, 1985).

Beckett, Ian, *The First World War: The Essential Guide to Sources in the National Archives*, (London: Public Records Office, 2002).

Beckett, Ian, *Home Front: 1914–1918: How Britain Survived the Great War*, (National Archives, 2006).

Betancourt, Romulo, *Venezuela, Política y Petróleo* (Monte Avila Editores Latinoamericana, 2001), accessed via Google Books.

Bilton, David, *The Home Front in the Great War*, (Barnsley: Leo Cooper, 2003).

Blumberg, General Sir H.E., *Britain's Sea-Soldiers: A Record of the Royal Marines During the War 1914–1919*, (Devonport: Naval and Military Printers and Publishers, 1927).

Bonney, George, *The Battle of Jutland 1916*, (Stroud: The History Press, 2010).

Bourne, John, *Britain and the Great War 1914–1918*, (London: Hodder and Stoughton, 1989).

Bridger, Geoff, *The Great War Handbook: A Guide for Family Historians and Students of the Conflict*, (Barnsley: Pen and Sword, 2009).

British Commission for Military History, *Look to Your Front: Studies in the First World War*, (Stroud: The History Press, 1999).

Brooks, Richard, *The Royal Marines: History of the Royal Marines 1664–2000*, (London: Constable, 2002).

Brown, Malcolm and Seaton, Shirley, *Christmas Truce: The Western Front December 1914*, (London: Pan, 2001).

Brown, Malcolm, *The Imperial War Museum Book of the Western Front*, (Pan, 2004).

Butler, Simon, *The War Horses: The Tragic Fate of a Million Horses Sacrificed in the First World War*, (Wellington: Halsgrove, 2001).

Campbell, Christy, *Band of Brigands: The Extraordinary Story of the First Men in Tanks*, (Harper Perennial, 2008).

Campbell, John, *Jutland: An Analysis of the Fighting*, (London: Conway Naval and Military Press, 1986).

Carradice, Phil, *The First World War in the Air*, (Chalford: Amberley, 2012).

Carver, Field Marshal Lord, *The National Army Museum Book of the Turkish Front 1914–1918: the Campaigns at Gallipoli, in Mesopotamia and in Palestine*, (London: Pan, 2004).

Cave, Nigel, *Somme: Beaumont Hamel*, (Barnsley: Leo Cooper, 1994).

Cave, Nigel, *Vimy Ridge: Arras*, (Barnsley: Leo Cooper, 1996).

Chambers, Stephen, *Gallipoli: Gully Ravine*, (Barnsley: Leo Cooper, 2003).

City of Portsmouth, *Records of the Corporation*, 1966–74, (1978).

Clayton, Anthony, *The British Officer: Leading the Army from 1660 to the Present*, (Longman, 2007).

Cooksley, Peter, *The Home Front: Civilian life in World War One*, (Stroud: Tempus, 2006).

Compton-Hall, Richard, *Submarines and the War at Sea, 1914–18*, (London: Macmillan, 1991).

Corrigan, Gordon, *Mud, Blood and Poppycock: Britain and the Great War*, (London: Phoenix, 2004).

Crowley, Patrick, *Kut 1916: Courage and Failure in Iraq*, (Stroud: The History Press, 2009).

Delve, Ken, *The Military Airfields of Britain: Southern England: Kent, Hampshire, Surrey, Sussex*, (Ramsbury: Crowood Press, 2002).

Doyle, Peter, *Gallipoli 1915*, (Stroud: The History Press, 2011).

Dwyer, Lieutenant Denis John, *History of the Royal Naval Barracks, Portsmouth*, (Gale and Polden, 1961).

Ferguson, Niall, *The Pity of War: 1914–1918*, (London: Penguin, 2009).

Fletcher, David and Tait, Janice, *Tracing your Tank Ancestors*, (Barnsley: Pen and Sword, 2011).

Ford, R., *Eden to Armageddon: World War I in the Middle East*, (London: Weidenfeld and Nicolson, 2009).

Friedman, Norman, *Naval Weapons of World War One*, (Yorkshire: Seaforth, 2011).

Fussell, Paul, *The Great War and Modern Memory*, (New York: Oxford University Press, 2000).

Gilbert, Martin, *Somme: The Heroism and Horror of War*, (London: John Murray, 2007).

Gittins, Sandra, *The Great Western Railway in the First World War*, (Stroud: The History Press, 2010).

Gray, Edwyn, *British Submarines in the Great War: a Damned Un-English Weapon*, (Barnsley: Leo Cooper, 2001).

Gregory, Adrian, *The Silence of Memory: Armistice Day, 1919–1946*, (Oxford: Berg, 1994).

Hans, Patrick and Hodges, Flavia, *A Dictionary of Surnames*, (Oxford: University Press, 1988).

Hart, Peter and Steel, Nigel, *Jutland 1916: Death in the Grey Wastes*, (London: Cassell Military, 2003).

Holmes, Richard, *The Western Front*, (London: BBC Books, 1999).

Holmes, Richard, *Tommy: The British Soldier on the Western Front*, (London: Harper Perrenial, 2005).

Howarth, Stephen, *The Royal Navy's Reserves in War and Peace 1903–2003*, (Barnsley: Leo Cooper, 2003).

Jackson, Robert, *Prisoners, 1914–1918*, (Routledge, 1989).

Jerrold, Douglas, *The Royal Naval Division*, (Hutchinson, 1923).

Keegan, John, *The Face of Battle: A Study of Agincourt, Waterloo and the Somme*, (London: Pimlico, 1991).

Kemp, Paul, *The Admiralty Regrets: British Warship Losses of the 20th Century*, (Stroud: Sutton, 1999).

Kenyon, David, *Horsemen in No Man's Land: British Cavalry and Trench Warfare 1914–1918*, (Barnsley: Pen and Sword, 2011).

Lavery, Brian, *Able Seamen: The Lower Deck of the Royal Navy, 1850 to 1939*, (London: Conway Maritime Press, 2011).

Lipscomb, Frank W., *British Submarine*, (A. & C. Black, 1954).

Mallinson, Allan, *The Making of the British Army: From the English Civil War to the War on Terror*, (Bantam, 2011).

Marix-Evans, Martin, *Somme 1914–18: Lessons in War*, (Stroud: The History Press, 2010).

Marwick, Arthur, *The Deluge: British Society and the First World War*, (Macmillan, 1991).

Massie, Robert K., *Castles of Steel: Britain, Germany and the Winning of the Great War at Sea*, (London: Vintage, 2007).

Massie, Robert K., *Dreadnought: Britain, Germany and the Coming of the Great War*, (London: Vintage, 2007).

McCarthy, Chris, *The Somme: The Day-by-day Account*, (London: Brockhampton Press, 2000).

McDonald, Lyn, *They Called it Passchendaele: The Story of the Battle of Ypres and of the Men Who Fought in it*, (Penguin, 1993).

Messenger, Charles, *Call to Arms: The British Army 1914–18*, (London: Weidenfeld Military, 2005).

Middlebrook, Martin, *The First Day on the Somme*, (Barnsley: Leo Cooper, 2003).

Moore-Bick, Christopher, *Playing the Game: The British Junior Infantry Officer on the Western Front 1914–1918*, (Hellion, 2011).

Moran, Lord, *The Anatomy of Courage*, (Constable, 2007).

Moulton, J.L., *The Royal Marines*, (Barnsley: Leo Cooper, 1972).

Murland, Jerry, *Retreat and Rearguard 1914: The BEF's Actions from Mons to the Marne*, (Barnsley: Pen and Sword, 2011).

Neasom, Mike, Cooper, Mick and Robinson, Doug, *Pompey: The History of Portsmouth Football Club*, (Horndean: Milestone, 1984).

Nicholson, G.W.L., *Official History of the Canadian Army in the First World War: Canadian Expeditionary Force 1914–1919*, (1964).

Oakley, Derek, *Royal Marines and Eastney*, (Supplement to the Globe and Laurel, 1991).

Oliver, Neil, *Not Forgotten*, (Hodder and Stoughton, 2005).

Phillipson, David, *Band of Brothers: Boy Seamen in the Royal Navy, 1800–1956*, (Stroud: Sutton, 1996).

Pidgeon, Trevor, *Flers: 15–26 September 1916*, (Barnsley: Leo Cooper, 2001).

Rawson, Andrew, *British Army Handbook 1914–1918*, (The History Press, 2006).

Reed, Paul, *Great War Lives: A Guide for Family Historians*, (Barnsley: Pen and Sword, 2010).

Robertshaw, Andrew, *24 Hour Trench: A Day in the Life of a Frontline Tommy*, (Stroud: The History Press, 2012).

Rodge, Huw and Jill, *Gallipoli: The Landings at Helles*, (Barnsley: Leo Cooper, 2003).

Sadden, John, *Keep the Home Fires Burning: The Story of Portsmouth and Gosport in World War I*, (Portsmouth: Evening News, 1990).

Sadden, John, *Portsmouth: In Defence of the Realm*, (Stroud: Phillimore, 2010).

Sellers, Leonard, *The Hood Battalion: Royal Naval Division: Antwerp, Gallipoli, France 1914–1918*, (Barnsley: Leo Cooper, 1995).

Sheffield, Gary, *Forgotten Victory: The First World War: Myths and Realities*, (Headline Review, 2002).

Sheffield, Gary, *The Somme: A New History*, (Phoenix, 2004).

Simkins, Peter, *Kitchener's Army: The Raising of the New Armies 1914–1916*, (Barnsley: Pen and Sword, 2007).

Simkins, Peter, Jukes, Geoffrey and Hickey, Michael, *The First World War: The War to End All Wars*, (Osprey, 2013).

Simpson, Andy, *Hot Blood and Cold Steel: Life and Death in the Trenches of the First World War*, (Brighton: Tom Donovan, 1993).

Snelling, Stephen, *VCs of the First World War: Passchendaele 1917*, (Stroud: The History Press, 2012).

Sparrow, Geoffrey and Macbean-Ross, J.N., *On Four Fronts with the Royal Naval Division*, (Hodder & Stoughton, 1918).

Stapleton, Barry and Thomas, James H. (eds), *The Portsmouth Region*, (Stroud: Sutton, 1989).

Stedman, Michael, *Thiepval*, (Barnsley: Leo Cooper, 1995).

Steel, Nigel and Hart, Peter, *Tumult in the Clouds: the British Experience of War in the Air, 1914–1918*, (London: Hodder and Staughton, 1997).

Terraine, John, *Business in Great Waters: the U-boat Wars 1916–1945*, (Barnsley: Pen and Sword, 2009).

Terraine, John, *Mons: The Retreat to Victory*, (Barnsley: Pen and Sword, 2010).

Thompson, Julian, *History of the Royal Marines: From Sea Soldiers to a Special Force*, (London: Sidgwick and Jackson, 2000).

Thompson, Julian, *The Imperial War Museum Book of the War at Sea, 1914–1918*, (London: Sidgwick and Jackson, 2005).

Todman, Dan, *The Great War: Myth and Memory*, (London: Hambledon Continuum, 2006).

Travers, Tim, *The Killing Ground: The British Army, the Western Front and the Emergence of Modern Warfare 1900–1918*, (Barnsley: Pen and Sword, 2009).

Van Emden, Richard, *Boy Soldiers of the Great War*, (London: Headline, 2006).

Van Emden, Richard, *Prisoners of the Kaiser: The Last POWs of the Great War*, (Barnsley: Pen and Sword, 2009).

Van Emden, Richard, *Tommy's Ark: Soldiers and Their Animals in the Great War*, (London: Bloomsbury, 2010).

Wakefield, Alan, and Moody, Simon, *Under the Devil's Eye: The British Military Experience in Macedonia 1915–18*, (Barnsley: Pen and Sword, 2010).

Webb, J., Quail, S., Haskell, P., Riley, R., *The Spirit of Portsmouth: A History*, (Stroud: Phillimore, 1989).

Westlake, Ray, *British Battalions on the Somme 1916*, (Barnsley: Leo Cooper, 1994).

Westlake, Ray, *Kitchener's Army*, (Gloucestershire: Spellmount, 1998).

Wilcox, Ron, *Battles on the Tigris: The Mesopotamian Campaign of the First World War*, (Barnsley: Pen and Sword, 2006).

Wilkinson, Roni, *Pals on the Somme: Kitchener's New Army Battalions Raised by Local Authorities During the Great War*, (Barnsley: Pen and Sword, 2006).

Winter, J.M., *The Great War and the British people*, (Macmillan Education, 1986).

Wragg, David, *Royal Navy Handbook 1914–1918*, (Stroud: Sutton, 2006).

Yates, Keith, *Flawed Victory: Jutland, 1916*, (London: Chatham, 2003).

Journal Articles

Ashworth, G.J., 'Portsmouth's Political Patterns 1885–1945', *The Portsmouth Papers*, 24, (1976).

Course, Edwin, 'Portsmouth Corporation Tramways, 1896–1936', *The Portsmouth Papers*, 45, (1986).

Eley, Phillip, 'Portsmouth Breweries', *The Portsmouth Papers*, 51, (1988).

Eley, Phillip and Riley, R.C., 'The Demise of Demon Drink? Portsmouth Pubs 1900–1950', *The Portsmouth Papers*, 58, (1991).

Grundy, Nigel J.H., 'W.L. Wyllie, The Portsmouth Years, 1996', *The Portsmouth Papers*, 68, (1998).

Hoad, Margaret J., 'Portsmouth – As Others Had Seen It' (Part II 1790–1900), *The Portsmouth Papers*, 20, (1973).

Hubbuck, Rodney, 'Portsea Island Churches', *The Portsmouth Papers*, 8, (1969).

MacDougall, Phillip, 'Settlers, Visitors and Asylum Seekers: Diversity in Portsmouth Since the Late 18th Century', *The Portsmouth Papers*, 75, (2007).

Peacock, Sarah E., 'Borough Government in Portsmouth, 1835–1974', *The Portsmouth Papers*, 23, (1975).

Peacock, Sarah, 'Votes for Women: The Women's Fight in Portsmouth', *The Portsmouth Papers*, 39, (1983).

Quail, Sarah, 'Origins of Portsmouth and the First Charter', *The Portsmouth Papers*, 65, (1994).

Riley, R.C., 'The Growth of Southsea as a Naval Satellite and Victorian Resort', *The Portsmouth Papers*, 16, (1972).

Riley, R.C., 'The Industries of Portsmouth in the Nineteenth Century', *The Portsmouth Papers*, 25, (1976).

Riley, R.C., 'The Houses and Inhabitants of Thomas Ellis Owen's Southsea', *The Portsmouth Papers*, 32, (1980).

Riley, R.C., 'Railways and Portsmouth Society, 1847–1947', *The Portsmouth Papers*, 70, (2000).

Riley, R.C. and Eley, Phillip, 'Public Houses and Beerhouses in Nineteenth-Century Portsmouth', *The Portsmouth Papers*, 38, (1983).

Shuttleworth, Suzanne, 'Farms and Market Gardens on Portsea Island 1770–1880', *The Portsmouth Papers*, 61, (1993).

Stedman, John, 'Portsmouth Reborn: Destruction and Reconstruction 1939–1974', *The Portsmouth Papers*, 66, (1995).

Washington, E.S, 'Local Battles in Fact and Fiction: The Portsmouth Election of 1895', *The Portsmouth Papers*, 43, (1985).

Yates, Nigel, 'The Anglican Revival in Victorian Portsmouth', *The Portsmouth Papers*, 37, (1983).

Newspapers and Periodicals

Army List
Flight
Guardian
Kelly's Portsmouth Directories
London Gazette
Montreal Gazette
Navy List
Portmuthian
Portsmouth Evening News
The Times

Websites

Find My Past: www.findmypast.co.uk
FreeBMD: www.freebmd.org.uk
Great War Forum: www.1914-1918.invasionzone.com
Library and Archives Canada: www.collectionscanada.gc.ca
The Long, Long Trail: www.1914-1918.net
Memorials in Portsmouth: www.memorialsinportsmouth.co.uk
National Archives: www.nationalarchives.gov.uk
National Archives of Australia: www.naa.gov.au
Naval History: www.naval-history.net
Photos of the Great War: www.gwpda.org/photos
Sandhurst Collections: www.sandhurstcollection.co.uk

Index

If you enjoyed this book, you may also be interested in…

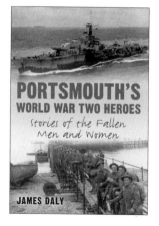

Portsmouth's World War Two Heroes
JAMES DALY

During the Second World War 2,549 service men and women from Portsmouth were killed in their various wartime occupations. Now this book uncovers their stories; stories that have never been told before: a bomb disposal petty officer awarded the George Cross; a 16-year-old paratrooper; a Battle of Britain hero; men killed in battleships, submarines, bombers and tanks throughout Europe, Africa, the Middle East and Asia. Although a touching exploration of the stories of individuals and units, here Daly makes it possible for the reader to build a picture of the effect that the Second World War had on the people of Portsmouth and the community at large.

978 0 7524 6351 3

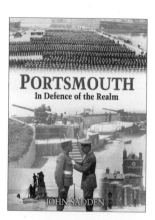

Portsmouth
JOHN SADDEN

Portsmouth was an important naval base by the early Middle Ages, but during the eighteenth century it began its rapid rise to pre-eminence. Many establishments sprang up to support this growth, on both sides of the harbour, for naval, military and marine services. All are fully featured in this comprehensive yet compelling book. Not confined to the evolution of facilities and fortifications, the many defensive and offensive innovations that were developed locally are also explored, as well as the parts played by individuals. Well illustrated with rare photographs, this book is essential to interested residents and visitors and of great value to naval and military historians everywhere.

978 1 8607 7649 6

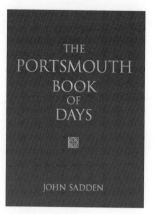

The Portsmouth Book of Days
JOHN SADDEN

Taking you through the year day by day, *The Portsmouth Book of Days* contains a quirky, eccentric, amusing or important event or fact from different periods of history, many of which had a major impact on the religious and political history of England as a whole. Ideal for dipping into, this addictive little book will keep you entertained and informed. Featuring hundreds of snippets of information gleaned from the vaults of Portsmouth's archives, it will delight residents and visitors alike.

978 0 7524 5765 9

Visit our website and discover thousands of other History Press books.

www.thehistorypress.co.uk